TABLE OF CONTENTS

SUMMER 2026
VOLUME VI, ISSUE 4

LIBERTIES: A JOURNAL OF CULTURE AND POLITICS is published quarterly in Fall, Winter, Spring, and Summer by the Liberties Journal Foundation.

LIBERTIES JOURNAL FOUNDATION is a nonpartisan 501(c)(3) organization based in Washington, D.C., devoted to educating the general public about the history, current trends, and possibilities of culture and politics. The Foundation seeks to inform today's cultural and political leaders, deepen the understanding of citizens, and inspire the next generation to participate in the democratic process and public service.

EDITORIAL OFFICES
1101 30th Street NW, Suite 310
Washington, DC 20007

ISBN 979-8-9922010-3-1
ISSN 2692-3904

@READLIBERTIES
LIBERTIESJOURNAL.COM

Liberties

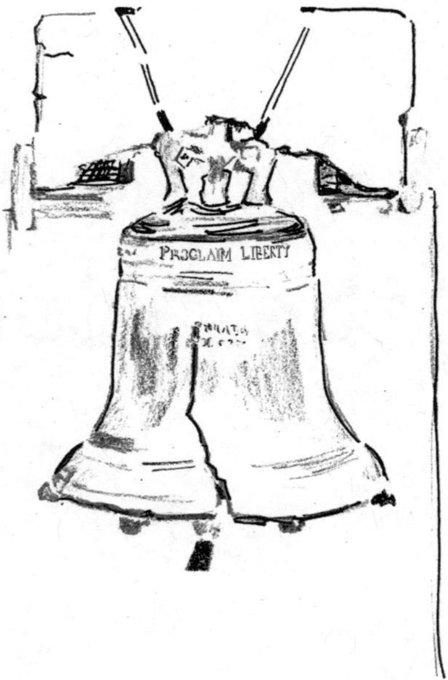

Liberties

SEAN WILENTZ

Untruth and Insanity in American History

Five weeks into his second term, President Donald J. Trump issued Executive Order 14253, entitled "Restoring Truth and Sanity to American History." For more than a decade, the order declared, a "concerted and widespread effort to rewrite our Nation's history" had been "replacing objective facts with a distorted narrative driven by ideology rather than truth." Trump singled out the Smithsonian Institution and the National Park Service, institutions under federal purview, for portraying American (and Western) values as inherently harmful and oppressive. True to form, he blamed the Biden administration for advancing "this corrosive ideology."

The order then instructed Vice President J. D. Vance, the Assistant to the President on Domestic Policy Vince Haley (a former speechwriter and advisor to Newt Gingrich as well as Trump), the Office of Management and Budget director Russell

Vought, and Secretary of the Interior Doug Burgum to conduct an overhaul of the Smithsonian. These four authorities on American history would work closely with the policy's West Wing overseer, Senior Associate Staff Secretary Lindsey Halligan, the former Florida insurance lawyer and Trump loyalist who went on to serve illegally as interim U.S. Attorney for the Eastern District of Virginia until she was removed by a federal court order early in 2026. Trump's historiographical diktat further instructed Secretary Burgum "to reinstate the pre-existing monuments, memorials, statues, markers, or similar properties" that had been removed to "inappropriately minimize the value of certain historical events or figures," which sounded like a euphemism for placing disgraced Confederate soldiers and politicians back on their pedestals.

Right-wing outcries about left-wing historical distortions, predictably exaggerated and partial to conspiratorial thinking, are by no means uniformly meretricious, which thwarts any blanket condemnation of Trump's order. The reluctance of liberals and progressives to call out those distortions on their own terms, a distortion of their own, is an abiding intellectual deformation that gives political hostages to the right. In making a federal case out of wokeness, however, the Trump White House, while exploiting a convenient target to arouse its political base and its band of academic acolytes, chiefly intends to expand presidential power further by commandeering and subjugating previously autonomous or semi-autonomous public institutions that have anything to do with history, including the National Archives. Not only will the administration control, as far as possible, how history is conveyed; it will also control the information upon which future generations — or, in the shorter run, potential grand juries — will judge Donald Trump and his associates. The "unitary executive" theory evidently extends to authorizing the president and his underlings to determine as far as possible not just which versions of our past should be honored and which repudiated, but also the materials from which future historians will treat the present. *L'histoire, c'est moi.*

In their rebuttals to Executive Order 14253, the professional historians' associations conjured visions of a Trump administration hellbent on imposing, to the limits of its powers, an atavistic account of the American past. Sanitized Trumpian history, the Organization of American Historians declared, would "reflect a glorified narrative that downplays or disappears elements of America's history — slavery, segregation, discrimination, division — while suppressing the voices of historically excluded groups." Put differently, the administration aims to suppress the history writing of the last sixty years, which was significantly inspired by the civil rights movement, and revive a worshipful pre-1960s view of the American past in line with its restorationist vision of the American future.

If only that was all that the Trump regime has in mind.

Although no student of history, President Trump has very strong views of his place in it, which offer clues about his regime's actual historical significance. That self-image is fully displayed on the wall of the West Colonnade of the White House, now dubbed (with a Hollywood touch) the Presidential Walk of Fame, in a series of newly installed bronze plaques that describe each American president.

Complementing the dictator chic of the proposed Trump ballroom and the redecorated Oval Office festooned with gold appliqués, the Walk of Fame conveys a faux authority, as if the plaques were wrought by Clio herself. Relatively few people will ever see them except for Trump — who can see them daily, even several times a day, as long he is not at Mar-a-Lago or holed up in the private residence upstairs — along with visiting dignitaries whom the president wants to impress. The exclusivity, though, is in part the point. Housed in an inner temple of the White House, the plaques and their accompanying portraits stand as tablets of revealed historical truth with official authorization, banishing all doubts, fears, and confusions about the standing of presidents past and present and Trump's place among them. For its chief audience of one, it is the ultimate in the ego-fortifying branding that he craves. For his guests, it is a firm reminder of who's in charge. As much as the texts on the plaques, the narcissism of the display's privileged venue reflects the narcissism of its creator.

Fifty-one plaques describe forty-five presidents. From George Washington through George W. Bush, each man receives one plaque, except for Grover Cleveland, whose nonconsecutive terms get two. Suddenly, though, Barack Obama rates two plaques, apparently because one did not suffice to include all of the abuse heaped upon him: "the highly ineffective 'Unaffordable Care Act';" "a stagnant economy;" "the terrible Iran Nuclear Deal;" topped off by how Obama "spied on the Presidential Campaign of Donald J. Trump, and presided over the creation of the Russia, Russia, Russia Hoax, the worst political scandal in American History." The same need to pile on the invective explains why "Sleepy Joe Biden . . . by far the worst President in American History" who "brought our Nation to the brink of destruction" also gets two plaques, his portrait contemptuously replaced by a picture of an autopen.

The two plaques devoted to Trump's first term consist, naturally, of a series of superlatives, among other things crediting him, preposterously, for creating (in Truth Social caps) "the Greatest Economy in the History of the World." More strikingly, the first year of his second term gets two plaques all to itself, concluding with the demolition of the East Wing and the construction, "right here at the White House, the magnificent Trump Presidential Ballroom after a 225-year wait — but THE BEST IS YET TO COME!" To get some perspective on these proportions: the Presidential Walk of Fame devotes more attention to that first year of Trump's second reign, 2025, than it does to the entire presidencies of Abraham Lincoln and Franklin D. Roosevelt combined.

The pathetic grandiloquence is predictable, as are the falsehoods and the slanders. More telling is how the custom-made running narrative connects Trump with his more distant predecessors. Time and again, when describing major and minor

presidents alike, the plaques cast the history of the presidency as an inevitable anticipation of Trump himself, all the while taking care to avoid all embarrassing similarities and contrasts. He is, in his person, the American telos.

Andrew Jackson, for example, in an inartful bit of writing, "was unjustifiably treated unfairly by the press, but not as viciously as President Abraham Lincoln and President Donald J. Trump would, in the future, be." The plaques approvingly highlight presidents who "raised Tariffs," in most cases suggesting falsely that they did so unilaterally much as Trump tried to do. (The plaque on William McKinley does praise him for authoring, as a congressman, the tariff of 1890, while ignoring that measure's disastrous economic — and for McKinley's fellow Republicans, political — effects.) The plaques even manage to rope John Tyler in as a pro-tariff man, and never mind that he approved a hike in rates very reluctantly; Tyler is also noted for being the first president for whom Congress drew up articles of impeachment to no avail, another Trumpian connection. Tyler's pro-slavery politics and eventual defection to the Confederacy go unmentioned. Warren G. Harding comes off better than most for having "cut Taxes, raised Tariffs, and restricted immigration," the Trump trifecta. Harding's plaque omits the Teapot Dome Scandal, lest it prefigure the Trump kleptocracy.

Going back to the earliest days of the republic, George Washington's plaque, not surprisingly, elides how Washington, far from inciting an armed insurrection against federal authority, personally led the forces that crushed one, the Whiskey Rebellion in 1794. John Adams' plaque, however, misses the opportunity to mention the repressive Alien and Sedition Acts of 1798, from which Trump has haphazardly borrowed the only one still on the books, the Alien Enemies Act, to launch his mass deportations.

The plaques do not explicitly call Trump The Greatest President of All Time, although they could easily be mistaken for doing do. Collectively, though, they leave little doubt that he is right up there with Washington and Lincoln. More to the point, they present American history, or at least the history of the

American presidency, as two and a half centuries of prologue that culminate in the ascendancy of Donald J. Trump, the hero who not only made America great again but ushered in a golden age, making America greater than it ever was before.

There is every reason to think that Trump has come to view American history this way. But so, now, do tens of millions of other Americans who need not visit the Presidential Walk of Fame to regard his presidency as a providential, even divine, dispensation. And in important ways that Trump cannot possibly understand, his regime, while aberrant in many respects, truly is the culmination of important currents in our past.

Trump's monomania, along with his royalist pretensions, come into sharper focus with his attempts to self-brand the nation's currency. Here, though, his schemes have run into trouble, owing to an obscure bit of history connected to the Civil War era exploits of a certain Spencer M. Clark.

From the nation's founding until the war, the U.S. Treasury and U.S. Mint deliberately avoided placing actual individuals, let alone living ones, on its coinage, lest it imitate Old World and especially British currency that depicted the reigning monarch. (Americans repeated, into the 1860s, an apocryphal story that when George Washington learned that the first silver dollar was to bear his likeness, he ordered the die destroyed.) Coin designers instead opted for allegorical figures, such as the bust of a female with flowing long hair representing Liberty. But during Abraham Lincoln's presidency, the government's issuance of so-called greenback paper currency as legal tender, a part of its effort to crush the slaveholders' rebellion, opened fresh opportunities for personal glorification. In 1862, Treasury Secretary Salmon P. Chase, a stalwart abolitionist but also an ambitious politician who would have preferred to see himself and not Lincoln in the White House, approved and probably encouraged having his likeness appear on the first one-dollar greenback. Critics assailed Chase's impudence. The issue of currency portraiture, however, did not become a controversy until four years later, by which time Chase had resigned from the Treasury Department and been named Chief Justice of the U.S. Supreme Court.

This brings us to Spencer Morton Clark. He was a Vermont-born small businessman who at some point moved to Washington and in 1856 obtained work as a clerk in the Bureau of Construction of the Treasury Department. Interested in the design of notes and securities, he gradually assumed greater responsibilities and became an advocate for establishing a separate office for overseeing the design and production of department paper. Although he lacked any experience as an engraving engineer, in 1862, having won the confidence of Secretary Chase, he was named superintendent of the first division of the new Bureau of the Currency, which over the decades would evolve into the Bureau of Engraving and Printing.

Working at first with a male assistant and four female operatives, Clark was credited with, among other innovations, designing the first so-called Treasury Seal, a version of which still appears on American paper money, as well as for proposing that a facsimile signature of the Treasurer of the United States appear on department notes instead of relying on the battalions of clerks that had hitherto signed the notes. Clark's early tenure, though, was marred by allegations of scandal, including charges that he was "hiring women based on their looks rather than their ability" and that his department had become, one congressman claimed, "a house for orgies and bacchanals."

As it happened, the Treasury Department was becoming the first federal agency to hire large numbers of female clerks, many of them teenagers and young women whose fathers were either in the military service or had been killed — a vulnerable workforce whose wages were essential to support their families. Short of the extravagant Dionysian rhetoric, substantial evidence surfaced of rampant sexual exploitation, including detailed testimony from at least one employee affirming that Clark had offered her $100 and then $1,000 to have sex with him. A congressional inquiry

— conducted by a panel of House members friendly to Secretary Chase — cleared Clark of misconduct, calling him the victim of a conspiracy; and so he kept his job to the end of the war and beyond.

Clark duly oversaw production of a new form of currency for public circulation, the so-called fractional notes for amounts less than a dollar, which were needed because of the public's widespread hoarding of specie coins. The initial fractional notes bore the likenesses of George Washington and Thomas Jefferson, "illustrious men of our country," a later journalist remarked, "long since gathered to their fathers." But when an issue of five-cent notes appeared in 1866, reckoned likely to be, in future, the most widely used fractional note of all, they featured a portrait not of a departed Benjamin Franklin or Paul Revere but of the bearded, exceedingly un-illustrious, and very much living Spencer M. Clark. For good measure, Clark, unfailing in his efforts to curry favor, had the portraits of Chase's successor, William Fessenden, and the current Treasurer of the United States, Frances Spinner, placed, respectively, on the twenty-five- and fifty-cent notes.

There are differing versions of what happened. By one account, Superintendent Clark asked Treasurer of the United States Francis Spinner if, apart from the others, it would be all right to have "Clark" appear on the note, and Spinner, assuming he meant the explorer William Clark of Lewis and Clark fame, assented. Only after proofs of the bills appeared, so the story goes, was it discovered that the superintendent had already had a die cut with his portrait, which duly appeared on the new bills; and, supposedly, Clark lamely blamed a "misunderstanding." No matter what actually happened, though, demand for the notes was so great and time had grown so short that the Treasury Department approved production and release of the Spencer M. Clark five-cent bill.

The appearance of a relatively minor and long suspect federal official on currency over which he was largely responsible caused a furor from which Clark, this time, could not entirely escape. (He would resign two years later, his reputation precarious when yet another scandal broke, this one over alleged financial irregularities.) Elevating Fessenden and Spinner was bad enough, but plastering Clark's portrait on legal tender was ridiculous. Congress duly amended an appropriations bill to include a provision, known as the Thayer Amendment, that forbade the visage of any living person from appearing on legal tender notes and securities. That amendment remains on the books, since enlarged to state that "only the portrait of a deceased individual may appear on United States currency and securities" (31 U.S.C. § 5114[b]).

It would be fine historical justice if a scoundrel like Spencer Clark, the plausibly accused sexual predator, con man, and confirmed egomaniac, were responsible for now keeping Donald Trump's mug off our money. When it comes to branding, though, Trump never says die, and his army of GOP sycophants rush to flatter him. Trump has already succeeded in arranging to have his signature replace that of the Treasurer of the United States on paper legal tender, overturning the rule that dates to Clark's tenure. In 2024–2025, Representative Joe Wilson, Republican of South Carolina — previously best known for interrupting a presidential address to a joint session of Congress in 2009 by shouting "You lie!" at Barack Obama — floated a proposal to put Trump's portrait on a new $250 bill, a clear violation of the Thayer Amendment that got nowhere. During the 2024 campaign, however, the Trump fundraising operation issued $100 commemorative coins designed to look official, displaying an image of the White House and the words "In God We Trust" as well as Trump's profile. Although they were just mementos, subsequent developments suggest that those coins may have been mock-ups for something much closer to official.

On March 19, 2026, the United States Commission on Fine Arts — a federal body purged in 2025 and restocked with individuals, the White House announced, "more aligned with President Trump's America First policies" — unanimously approved the design of a 24-carat-gold commemorative 250th-anniversary coin bearing Trump's glowering likeness, an official piece of currency from the U.S. Mint, physical size and denomination to be determined. To complaints that this is yet another obvious violation of the Thayer Amendment, Scott Bessent's Treasury Department claims it has found a loophole in 31 U.S. Code § 5112, giving the Treasury Secretary authority to "adopt and prepare new designs" — as if that provision superseded the Thayer Amendment, which it emphatically does not. Where the forgotten Spencer Clark failed in getting his portrait permanently affixed to a five-cent paper piece, Donald Trump may well succeed in being inscribed on a gold coin commemorating American Independence — currency to celebrate monarchy's overthrow that is truly fit for a king.

Other projected Trump historical markers have less troubled American precedents. To greet George Washington on his journey from Mount Vernon to New York for his first inauguration in 1789, individual towns and cities built temporary arches, republicanized variants of décor for a royal procession. Into the nineteenth century, Americans designed permanent memorial arches, nowhere more often than in New York City. These monuments include my own favorite, the Soldiers and Sailors Arch at Grand Army Plaza in Brooklyn, honoring the Union victory over the slaveholders in 1865.

As far as urban memorials go, the Brooklyn arch, standing eighty feet above ground, is as close as it gets in the United States to a European-style triumphal edifice, centering the plaza designed by Frederick Law Olmstead and Calvert Vaux at the entrance to Prospect Park much as Napoleon's Arc de Triomphe centers a radial street axis off the Champs-Élysées. Indeed, the Brooklyn arch, with its statuary paying homage to the Union dead, including an equestrian bas-relief of Abraham Lincoln, was deliberately modeled on the Arc de Triomphe (though the latter, with its glorification of the Napoleonic imperium, strikes a different thematic tone). Imposing as it is, however, the Soldiers and Sailors Arch is less than half the height of its 164-foot Paris counterpart. Adapted to an American civic space, commemorating the destruction of slavery as well as the salvation of the Union, the Brooklyn arch reimagines the form as a more modest republican monument; grandeur but not grandiosity.

Trump and his supporters have a bigger and, of course, much glitzier idea, driven by his unfathomable version of the status anxiety common among *arriviste* robber barons. Reportedly, Trump began musing about building a triumphal arch when he visited Paris in 2017 at the invitation of President Emmanuel Macron and attended the Bastille Day parade at the Arc de Triomphe. Informal proposals for a Trump-themed arch in Washington began to surface later in his first term, more as a gesture of undying support or perhaps a provocation in anticipation of the 2020 election than a serious suggestion. More substantive plans appeared in the aftermath of Trump's second inauguration.

In April 2025, the *American Mind*, the online journal of the Claremont Institute, not previously known as an authority on architectural criticism or urban design, published an essay called "Washington Needs an Arch" by Catesby Leigh. A longtime journalist turned architecture expert, the Washington, DC-based Leigh had earlier made a name for himself in publications such as *National Review*, *First Things*, and the *New York Post* as well as *Arts and Antiques* and *American Arts Quarterly*, and as a co-founder of the National Civic Art Society, a non-profit organization dedicated in part to reviving traditional neoclassical styles in the nation's capital. His article observed that Washington is the only major Western capital lacking a monumental arch, which in his view is a distinctive marker of national greatness and a proper gateway for civic space. Leigh advocated correcting that glaring flaw, and he knew just where to build it — what he called the "conspicuous dead space" at Memorial Circle at the west end of the Arlington Memorial Bridge, across the Potomac from the Lincoln Memorial. (That space is of course not dead: it is the cobbled and gently affecting approach to Arlington National Cemetery, over which the Lee Mansion presides from a solemn height — a kind of antechamber of national meaning.)

Leigh had in mind a triumphal arch but in the modest American mode, about sixty feet tall (roughly the same height as the arch in New York's Washington Square Park), built to honor the semiquincentennial of the Declaration of Independence. Although the design was compatible with conservative sensibilities, Leigh couched his proposal in architectural and civic terms, not in political terms, as a completion of Washington's coherent classical design. He explicitly connected his monument to the abstract principles of the Declaration of Independence and not to any individual, let alone to Donald Trump. In reclaiming neoclassical precepts, he had no intention of disrupting the existing sightlines but aimed to complement them, providing, as he sees it, a long missing counterpart to the Lincoln Memorial.

There is no evidence that Trump's circle drew directly on Leigh's suggestion, but leading architects within that circle who have promoted the more recent Trump arch proposals, notably Justin Shubow and Duncan Stroik, are important figures in Leigh's conservative neoclassical milieu and were almost certainly aware of his essay. Leigh, however, without withdrawing his original proposal, has expressed dismay at what the Trumpists now envisage, an arch that is "way too big" and out of scale for the site — that is, an arch consonant with Trump's view of history and his place within it.

As of this April, the design proposal, prepared by Harrison Design, calls for a 190-foot-high main structure topped by a 60-foot gold statue of Lady Liberty — 250 feet in all, tacky symbolism for one foot per year since 1776. The main structure alone is taller than the Arc de Triomphe; with the statue on the arch's roof, it will stretch nearly half as high as the heaven-scraping Washington Monument obelisk, meaning that it will dwarf every other structure in the city, completely disrupting the DC skyline. (Since it will be built in Virginia, the arch will sidestep the District of Columbia's strict restrictions on the heights of buildings.) Viewed from the Virginia side, it will frame and completely dominate the Lincoln Memorial, off in the distance. Approached from the DC side, it will overwhelm the venerable rows of simple headstones in

Arlington Cemetery.

The design is unmistakably Trumpian, with gold rococo accents near the roof of the arch along with golden statues of two eagles in flight flanking the enormous statue up top. Gilded details evoke New York City not so much in imitation as to outdo Trump's hometown, where the elite never quite accepted him: the resplendent gold statue is a replica of the green oxidized copper Statue of Liberty, this time sporting wings, while a pair of lions atop stone pedestals guards the arch on the DC side just as their originals guard at the New York Public Library — only these lions are gold, not pink marble. (That marble gives the Library lions their serene grace atop unmistakable power; whereas Trump's worship of gold appears, to a layman, pathological.)

To be sure, the formal plans presented by Harrison Design state that the arch is simply a commemoration of the Declaration of Independence at 250, the same as Catesby Leigh's original proposal. But the grandiosity as well as the flashy details make its provenance as unmistakable as that of any Trump real-estate project. In any case, Trump is clear about whose monument it really is. Asked by a reporter back in October who the monument is for, the ever-unguarded Trump replied, "Me. It's going to be beautiful." (The man gives candor a bad name.) And just in case anybody tried messing around with who's in charge and what the arch is for, and who or what it may end up honoring, Trump named as overseer of the project Vince Haley, the same ex-speechwriter loyalist he appointed as part of the team to overhaul the offerings at the Smithsonian.

The gargantuan ballroom that is to replace the razed East Wing of the White House is another example of Trump's edifice complex run amok. Early renditions look as if the plans were inspired more by Albert Speer than by Richard Morris Hunt. The privately funded project is also an enormous public show of subservient allegiance from a billionaire class falling over itself to render unto their new

Caesar whatever it takes to get on his good side, whether out of fear or opportunism or both. Of course, the building contract went to a firm, Clark Construction, that is very much a Trump favorite, having also wangled a hugely inflated no-bid deal to repair two fountains in Lafayette Park at a cost to the taxpayers of $11.9 million, with add-ons that will bring the bill to $17.4 million.

Beyond the imperial pretentions and kleptocracy of Trump's second term, however, there is an additional explanation for his insistence on building this thing. As it happens, Trump's desire to construct a new presidential ballroom antedates his own presidency. In 2010, Obama's former strategist David Axelrod recounts, private citizen Trump approached him saying, "I see you have these state dinners on the lawn there in these shitty little tents. Let me build you a ballroom you can assemble and take apart. Trust me. It'll look great." Trump was not wrong about those tents, but Obama evidently lacked enough trust in him to take up the offer. It would take fifteen years, but Trump, who never forgets a slight, would get his way, and not with anything so humble that it could be easily taken down and reassembled. It appears that he has made himself comfortable in the presidency by going back to the construction business. He is a human wrecking ball. For a developer, rubble is a sign that things are looking up.

Another of Trump's proposals with historical resonance, or at least the idea behind it, has at first glance a perfectly American pedigree. Perhaps his most sizable project, to build a National Garden of American Heroes, might have been conceived as a complement to the Hall of Fame of Great Americans designed by Stanford White, a loggia overlooking the Hudson and opened in 1901 on what was then the campus of New York University and is now the home of Bronx Community College. Starting with a group of thirty eminences chosen by a national board selected by NYU, the hall added new honorees every five years until the process halted in 2000; now, 102 greats are included in seven categories ranging from statesmen and writers to theologians and military leaders.

I confess to a personal attachment, a sentimental attachment, to that old hall, mainly because my father, who grew up nearby, took me there when I was a boy. In that majestic setting, the displays spoke to me of great battles and great poems and great deeds and great sacrifices as no teacher or textbook ever would. It was a shrine but a remarkably democratic one, featuring busts of ordinary-looking men and women who had done extraordinary things, each one a hero but presented simply, one by one, the unheroic design elevating their heroism. Every other hall of fame, including my other favorite in Cooperstown, is descended from that curving memorial in the Bronx.

But the plans for the National Garden of American Heroes, to be built on federal land near the National Mall, are something very different. Trump announced his garden as a political gesture, not a commemorative one, to counter the all-too-indiscriminate destruction of public statues that followed the murder of George Floyd at the hands of Minneapolis policemen in 2020. In place of iconoclasm Trump offered iconophilia, and there was every reason to be suspicious, lest Trump's statue park complement his efforts to restore honor to the names and images of disgraced Confederate traitors.

In fairness, while the selection process remains opaque, the list of the Americans who have made the cut (projected, when completed, to be 250: that number again) is for the most part not as bad as one would have rightly feared. To be sure, there is some obvious right-wing influence to go along with sheer boorishness. Only political bias can explain selecting Jeane J. Kirkpatrick as a hero, but not Daniel Patrick Moynihan, just as only politics can account for why Russell Kirk deserves inclusion. The list of visual artists is thin — John James Audubon and Charles Willson Peale but not Winslow Homer or Jackson Pollock. Most egregious is the selection of just two men under the category of journalists, Trump's "enemies of the people": Edward R. Murrow and, bizarrely, Alex Trebek, the host of the television game show *Jeopardy!*

Still, right-wing partisanship cannot explain why the Supreme Court justice named Marshall who made the grade is Thurgood and not John, or why Phillis Wheatley is included but Marianne Moore is left out. Most notably, Ulysses S. Grant is present but Robert E. Lee is not; nor, for that matter, is any other Confederate. Somebody clearly made an effort. Given the project's origins, what seems to have been the studied exclusion of any Slave Power traitor comes not simply as a relief but as a signal that the Lost Cause may at long last have been firmly denied any claim whatsoever to honor in the national memory. The exclusion in fact quietly endorses the spirit behind the Confederate removals in 2020.

But don't be fooled by the list of names alone: far from updating the old Hall of Fame of Great Americans in the Bronx, the Garden of American Heroes will be yet another Trumpian attempt to outdo his hometown with as much grandiosity as possible, and with further self-glorification in the offing. Last July, when Trump signed his larcenous so-called "One Big Beautiful Bill," the measure set aside $40 million to "establish and maintain" the garden, which strongly suggested that, as with everything else this White House touches, there is some serious grifting afoot. But we ain't seen nothing yet — literally in terms of anything built, figuratively in terms of the scale of potential corruption. Subsequent reporting has disclosed a far huger enterprise, with reflecting pools and dining facilities and an amphitheater, and life-sized statues (no modest busts here) commissioned at a cost of $250,000 each, which alone would bring the total to $10 million more than Congress has already appropriated.

As with the Presidential Walk of Fame, meanwhile, the true test of the garden's historical significance will lie in the biographical material identifying each hero. An official White House statement has described the project as being "built to reflect the awesome splendor of our country's timeless exceptionalism," a sure sign of anti-historical boosterism. And the biographical descriptions that accompanied the original list of names were so vapid that they drained most of the heroes of their heroism while pushing a false and treacly view of an American past where never was heard a discouraging word. The great abolitionist Frederick

Douglass, for example, is rendered as "a proud patriot who loved his country and wanted to see it become the best version of itself." A more accurate summary would have quoted Douglass' own words on the subject of patriotism, that "the best friend of a nation is he who most faithfully rebukes her for her sins."

Most sinister of all, the list of honorees released thus far consists of 245 names, not 250. It's a dead giveaway: the only mystery here is about who the other four honorees will be who will stand beside Donald John Trump. Roy Cohn would be a pretty safe bet. The late Charlie Kirk of Turning Point USA will almost certainly be there. But who else? Witkoff? Giuliani? Hulk Hogan? Or maybe, realizing the omission, they will smuggle in Robert E. Lee or Stonewall Jackson or Jefferson Davis after all.

Should Trump's Garden of American Heroes ever turn into something more than a political gambit, it is just possible that under another administration it could be revised into an updated Hall of Fame, built to properly American scale — the slightest of vindications for Trump. The same cannot be said for Trump's other main response to the troubles of 2020, his 1776 Commission, announced two days before the November election, which delivered its report on American history during the waning days of Trump's first term.

Created in part as a counter to the *New York Times*' tendentious and erroneous 1619 Project and the influential Manichean writings of the historian Howard Zinn, the commission was charged with finding ways to promote what Trump called "patriotic education" by refuting what he contended was "a twisted web of lies" about America's historically systemic racism. The eighteen-member commission, chaired by Larry Arnn, co-founder of the Claremont Institute and president of Hillsdale College, and joined by a grab bag of Trump-aligned professors and less-than-qualified public figures, including Charlie Kirk, provided Trump with what he asked for and more.

The most telling section of the commission's report had nothing to do with 1619 or 1776 but everything to do with early-twentieth-century America and the rise of Progressivism — in the commissioners' view a great anti-American heresy, which has posed a challenge to the nation's fundamental values akin to the challenges posed by slavery, fascism, and communism. Progressives, the commission reported, were elitists who "rejected the self-evident truth of the Declaration that all men are created equal and are endowed equally, either by nature or by God, with unchanging rights." Instead, they "believed there were only group rights that are constantly redefined and change with the times." The commission singled out Woodrow Wilson as a Progressive mastermind, who, it claims, even before he became president, laid out "a new system of government" sometimes called "the administrative state," a government "unaccountable to the people and without constitutional restraint."

What a Progressive such as Louis Brandeis — who described "the final end of the state" as making "men free to develop their faculties" — would have made of such an account is not too difficult to imagine. In 1862, Abraham Lincoln established the United States Department of Agriculture, an independent agency charged with protecting a specific group, the nation's farmers, conducting agricultural research, and securing the nation's food supply. Was Lincoln, then, and not Wilson, the original avatar of group rights and the father of the unaccountable administrative state? In demonizing, under the label of Progressivism, modern American liberalism as an alien force, the commission report restated, in a softer form, the right-wing animus that has long dated the downfall of the American republic to the creation, under Wilson, of the graduated federal income tax and the Federal Reserve. It is but a step or two away from the more crackpot theories of American history, some of them recently propounded by Supreme Court Justice Clarence Thomas, that conflate modern liberalism with totalitarianism and describe Progressivism as not merely the equivalent of but also the progenitor of Hitler, Mussolini, and Stalin. Really.

Yet this is the history that the first Trump White House endorsed, and it is the nearest thing available to what American history will look like when Trumpian truth and Trumpian sanity are restored.

Trump's authoritarian second term — and even, for that matter, his more chaotic first term — has had a vertiginous effect that leads many to look for some historical precedent for this wild turn of events, to regain balance if not necessarily to find reassurance. Historians get asked the question all the time: has there been anything before in American history even remotely like the Trump regime? The answer, on the narrowest of grounds, is no: even down in the depths of James Buchanan and Andrew Johnson, no American president or White House administration has shown such disregard, even open contempt, for the Constitution and the rule of law as we now witness nearly every day.

Yet this fact can be misleading, causing commentators to look abroad, usually to one variety or another of European fascism, for similarities. These are easy enough to find: it is difficult, for example, to notice the rising influence of Opus Dei and reactionary Catholicism generally in Washington, as well as among MAGA intellectuals such as Patrick Deneen and Adrian Vermeule, and not be reminded of Francisco Franco's Falange Española Tradicionalista. But no matter how close the foreign analogies, they egregiously overlook our homegrown evils, the deeply illiberal strains in the entirety of American history, which are obscured by limiting the search for analogies to past occupants of the White House.

We are prone to approach Trumpism with thoughts of *It Can't Happen Here*, Sinclair Lewis' second-rate but influential nightmare fantasy from 1935, as well as Philip Roth's much superior *The Plot Against America*. At long last, supposedly, where Charles Lindbergh's America First failed, Trump is now forcing Americans to deal with the fact that it *can* happen here. Even holding aside slavery and the Confederacy, though, we knew this already, or we should have known it. Consider the experience of any black American in the South under the Jim Crow police-state regime, and the facileness of such prettifying thinking about American history becomes obvious: factually speaking, it *has* happened here. Then trace the history of what became of that evil after Jim Crow's formal collapse: the shift of the solid segregationist South into the Republican Party, the rise of the Christian Right and then the Christian Nationalist Right out of the ruins of massive resistance, the political flirtations and more than flirtations with the likes of the cleaned-up Klansman David Duke, the right-wing militia paranoia of the 1990s that drove Timothy McVeigh to terrorism, the political careers of George Wallace and Pat Buchanan and Jesse Helms and Strom Thurmond, and finally add the internet and social media — ponder all this and you begin to have a handle on the origins of a powerful all-American authoritarian current that has fed into MAGA.

Trump, of course, could not care less about the history of what paved his way to power. Our history-obsessed and legacy-addled president is phenomenally ignorant of our actual past. The ideologues around him will continue to push hard to impose an eviscerated version of our history that consigns the long and consequential career of American liberalism to history's dustbin. For Trump, though, American history is just a lot of gold leaf, just more fodder for his self-glorification. And in that respect, certainly, he bears an indisputable resemblance to every caesar, generalissimo, caudillo, duce, führer, jefe, *vozhd*, Dear Leader, and Great Helmsman who ever walked the earth.

BENJAMIN FRANKLIN

Drinking Song

To the Abbé de la Roche, at Auteuil

Singer

Fair Venus calls, her voice obey,
In beauty's arms spend night and day.
The joys of love, all joys excel,
And loving' s certainly doing well.

Chorus

Oh! no!
Not so!
For honest souls know,
Friends and a bottle still bear the bell.

Singer

Then let us get money, like bees lay up honey;
We'll build us new hives, and store each cell.
The sight of our treasure shall yield us great pleasure;
We'll count it, and chink it, and jingle it well.

Chorus

Oh! no!
Not so!
For honest souls know,
Friends and a bottle still bear the bell.

Singer

If this does not fit ye, let's govern the city,
In power is pleasure no tongue can tell;
By crowds tho' you're teas'd your pride shall be pleas'd
And this can make Lucifer happy in hell!

Chorus

Oh! No!
Not so!
For honest souls know,
    Friends and a bottle still bear the bell.

Singer

Then toss of your glasses, and scorn the dull asses,
Who, missing the kernel still gnaw the shell;
What's love, rule, or riches? Wise Solomon teaches,
They're vanity, vanity, vanity still.

Chorus

That's true;
He knew;
He'd tried them all through;
Friends and a bottle still bore the bell.

(1779)

ANDREW DELBANCO

The Universities and Humility

"The very possibility of civilized human discourse rests upon the willingness of people to consider that they may be mistaken." Those words were spoken in June 1968 by the great historian Richard Hofstadter in his commencement address at Columbia, which had been convulsed that spring by violent arrests of students protesting the Vietnam War. Hofstadter defended the students' freedom to "confront difficult and inflammatory things," including "the most troublesome questions of politics and war, of sex and morals, and national loyalty." Speaking to both the enraged left and the bewildered right, however, he insisted that the willingness to think and rethink in view of new evidence and experience is indispensable to any civilized society.

This principle is today in urgent need of revival. For those of us who make our lives in universities, it should be self-evident because anyone with a will to learn knows that the best way to do so is with zeal leavened by humility. It should be self-evident, but alas it often is not.

The imperative to acknowledge our own fallibility has a long lineage. In the West it stretches back to Judaism, suffused with a dialectical spirit of self-questioning. In ancient Greece Plato subjected all claims to inconvenient questions from his teacher, Socrates, who confessed (as translated by Benjamin Jowett), "I neither know nor think I know." Early Christianity decried the sin of pride as a mark of reprobation.

Self-doubt is an uncomfortable condition that, for many people, cannot match the appeal of ideology in politics or dogma in religion. Yet it is a necessary precondition for curiosity, tolerance, and any form of open thought. This was a central insight of the Enlightenment, from which some two centuries ago there arose a new kind of educational institution committed to what my Columbia colleague Stuart Firestein, a distinguished neuroscientist, describes as "knowledgeable ignorance" — the recognition of how little one knows and that everything one thinks one knows is provisional pending further investigation. It was on that basis, in Berlin in 1810, that the modern university was founded as a site of free inquiry and teaching in which the pursuit of truth proceeds in a spirit of skepticism toward received certitudes and brooks no interference from prelates, princes, or any authority external to the university itself.

The functional principle of this new institution — academic freedom — was slow to take hold in the United States. Through most of the nineteenth century America's universities, such as they were, remained under denominational constraint if not control. In 1878, for example, the president of Vanderbilt University, a Methodist bishop, fired its professor of geology for teaching evolution in defiance of "the plan of redemption." Soon the clergy were supplanted by men of wealth who had no problem with Darwin, at least not in the dubious form of Social Darwinism, whose doctrine of "survival of the fittest" flattered the thriving rich and justified the fate of the unworthy poor. But when it came to other unwelcome ideas, wealthy meddlers were ready to step in to exercise what Thorstein Veblen called "pecuniary surveillance" over "the permissible limits of learning." At the University of Wisconsin, in 1894, two leading faculty were dismissed for "teaching socialism."

It wouldn't be difficult to assemble an anthology of similar interventions first by men of the cloth and then by titans of industry. In retrospect all these efforts look like rearguard actions by a regime in retreat. In 1869, speaking at his inauguration as president of Harvard, Charles W. Eliot (a chemist descended from Puritan clergy) declared that "the winnowing breeze of freedom" had begun to "blow through all its chambers." Arguably the most ventilated of America's universities had been established four years earlier in upstate New York by the engineer and entrepreneur Ezra Cornell, who envisioned a new kind of university in which "any person can find instruction in any study." Soon several new institutions — including Johns Hopkins in 1876 and the University of Chicago in 1890 — were founded on the premise that no subject or point of view should be ruled *a priori* out of bounds.

Still, the fight over academic freedom continued into the twentieth century. In 1900, the Stanford sociologist Edward Ross gave a public lecture opposing the use of Asian immigrant labor by the railroads. Jane Stanford, the widow of the railroad tycoon who had founded the university and now its sole trustee, became enraged and Ross was fired. In 1915 a group of eminent scholars led by the Columbia philosopher John Dewey established an advocacy organization — the American Association of University Professors (AAUP) — whose "Declaration of Principles" defined and defended academic freedom as its cardinal value. Two years later, the Columbia trustees, unimpressed, prevailed upon the university president to dismiss several members of the history department for holding a view — opposition to America's entry into World War I — that was obnoxious to their own. With tacit consent from most faculty, he complied. Attempts at suppression continued during the "Red Scares" that followed both World War I and World War II, but by and large the forces of reaction grew weaker as the faculty's role in institutional governance, bolstered by the protections of tenure, grew stronger.

The shared premise of the new universities — as well as older ones that were attempting to renew themselves — was that the only route to knowledge is through restless discontent with received certitudes. To this end, using language both descriptive and aspirational, the AAUP defined the modern university as "an intellectual experiment station." At its best, that is what it became and what it continues to be.

From the start, however, even the most progressive academic leaders knew that universities could sustain their "searching function" (Hofstadter's phrase) only if they won support, or at least forbearance, from the public.

As a legal matter, private institutions were answerable only to themselves. As early as 1819, the principle of self-governance had been affirmed by the U.S. Supreme Court when it ruled that an attempt by the state of New Hampshire to alter the charter of Dartmouth College was unconstitutional. But while older institutions with private endowments were thus protected from government interference, by the early twentieth century they were becoming, in an extralegal sense, quasi-public. Through a series of laws enacted by Congress culminating with the War Revenue Act of 1917, the modern system of tax exemptions for nonprofit organizations and tax deductions for their donors was taking shape. The rationale for conferring tax advantage on institutions and on the philanthropic individuals who support them is that they serve the public interest. But when consensus breaks down over what constitutes that interest, tax advantage starts to look like tax evasion and politicians can be counted on to stress the resemblance.

Though the AAUP founders could hardly have been expected to foresee the crisis of trust in which higher education finds itself today, they were sensitive to the risks. They knew that American universities have always had to manage a distinctively American tension between government and private enterprise, including enterprises that do not operate for profit. They knew, too, that the right to autonomy must be balanced with some degree of deference to external forces — always a delicate balance because any true university, while ultimately dependent on public approval, must be a nursery and sanctuary for ideas that incur public disapproval.

Over the course of the twentieth century, this mutually wary relationship — now commonly referred to as a compact or contract between academia and society (Clark Kerr, the transformative president of the University of California, preferred the metaphor of a common-law marriage) — became more and more consequential, with a great deal at stake for both partners. Following World War II, the monetary value of the contract soared with the rapid expansion of the National Institutes of Health and, early in the Cold War, the establishment of the National Science Foundation, partially in response to technological and military competition from the Soviet Union. The government now invested huge sums in universities in the form of research grants, as well as grants and subsidized loans directed through the Department of Education to millions of students. And because the labor market increasingly rewarded holders of a college degree, the benefits of the compact were widely assumed to outstrip the costs.

But lately, for a host of reasons, notably the galloping sticker price of tuition, college education has come under attack as a foolish investment for young people seeking work in the trades or the service economy or even in white-collar jobs. In fact, because colleges provide significant financial aid, students are paying less on average in real dollars than a decade ago — but that hasn't changed the impression of skyrocketing cost. Some mega-wealthy entrepreneurs, almost all of whom benefited from attending college, now ridicule it as a time-wasting distraction. And despite the astonishing success of mRNA vaccines to prevent or mitigate COVID-19 infection, as well as countless other therapies and technologies developed in university labs, the reputation of academic scientists (and to some extent, economists) fell into sharp decline following the shocks of the pandemic — prolonged school closures, mask mandates, enforced isolation, along with persistent inflation triggered by shortages of staple goods and by the federal effort to stabilize the economy. Calls to "follow the science" now seem to many people to lead to perdition.

Meanwhile an even more damning narrative burst into prominence. This one says that universities, dominated by what the current president of the United States calls "Marxist maniacs and lunatics," have become un-American or even anti-American, intolerant of conservatism and capitalism itself, ruthless toward dissenters, incubators of antisemitism, and so on.

It is mostly a slander. With humanities enrollments declining and expectations rising that the main function of universities is to train students for the workplace, the number of students sitting in classrooms discussing such supposedly subversive authors as Karl Marx or Michel Foucault or Judith Butler is small and shrinking. And even for those who are asked to read them, there is no reason to assume that they are doing so with uniform assent. "The charge of widespread 'indoctrination' by left-wing faculty," writes the historian David A. Bell, a liberal centrist, "is nonsense, and, worse, a pretext being used shamelessly by the right to attack the university system and bring it under government control."

Still, there is no doubt that universities — especially the so-called elites — have made themselves easy targets by furnishing their critics with a rich repertoire of follies and scandals that cast doubt on their professed devotion to academic freedom. They have done too little to counter the view that they have become playgrounds of "virtue signaling" — trigger warnings, land acknowledgments, compulsory statements of fidelity to a narrow conception of "diversity," and so on. Even if this damning portrait of academic culture is an opportunistic exaggeration, there is enough truth in the caricature that the public is hard pressed to distinguish between reality and appearance.

After the monstrous attack by Hamas on Israeli civilians in October 2023, some universities, faced with the task of distinguishing between protected free speech and poisonous hate speech, made matters worse by bungling their response to protests over Israel's ferocious counterattack. At my own academic home, whose formal name is Columbia University in the City of New York, non-students seeking to bring toxic hatreds onto campus are only a subway ride away. The situation was managed poorly. But none of us who stood on the sidelines should be confident that we would have defused it before it spun out of control.

Well before those sad and damaging events, universities had been exposing themselves to attacks in the name of outraged patriotism. In the always contested terrain of American history, college courses once likely to conform to a triumphalist story inherited from antebellum and Gilded Age historians who celebrated America's "exceptionalism" now emphasize cruelties perpetrated against enslaved, indigenous, or exploited peoples who served involuntarily or resisted America's "Manifest Destiny." This is a belated corrective to the boosterish narrative that once marginalized millions of Americans in favor of a monochrome story of power and progress. Yet as Bill Readings warned three decades ago in a prescient book called *The University in Ruins*, it is at their own peril that universities abandon their role as "producer, protector, and inculcator of national culture" in the eyes of the broader public.

The charge that academia is a nest of insidious leftists has long roots. It reaches back to William F. Buckley (*God and Man at Yale*, 1951), and Allan Bloom (*The Closing of the American Mind*, 1987) and has been carried on with varying degrees of subtlety by conservative writers such as Roger Kimball, Bruce Bawer, and George F. Will, among many others. More recently, it has been taken up by liberals who write in a tone closer to that of disappointed friends, including Laura Kipnis, Jonathan Haidt, and Eboo Patel, all of them warriors against the excesses of "Woke," "DEI," "#MeToo," and "Cancel Culture."

I doubt that many people on left, center, or right (with a few exceptions such as Christopher Rufo and others involved in the Heritage Foundation's Project 2025) anticipated that with the second election of Donald Trump, critiques of the university — whether fanciful or well-founded or somewhere in between — would become grounds for suspending or canceling billions of dollars in research grants, curtailing the influx of international students, enforcing "viewpoint diversity" (on the weak premise, as Amanda Anderson of Brown University puts it, that "individuals occupy identifiable political positions aligned with stable and explicit beliefs that do not change over time") or "meritocratic" admissions and hiring, as if merit were an objective quality measurable in scores and grades or by counting publications or citations.

With the full force of government behind them, enemies of the university are now employing a strategy of divide and conquer. In the absence of a collective response remotely comparable to the defense led by AAUP a century ago, this strategy has proven to be highly effective. Columbia, Penn, Brown, Cornell, and Northwestern have made their deals. Harvard appears to be defying with one hand and dealing with the other. The Board of Visitors at the University of Virginia, buckling under fear of becoming the next target, forced out the university's president James Ryan, a person of luminous integrity. And even with hints of a truce in the air, it seems unlikely that research support will return to previous levels anytime soon. With the rise in taxation rates on endowment income and a likely decline in overhead support attached to federal grants, the damage promises to be difficult if not impossible to reverse. American universities already appear to be losing their preeminence in the international rankings, which are based overwhelmingly on research output in the sciences.

I have taken a historical approach to some of the issues now facing higher education on the premise — the premise, I think, of all historical writing — that knowledge of the past has value for confronting challenges in the present. I have focused on well-known research universities because they are the institutions most visibly under assault. It should be stressed, however, that collateral damage is rippling through the whole range of higher education — from regional public universities to liberal arts colleges and historically black colleges and universities, as well as community colleges, which collectively enroll vastly more students, including large numbers of low-income and first-generation students, than elite institutions do. Compensatory cuts in state subsidies to education seem likely to follow reductions in federal Medicaid support. Pell grants, designed to help low-income students pay for college, continue to lose their purchasing power in relation to the price of attendance. Federal funding for English language instruction, technical training, and other forms of adult education is threatened by restrictive provisions in the "Big Beautiful Bill" as well as by the dismantling of the Department of Education. In short, programs intended to help the most vulnerable students are on the chopping block.

Those mounting the attack on higher education have many rhetorical advantages. They have tapped into an ugly undercurrent of contempt not only toward privileged intellectuals but also toward people very much without privilege — immigrants, people of color, students from disadvantaged backgrounds deemed unprepared or unfit. They also benefit from the fact that the term "university" is an abstraction in which it is hard to discern the dedicated teachers, researchers, students, and support staff who do the day-to-day work in classrooms, laboratories, dormitories, recreational facilities, administrative offices, and all the rest, serving not only the academic community but neighbors as well. At my own university it has been heartbreaking to watch the gutting of Columbia's Double Discovery Center — the original model for the federal Upward Bound program — which is mainly dependent on now-canceled grants from the Department of Education. Having served thousands of vibrant high school and middle school students in northern Manhattan for more than sixty years with tutoring, mentoring, and counseling — a magnificent exception to the rule that elite institutions hold themselves aloof from their local communities — DDC is now fighting to survive on private benefactions.

In October 2025, nine universities in varying degrees of favor or disfavor with the current administration were invited to sign a "Compact for Academic Excellence in Higher Education." In exchange for acquiescing to its demands (among them, a five-year tuition freeze and limitations on foreign student enrollment), the compact promised "multiple positive benefits" such as "substantial and meaningful federal grants." To qualify for these benefits, the signatories were asked to ban anything that would "punish, belittle and even spark violence against conservative ideas."

Do "conservative ideas" include such features of the American past — which some people, it seems, hope to see restored in the future — as segregation, the prohibition of "mixed" marriages, and literacy tests at the polls? Do they include superseded conservative ideas such as free trade, limited government, and an independent judiciary? Its incendiary incoherence notwithstanding, the proffered compact, in the words of Erwin Chemerinsky, the dean of Berkeley's law school, amounts to a brazen attempt at "extortion, plain and simple." So far, thankfully, it is an offer that the invitees have been willing to refuse.

But universities continue to be under surveillance by Big Brother, who has demonstrated his willingness to punish transgressors and to do it again anytime he doesn't like what he sees. Meanwhile, state legislatures dominated by his followers — notably in Florida and Texas — have banned the teaching of "divisive concepts" and granted new powers to administrators and trustees to review, discipline, or even terminate tenured faculty. Students with grievances about course content or grades or disciplinary procedures now have allies outside the university itching for a fight — conservative media, watchdog organizations, legislators, even governors — to whom they can appeal and thereby threaten faculty or staff by whom they've been offended. We face the prospect, as Suzanne Nossel, the former director of PEN America, writes, of professors "walking on eggshells for fear of not just a viral video or student complaint, but one that triggers government reprisals."

What should we make of the charge that universities have brought these furies upon themselves? For the most part, comparing instances of intellectual intolerance on the left to the wholesale assault from the right amounts to an egregious case of false equivalence. Yet there are elements of truth in the backlash against "identity politics," or the sweeping claims of "Critical Race Theory," or the instinctive deployment of the term "social justice" as if everyone agrees on what it means, or the excoriation of "settler colonialism" as a proxy for antisemitism. Despite the current administration's mobster tactics, we in academia should consider that once we get through the current crisis, some of the shocks may prove salutary, and that serious self-searching is overdue.

To that end, the AAUP's "Declaration of Principles" remains a valuable resource. Its authors understood that universities, even though liberated in the previous century from control by the sects that founded them and from coercion by the governments that chartered them, bear ultimate responsibility for regulating themselves. In a society where hostility toward intellectuals is always latent and sometimes virulent (Hofstadter wrote the key book on this subject, *Anti-Intellectualism in American Life,* in 1962), they knew, too, that universities would always remain suspect. On the core issue of academic freedom, as the legal scholar Robert Post has remarked, if faculty were to construe that freedom as the right "to research and publish in any manner they see fit," it would not be long before public support "would vanish." Post made that comment sixteen years ago. Today we seem to be approaching the vanishing point.

Anyone concerned about the future of higher education would do well to recall that even as the authors of the "Declaration of Principles" defended academic freedom as essential for the search for truth, they devoted a section (cited much less frequently than its clarion call for freedom) to its "corresponding duties" and "correlative obligations." But what, exactly, did — and does — such a call for self-regulation mean?

In the natural sciences it has meant that hypotheses must be tested by experiment and experimental results put to the test of replication. In the so-called social and human sciences — where the line between argument and opinion is often thin and work can be ideologically tendentious — it takes the form of peer review of journal articles, book manuscripts, and nominations to tenure. These quality control methods are by no means immune to error or to abuse, but they do ensure that propositions and theories, to be taken seriously, must have something more than the status of unfounded claims.

But when most people think of the university, they don't think of the lab or the academic journal or the scholarly conference. They think of the classroom. When it comes to teaching, what can one say about how universities have been doing at monitoring themselves? Here is a frank answer from Leon Botstein, longtime president of Bard College and dauntless champion of liberal education, who has denounced Big Brother more fiercely than all but a very few college presidents while at the same time holding universities to account in a spirit of loyal opposition:

> Universities have retreated shamelessly from their obligation to teach, particularly undergraduates. Higher education has become a matter of lecture halls, seminars taught by graduate students, standardized testing, fully remote learning, and obscurantist pseudo-professionalism, notably in the humanities and social sciences. Universities have abandoned the act of serious teaching and learning and settled for anonymity and routine.

One need not agree in every particular with this list of indictments — in my experience graduate students can be very good teachers — but every honest observer of higher education knows that there is a lot of truth in it. Fifteen years ago, in their data-heavy book *Academically Adrift: Limited Learning on College Campuses*, the sociologists Richard Arum and Josipa Roksa argued in depressing detail that too many universities have been complacent as "students' academic effort has dramatically declined in recent decades." They made that argument long before the advent of artificial intelligence, which now invites students — at least those who wish to evade responsibility for their own learning — to substitute prefabricated writing and research for their own work.

Unfortunately, academia's loudest critics are generally concerned less with meeting the needs of unconfident or underprepared students and more with the putative problem of radical professors browbeating students with "woke" ideas. How credible is this charge? The University of California sociologist Steven Brint, another sober critic of academia from within the academic world, put it this way in a recent interview with the *Chronicle of Higher Education*:

> Those who are 'woke,' or social-justice oriented remain a fairly small part of the faculty, let's say twenty percent as a kind of rough approximation. . . . In some disciplines like gender studies and ethnic studies it approaches fifty percent but, in self-description at least, never gets to be a majority even there. So it exists, but it's not a majority tendency.

But even if most teachers remain open to a range of perspectives, less sanguine observers will say that students whose thinking does not align with "progressive" norms nevertheless feel compelled to censor themselves or risk ostracism by their peers. My impression, based on many conversations with students, is that they are less likely to feel constrained by teachers than by other students. The classroom thus gives itself up to "the tyranny of the prevailing opinion and feeling" by which a majority — more likely, an imperious minority — seeks to "impose . . . its own ideas and practices as rules of conduct on those who dissent from them," and thereby to "fetter the development and, if possible, prevent the formation of any individuality not in harmony with its ways, and compel all characters to fashion themselves upon the model of its own."

Those words come not from a contemporary writer but from the greatest exponent of free speech in the Anglo-American tradition, John Stuart Mill. In *On Liberty*, in 1859, Mill sounded the alarm at "a social tyranny more formidable than many kinds of political oppression." Today it is an article of faith among anti-academic pundits that even if teachers don't browbeat their students, universities are aiding and abetting the habit of self-censorship, which inhibits both faculty and students from saying — or even thinking — what they wish.

The "soft power" of conformity is impossible to measure, but it does exist. I confess that I have done a little self-censoring myself. In my course on early American literature, I had assigned for many years Benjamin Franklin's "Advice to a Young Man on the Choice of a Mistress," from 1745, in which he advises a young friend on the sexual advantages of older women. Ribald and deliberately outrageous, it guaranteed raucous laughter when I read it aloud, which I did partly for comic relief after a week of theological tracts and hellfire sermons by Franklin's contemporary Jonathan Edwards, but also because it illustrates the split (Edwards would have been scandalized had he read it) between pietism and rationalism in eighteenth-century America. Then, around a decade ago, the laughs died down and gave way to a few nervous chuckles or silent stares, so I decided to drop it from the syllabus. The last time I assigned it and read it in class, the only hearty laughter came from the one older student in the room, who asked me afterwards for the full citation so she could share it with her ex-husband.

I am still not sure where my decision falls on the spectrum between cowardice and good manners. One reason I appreciate the AAUP authors is that they advised continual self-monitoring. "The teacher," they wrote, "ought also to be especially on his guard against taking unfair advantage of the student's immaturity by indoctrinating him with the teacher's own opinions before the student has had an opportunity fairly to examine other opinions upon the matters in question." Then they added the admonition that professors should "refrain from intemperate or sensational modes of expression" not only in the classroom but in their extramural speech as well.

In fact, cool disinterest in the classroom is rarely desirable, especially when the subject entails judgments of value. Such detachment is a prescription for bland, dull, and bloodless teaching. Good teachers exemplify what it means to care passionately about whatever subject they are teaching — an idea or a historical episode or a work of art or any aspect of human experience. But good teachers also exemplify the habit of self-questioning, of taking seriously arguments that run counter to their own convictions, beginning with the obligation to make students aware that such arguments exist.

I find another aid to reflection in *The Education of Henry Adams*, that brilliant memoir and cultural history, from 1907, in which Adams recalls his brief stint teaching medieval history at Harvard and wishing that he could have "seated a rival Assistant Professor opposite him, whose business should be strictly limited to expressing opposite views." Owing to its prohibitive expense, team-teaching is rare even at lavish Harvard, so most of us are left without the benefit in class of a contrarian colleague to question our assertions. This means that teaching any subject that entails ethical, aesthetic, psychological, political, or historical questions — any subject, that is, that falls under the rubric of "the humanities" — requires an honest effort to argue against oneself. That is the surest way to instigate what Adams called "conflicts of thought" not only among one's students but within the mind of each.

Recent attacks on academia have taken on a tone of hot indignation, and though they have been met with reciprocal outrage — most of it well warranted — there are also signs within universities of chastened self-reflection. The strategically self-flagellating Yale

"Report on the Committee on Trust in Higher Education" has been received warmly by commentators on the right as a sign of *mea culpa*. Another such sign is the sprouting up of organizations with the irreproachable aim of encouraging students to regard adversaries as interlocutors rather than as enemies. Some are campus-based, such as Duke's "Civil Discourse Project" or Vanderbilt's "Collaborative for Campus Dialogue." Others are consultants-for-hire with irenic names — "Braver Angels," "Interfaith America," "Constructive Dialogue Institute" — all of them intended, as the latter explains, to "equip the next generation of Americans with the skills to bridge divides."

Most of these initiatives have a flavor of sensitivity training that is reminiscent of the heyday of DEI. They tend to be long on method ("we host skill-building workshops," explains "Dartmouth Dialogues") but short on content. And to the extent that they are peripheral to the academic work of the university, they are likely to be ephemeral. Surely the best constructive dialogue institute remains the classroom itself, where students, under the guidance of a teacher with earned knowledge of the matter at hand — the history of the Middle East, or the First and Fourth Amendment rights of noncitizens, or any contested issue past or present — learn the difference between informed argument and instinctive opinion.

We are also seeing the proliferation of centers, institutes, and schools of "Civic Thought." The first such center, the James Madison Program in American Ideals and Institutions, was founded long before the present fraught moment, at Princeton in 2000, by the conservative political philosopher Robert George. More recently, driven by the implausible panic that tenured radicals have seized the universities and by the plausible concern that few students graduate with a basic understanding of the founding principles of the American republic, the "civic thought" effort seems poised to become a movement. So far it has been making headway mainly at public institutions in red states. It picked up speed in 2016 with the establishment by the Arizona state legislature of a School of Civic & Economic Thought and

Leadership at Arizona State University under the direction of the historian of political philosophy Paul Carrese. Since then, other centers and schools have been created by legislative fiat at state flagship universities, including the University of Texas at Austin, the University of Florida, the University of North Carolina at Chapel Hill, and Ohio State (now one of five such programs in Ohio). Three other states (Iowa, West Virginia, and Utah) have passed legislation to create similar programs in the past year alone.

For the moment, these schools and institutes enjoy considerable independence and run on separate budget lines not generally subject to shared faculty governance. Writing in the *Washington Post*, George F. Will has hailed them as agents of salvation that are "reviving universities' civic seriousness . . . reinvigorating the humanities, inspiring students eager to grapple with big questions, and reversing academia's forfeiture of its prestige." But this seems overheated and premature.

For one thing, many faculty regard them with suspicion, for good reason, as fronts for conservative state legislatures seeking to influence university hiring and decision-making. The historian Timothy Messer-Kruse, who points out that "civics" can mean anything from learning good behavior to "teaching the structure of government," describes the movement with cutting irony as "a New Deal jobs program for conservatives." It is also true that any program originating from outside existing institutions rather than arising organically from within risks becoming — to use the prevailing term of opprobrium for the territorialism of academic life — just another "silo" in which faculty and students seek solidarity in the company of like-minded peers. Most of the new centers depend, moreover, on a scarce supply of faculty qualified to teach, say, constitutional law or Middle East history. They also depend on funding streams from legislatures that may become less friendly with a shift in the political winds.

Still, we seem to be witnessing a determined and, one hopes, good-faith effort to renew something first attempted some two hundred fifty years ago by the nation's founders, who tried but failed to establish a new academic institution explicitly designed to prepare young people (exclusively young men, at the time) for citizenship in the new republic. Distrustful of the old sectarian colleges with roots in this or that Protestant denomination, the founders envisioned a federal university whose mission would be essentially secular — to teach what Benjamin Rush called "the principles and forms of government, applied in a particular manner to the explanation of every part of the Constitution and laws of the United States." George Washington told Congress that such a federal institution would teach "the people themselves to know and to value their own rights; to discern and provide against invasions of them; to distinguish between oppression and the necessary exercise of lawful authority" so they will obtain a "temperate vigilance against encroachments, with an inviolable respect for the Laws."

In the twentieth century, similar motives animated the creation of general education curricula such as the Columbia Core, which began as a "War Issues" course during World War I, and the Harvard "Red Book" curriculum, conceived as an "education in a common heritage and toward a common citizenship" following World War II. The authors of these curricula anticipated an influx of students from outside the prep school pipeline — students of lesser means (thanks in part to the G.I. Bill) and more varied backgrounds, including Jews (despite strenuous efforts by Ivy League presidents to keep them out) — who would break the homogeneity of even the most venerable and clubby institutions. It remains to be seen whether the new twenty-first-century civic thought institutes manage to adapt and advance those erstwhile attempts at civic education, or whether they devolve into just another cluster of battle stations in the culture wars.

Whatever the future of these interventions, one thing is certain: reading and discussing challenging texts — once at the core of a college education — has been disappearing from the experience of most college students. This is an inestimable loss: whether the text on the table is concerned with public life such as *The Federalist Papers* or *Letter from a Birmingham Jail*, or a meditation on private life such as *The Beast in the Jungle* or the poems of Sylvia Plath, there is irreplaceable value in confronting privately (reading) or publicly (discussing) any work that pushes readers to grapple with the kinds of antinomies — law and justice, majority rule and minority rights, altruism and ambition, love and desire — that sooner or later confront us all.

I am tempted to say that the task before us is to Make the Classroom Great Again. I mean this not in a spirit of nostalgia for some mythic past when universities had their values straight and academics lived by them. I mean it to celebrate the countless teachers in the present who — under hostile surveillance and often without the protections of tenure — are determined to give their students an experience larger than mere credential acquisition.

At stake in the present moment is nothing less than the fate of such an education — one that requires wrestling with contradictory claims to truth — which is properly called a liberal education. Such an education is best advanced in a classroom that is a place of genuine diversity in every sense of the word (now, alas, a taboo word) in accord with Mill's conviction that "the only path to knowledge of any subject — including that most mysterious subject, the self, is by hearing what can be said about it by persons of every variety of opinion, and studying all modes in which it can be looked at by every character of mind." No one has stated better what a good classroom in a good university should be.

No one, that is, unless it was Philip Roth (who did a good deal of teaching through his career) in *The Professor of Desire*, in 1977, a novel both raunchy and tender about a professor who introduces his students to such masterworks as *Anna Karenina*, *Madame Bovary*, and *Death in Venice*, in which tormented souls struggle to reconcile social norms with the imperatives of their inner lives. For the first meeting of his class, he drafts some remarks by which to prepare his students for what they are about to encounter. The result is a homily that might once have seemed mawkish but that now, to anyone familiar with what goes on (or doesn't) in our universities, will sound wistful, even elegiac:

> There is nothing quite like the classroom in all of life . . . Why? Because once you have left here people are rarely, if ever, going to talk to you or listen to you the way you talk and listen to one another and to me in this bright and barren little room . . . I doubt that you know how very affecting it is to hear you speak thoughtfully and in all earnestness about solitude, illness, longing, loss, suffering, delusion, hope, passion, love, terror, corruption, calamity, and death . . . because, oddly and sadly, this may be the last occasion you will ever have to reflect in any sustained and serious way upon the unrelenting forces with which in time you will all contend, like it or not.

Over the half century since Roth wrote those words, reading and discussing vital texts has become a puzzling rumor for most college students, including those at our most exalted (now reviled) institutions. Literature — characterized by Hofstadter's colleague Lionel Trilling as "the human activity that takes the fullest and most precise account of variousness, possibility, complexity, and difficulty" — now tends to be marginalized in college as a subject of arcane or eccentric interest. This is a terrible loss for students who will never discover that writers who differ from themselves in gender, race, religion, class, or any other confining category can open their minds to the commonality of human experience, including the self-doubt and even the self-loathing from which no honest young person is spared in their own lives.

To restore this form of education will require overcoming many countervailing forces. These obstacles include incentives and rewards that drive faculty to focus on research and relentless publication at the expense of teaching; a growing truancy problem, by which students regard class attendance as optional; the incursion of AI into every aspect of life, which leaves students unprepared for the low-tech methods of reading closely and speaking carefully; the contraction of graduate education, in which teaching is regarded as a tiresome obligation rather than a calling; the budgetary challenge of preserving small classes that can never deliver the economies of scale provided by online instruction or big lectures — not to mention the need for inexperienced faculty to learn how to conduct a discussion that has both spontaneity and structure.

Against all odds, there are signs of progress. Institutions ranging from Purdue, Stanford, and Vanderbilt universities to SUNY Onondaga and Austin community colleges (full disclosure: all are grantees of the Teagle Foundation, which I lead), are restoring major literary and philosophical texts to the "gateway" experience for most if not all incoming students. The Yale report laments that "there is no single course, book, work of art, or scientific experiment that every Yale student is guaranteed to explore before graduation." The revival of interest in core education is not being driven by ideologues of any political stripe. At the institutions I know best it is being carried on — in the words of Roosevelt Montás, a legatee of the Hofstadter-Trilling tradition, longtime director of Columbia's Core Curriculum, and now director of the new Chang-Chavkin Center for Liberal Education and Civic Life at Bard — with the aim of "complicating the answers" and "unsettling the certainties" proffered by any closed mode of thought, and to make this experience available to as many students as possible.

I want to conclude these reflections in the same way I began them, with somebody else's words — this time not from a renowned historian but from a current college student who wrote a column last year in my university's student newspaper, the *Columbia Daily Spectator*, about the tone and the atmosphere that he values when in class with a good teacher and engaged peers. It was written by Salvatore Mannella, a college senior and officer of Columbia's chapter of College Republicans, in the wake of the assassination of Charlie Kirk: "We are students. Every day, we sit and listen to those who know things that we do not. But something changes when we leave the classroom: suddenly we have all the answers." He then offers the modest suggestion that "we should approach our discussions with one another with the same openness and humility with which we approach our studies." This, in substance, is the same plea that Hofstadter made on the same campus nearly sixty years ago.

However much we may disagree on who or what is to blame for the fractious state of our universities, surely if the norms of the well-led classroom, the open classroom, the liberal classroom — taking hard questions seriously, thinking before speaking, honoring the right of others to speak and be heard — were to supplant the hissing and howling that now pass for public discourse, and such a classroom were to become a model for a whole society, we would all be better off. Who can argue with that?

PHILIP FRENEAU

Wild Honeysuckle

Fair flower, that dost so comely grow,
Hid in this silent, dull retreat,
Untouch'd thy honey'd blossoms blow,
Unseen thy little branches greet:
    No roving foot shall crush thee here,
    No busy hand provoke a tear.
By Nature's self in white array'd,
She bade thee shun the vulgar eye,
And planted here the guardian shade,
And sent soft waters murmuring by;
    Thus quietly thy summer goes,
    Thy days declining to repose.

Smit with those charms, that must decay,
I grieve to see thy future doom;
They died—nor were those flowers more gay,
(The flowers that did in Eden bloom)
    Unpitying frosts and Autumn's power
    Shall leave no vestige of this flower.

From morning suns and evening dews
At first thy little being came:
If nothing once, you nothing lose,
For when you die you are the same;
    The space between is but an hour,
    The mere idea of a flower.

(1786)

LEWIS HYDE

Immigrants and Abolitionists

At last it occurred to me that what I had lost was a country.

THOREAU

Then

I recently reread "Slavery in Massachusetts," the angriest essay that Henry David Thoreau ever wrote, and now I can't get it out of my head. A fugitive slave had been captured in Boston and, despite abolitionist resistance, shipped back to his enslaver in Virginia. Everything about the case enraged Thoreau. He was angry that federal troops had occupied the city, angry that the governor allowed the president to seize control of the state militia. He was angry that no one enforced state laws giving fugitives their civil rights, and angry at state officials who obeyed the laws of slavery and ignored one of their own that commanded resistance. In the face of a government dominated by slave-holding states, Massachusetts should have defended its sovereignty, even if blood should flow and the Union itself be dissolved. "My thoughts are murder to the State."

Thoreau initially delivered "Slavery in Massachusetts" at a Fourth of July rally in 1854. Even today it gives off enough heat to light the tinder of my own anger and despair. There are too many parallels between the rendition of slaves and the Trump rendition of immigrants, too many similarities between the troops then occupying Boston and the Marines and Immigration and Customs Enforcement (ICE) agents recently deployed to our cities. Behind both of these — the treatment of immigrants and the control of armies — lie questions of states' rights, a term I have long held in contempt but now hold up as a stay against the loss of my country. Can a state that protects its immigrants with sanctuary laws resist a government that sues to quash them? Who, at the end of the day, controls the National Guard, the governors, or the president? Is the structure of the republic robust enough to settle such questions peacefully, or will the current regime's taste for violence lead to settlement by other means?

The events that got Thoreau so hopping mad began in May 1854, when the fugitive slave Anthony Burns was jailed in Boston, pending rendition to Virginia. Two days after his arrest, a poorly organized mob tried and failed to free him from the Court House. President Franklin Pierce then ordered five companies of U.S. Marines and artillery to enter the city while the U.S. marshal, authorized by law to command assistance from "bystanders, or *posse comitatus*," enlisted several hundred "specials," arming them with cutlasses, pistols, and clubs.

Boston's mayor called out the state militia to help, encouraged by a telegraph from the White House agreeing to pay all expenses (a sum exceeding $500,000 in today's dollars). The militia, effectively federalized, consisted of a thousand rank and file, eight companies of artillery, eleven of light infantry, and several of cavalry — the National Lancers and the Light Dragoons. Federal troops, with permission to fire without warning, mounted a brass cannon by the Court House, loaded it to the muzzle with grapeshot and pointed it at the crowd.

This show of force culminated several days later when the marshal's posse marched Anthony Burns to the ship that would carry him south. With a crowd of over 50,000 people bearing witness, Burns walked surrounded by marshals with drawn swords. Ahead marched the Marines, the infantry, and the National Lancers on horseback. Behind marched more Marines, a horse-drawn cannon, and the mounted Light Dragoons. As they neared the city docks, some of the militia, now drunk, taunted the crowd with a chorus of "Carry Me Back to Ole Virginny."

One witness to the rendition of Anthony Burns wrote that, in meeting "the armed power of the United States," citizens were made painfully aware of "the fact, before unfelt, that they were the subjects of two governments." That would have come as no surprise had they been more familiar with the Constitution, for its framers had indeed bestowed a species of dual citizenship on its subjects. As James Madison explained in Federalist No. 28, published during the debates over the Constitution, the envisioned government would not be "a *national* one;" it would have power over only "certain enumerated objects" and leave "to the several States a residuary and inviolable sovereignty" over all others. Before the Civil War, civil rights laws in Northern states were at times described in just such terms, as in 1857, when a Milwaukee newspaper declared that a law defending fugitive slaves "holds up the shield of State Sovereignty to protect citizens of Wisconsin from the aggressions of Slave Power."

The Framers had good reason to bestow sovereignty on the states. Well-acquainted with monarchy, the generation that brought this nation into being was exceedingly wary of what we now describe as a unitary executive. Influential men, wrote one New England minister in 1775, have "an insatiable lust of power"; in every age they lead "their blind confiding country-men into the very jaws of slavery, vassalage, and ruin."

The divided nature of American federalism was designed to check that grievous appetite. "Federalism was our Nation's own discovery," wrote Justice Anthony Kennedy in 1995. "The

Framers split the atom of sovereignty." Indeed, I would say that they split it twice over, not just into the triarchy of the legislature, the executive, and the judiciary, but also into the diarchy of state power and federal power, all with the explicit intention of destroying the monarchy of their youth.

The rendition of Anthony Burns vividly demonstrates the tension inherent in the split atom of state and federal power. Early in his angry essay, Thoreau calls the reader's attention to two laws with which Massachusetts intended to express its sovereignty, and which, had they been obeyed, might have prevented Burns' removal. The first of these was a statute in 1837 meant to guarantee trial by jury to an alleged fugitive; the second, from 1843, made it illegal for state officials to help detain anyone claimed as a fugitive slave.

These two laws are typical of the many "personal liberty laws" that all Northern states adopted before the Civil War in response to the Constitution's fugitive slave clause:

> No Person held to . . . Labour in one State . . . escaping into another, shall . . . be discharged from such . . . Labour, but shall be delivered up on Claim of the Party to whom such . . . Labour may be due.

Written in the passive voice, the clause says nothing about how or by whom the fugitive should be "delivered up"; it simply grants "the Party" a general right of recaption by self-help alone. As for fugitives themselves, they appear only as the objects of capture; no mention is made of their rights or those of free blacks who might be kidnapped into slavery. Personal liberty laws broke that silence, drawing their substance from the rights elsewhere enumerated in the Constitution: the right to trial by jury, to testify on one's own behalf, to *habeas corpus*, to the assistance of counsel, and so forth.

The 1837 law cited by Thoreau — an "Act to restore the Trial by Jury, on questions of personal freedom" — specifically addressed the jury question. It declared that any person "imprisoned, restrained of his liberty, or held in duress . . . shall be entitled to the writ of personal replevin." A writ of replevin is a legal mechanism whereby, in normal circumstances, a hearing is held to return an unlawfully seized good to its owner. In the days of chattel slavery, when the "good" in question was a slave, that hearing would be before a jury, and in Massachusetts, where slavery had been illegal since 1783, no jury could be trusted to honor the claim of the fugitive's "owner."

Today there are parallel examples of state laws adopted in the face of federal power. To take just two of the many recently passed: Illinois' recent Bivens Act empowers individuals to sue and seek damages against ICE agents who violate their constitutional rights, and California's "No Secret Police Act" bans law enforcement from wearing masks while on duty. Illinois passed its law December 9, 2025; the Justice Department sued to block it on December 22. California passed its anti-mask law September 20, 2025; the Justice Department filed suit against it on November 17. Regardless of whether either law survives, both are well worth having public fights over. If the states win, they are rewarded with an affirmation of their rights. If they lose, the voters get clear confirmation that ICE is a paramilitary force operating outside the Constitution and that the masking of agents means they answer to no one but the president.

Back in the nineteenth century, when Northern states got into fights over personal liberty laws, they lost. The Supreme Court struck them all down in 1842. The case leading to that decision began when one Edward Prigg, agent for a slaveholder in Maryland, arrested the alleged runaways Margaret Morgan and her children and brought them before a justice of the peace in York County, Pennsylvania, seeking a warrant for rendition. The justice, however, pursuant to Pennsylvania's own personal liberty laws, refused to consider the matter. Finding that he had no recourse to law, Prigg then took his captives back to Maryland, whereupon a Pennsylvania grand jury indicted him for kidnapping.

Prigg's challenge to that charge made its way to the U.S. Supreme Court, where Justice Joseph Story delivered the opinion. *Prigg v. Pennsylvania* upheld an absolute right of recaption and declared void all state laws interfering with that right. The Constitution's fugitive slave clause, Story wrote, extended "a new and positive right . . . confined to no territorial limits, and bounded by no State institutions or policy." Any law that "interrupts, limits, delays, or postpones" the enjoyment of that right "is repugnant to the provisions of the Constitution of the United States, and is therefore void."

Sweeping away all rights that Northern states had sought to secure for free blacks and fugitives, Story's decision closed out the pro-civil rights phase of this history and initiated a new one, the noncooperation phase, well exemplified by the second of the two laws that Thoreau cited: in 1843, Massachusetts passed a statute explicitly "making it penal for any officer of the 'Commonwealth' to 'detain or aid in the . . . detention . . . of any person . . . claimed as a fugitive slave.'" Behind the dry language of that law lay a case that began only a few months after Justice Story issued his opinion. In Boston, on October 19, 1842, a certain Constable Stratton arrested a young black man, George Latimer, claimed as a runaway by one James Gray of Virginia. Both Stratton's and Latimer's jailer, a man named Cunningham, were paid to act as Gray's agents. At first, despite the *Prigg* decision, Latimer's defenders sought to use the powers of the 1837 law guaranteeing a jury trial on questions of personal freedom. That went nowhere. The jailer Cunningham refused to deliver his prisoner and Massachusetts Chief Justice Lemuel Shaw, following *Prigg*, declared that Latimer had no rights under that or any other state law. Turning the tables in hopes of making their own use *Prigg*, Latimer's defenders then sought to have all local officials — the constable Stratton and the jailer Cunningham — stripped of their powers, given that, following Justice Story's logic, actions taken under color of state authority no longer had any place in fugitive slave cases.

During the weeks when all of this was going on, a tremendous outcry arose against the possible rendition. When Latimer was first detained, a crowd of hundreds of mostly black men almost immediately gathered and threatened to rescue him from the Court House. At the end of the month, at a mass biracial meeting in Faneuil Hall, curses were laid upon the Constitution while Frederick Douglass, William Lloyd Garrison, and others set about inciting the crowd to rescue the captive. A special *Latimer Journal* began to circulate, the editors declaring that "the slave shall never leave Boston even if . . . our streets pour with blood." Finally, a petition circulated demanding that the Suffolk County sheriff order his subordinate, Cunningham, to release his prisoner. The sheriff did so.

That did not make Latimer a free man, but it put the enslaver Gray in a fix. True, Massachusetts law could no longer help the fugitive, but this didn't mean that anyone in the state was obliged to help the claimant. Quite the opposite. If James Gray wanted to take Latimer back to Virginia, he would have to do so by self-help alone in a city fully primed to rescue him by force. Finally, on November 18, Gray released his claim for $400 ($15,000 today) and George Latimer walked free.

What became obvious during the Latimer case was an ironic consequence of *Prigg*: if personal liberty laws were "repugnant to the Constitution," if these laws were "void," then perhaps it was time to turn an inability to act into a refusal to act. Four months after Latimer was released, Massachusetts passed its first noncooperation law. In three brief paragraphs, "An Act to further protect Personal Liberty" prohibited the use of state jails to hold fugitives, forbade judges from issuing certificates of rendition, and made it punishable by fines and imprisonment for any state officer to aid in the detention of a runaway. A later extension of this act added more penalties: state officers could be impeached if they granted certificates of rendition, attorneys could no longer practice in Massachusetts if they helped claimants, and jailers who imprisoned alleged fugitives were themselves to be imprisoned and fined. These statutes do not merely suggest noncooperation with the laws of slavery, they require it. They are a codification of civil disobedience.

Two seemingly inevitable steps followed the shift in the 1840s to noncooperation. First, a new Federal Fugitive Slave Law was enacted in 1850, a forced-cooperation mirror image of the Latimer

Law. "All good citizens are hereby commanded to aid and assist" in the rendition of slaves, it reads, and those who hinder that process "shall" be subject to fines and imprisonment.

Second, when Northerners refused to honor that law, as they did in the Burns and many other cases, slaveholding states seceded from the Union, some directly citing personal liberty laws as a cause. South Carolina's "Declaration of Immediate Causes" is typical: "We assert that fourteen of the States have deliberately refused, for years past, to fulfill their constitutional obligations, and we refer to their own Statutes for the proof."

That was dated December 20, 1860. A month later the newly formed Confederate States bombarded Fort Sumter and the Civil War began.

Now

The threat of violence has always shadowed the promise of divided sovereignty. In describing the state-federal diarchy, Madison warned that fights would surely arise "between the two jurisdictions," and that "an appeal to the sword and a dissolution of the compact" could easily follow. When it came to the fight over slavery, those were exactly the appeals regularly heard, decade after decade, with states on both sides promising blood in the streets and civil war should their sovereignty be challenged.

Thoreau's speech after the rendition of Anthony Burns places him among those willing to call for violence in defense of states' rights. Abolitionists had failed to get Burns before a jury, not for want of effort, he said, but "for want of sufficient force": the state should have faced federal troops with troops of its own and met violence with violence. A Northern anti-slavery doctrine of states' right was pitted against a Southern pro-slavery doctrine of states' rights.

Thoreau was never an advocate of nonviolent action. He was an unapologetic defender of John Brown, saying, in regard to the raid on Harpers Ferry, "for once the Sharp's rifles and revolvers were employed in a righteous cause." In the Burns case, a deputy U.S. marshal had been killed by the mob trying to free Burns from the Court House, and Thoreau called their actions "heroic" and never mentioned the homicide. He strikes the same note toward the end of "Slavery in Massachusetts," framing it there in opposition to his more peaceful pursuits: "We walk to lakes to see our serenity reflected in them . . . Who can be serene in a country where both the rulers and the ruled are without principle? The remembrance of my country spoils my walk. My thoughts are murder to the State."

I doubt that Madison thought of his warning about violence and secession as prophetic; in context it appears mostly to highlight his optimistic suggestion that, when it came to conflicts between the sovereignties, some "tribunal" would be found to "impartially" adjudicate their differences. In the fullness of time that task has fallen to the Supreme Court which, before the Civil War, took the Constitution's Fugitive Slave Clause as the warrant for consistently ruling against the Northern states in conflicts over slavery.

In today's conflicts, the Trump administration has gone to great lengths to find some similar Constitutional basis to legitimize its encroachments on state sovereignty. To begin with the president federalizing the National Guard, an executive order issued on his first day in office declared that "a national emergency exists at the southern border of the United States" and that it was Trump's duty "to protect each of the States against invasion," a phrase lifted (oddly without attribution) from the Constitution. In addition, a clause in Article I gives Congress the power "to provide for calling forth the Militia to execute the Laws of the Union, suppress Insurrections and repel Invasions." In fact, that is one of the enumerated powers of Congress, not of the executive; but in an act in 1903 and its later amendments, Congress delegated their power to the president whenever there is "danger of invasion by a foreign nation," or "a rebellion or danger of a rebellion" against the government, or when the president "is unable with the regular forces" to execute the law.

Last year, with the day-one "emergency" and "invasion" in hand, and with permission seemingly granted by that 1903 statute, it was a small step for a memorandum on June 7 to state that the "violence and disorder" of the protests against ICE "constitute a form of rebellion" and thus require federalizing the National Guard. (And nationwide!) On the very next day Trump directed cabinet officials to take any action necessary "to liberate Los Angeles from the Migrant Invasion," and soon, over Governor Gavin Newsom's objections, U.S. Marines and the California National Guard were active in the city.

Newsom quickly filed suit, whereupon a federal District Judge issued a restraining order and returned control of the National Guard to the governor. The president's "actions were illegal," he wrote, "both exceeding the scope of his statutory authority and violating the Tenth Amendment." The protests in question "fall far short of 'rebellion,'" and to claim otherwise "is untenable and dangerous." In December, the Supreme Court issued its own narrow ruling: Trump failed "to show that [the 1903 statute] permits the President to federalize the Guard."

Score one for states' rights.

State and local "sanctuary" policies make for a second site of conflict "between the two jurisdictions," and a more critical one, given that the deportation crusade, with its haste, its shackles, and its daily body count, is so central to Trump's domestic policy. Adopted by states from New York to California and cities from Chicago to New Orleans, sanctuary policies echo the antebellum personal liberty laws in several ways: their purpose is to protect a vulnerable population, and their tactics amount to noncooperation. "Not" is the ruling modifier of their verbs. Law enforcement shall not stop, arrest, or search anyone solely for their immigration status; schools shall not ask students about their status; counties shall not lease out their jails to hold federal detainees, and so on.

One important legal distinction limits the range of this noncooperation. Contrary to Trump's propaganda, *sanctuary policies offer no sanctuary to actual criminals*. Being in the country unlawfully is a civil, not a criminal, offense and the policies therefore always have one proviso added to their negatives: "don't do this, don't do that," they say, "*except in response to a criminal warrant.*" California's sanctuary law, the "Values Act," even includes a long list of the crimes that might trigger such warrants, everything from assault and battery to torture and mayhem. The lesser violations of immigration law, however, are federal matters; locally, no action need be taken just because someone is an undocumented alien.

But why not cooperate? Why resist joining forces with Homeland Security and ICE? The answer is plain: both experience and research have shown, and common decency demands, that when it comes to community safety, health, and economic wellbeing, trust and common purpose make better foundations than cruelty and fearmongering. It matters that immigrants are not afraid to seek medical help, report a crime, go to church, or send their children to school. On the law enforcement side, it matters that scarce resources stay focused on local crime and that the lines of accountability and liability between the two sovereignties remain clear.

It is an added benefit that sanctuary policies protect the labor and taxes that immigrants contribute to the community. In 2022, nationwide, over $37 billion tax dollars from the undocumented helped fund schools, hospitals, and social services. In communities that adopt sanctuary policies, employment and income are higher, and poverty and public assistance needs are lower. Above all, crime is lower — a fact that should come as no surprise given that, sanctuary or not, crime rates of the undocumented are well below those of native-born Americans.

In one executive order, Trump claimed that sanctuary policies amount to "a lawless insurrection," ignoring the fact that, by constitutional design, the states have no role to play in immigration enforcement. (Arizona once tried to write its own immigration laws and the Supreme Court struck them down.) The federal government may request help from the states, but it cannot command it. As Justice Antonin Scalia wrote in 1997, "the Federal Government may not compel the States to implement, by legislation or executive action, federal regulatory programs." Last year a U.S. District Judge agreed when dismissing the Justice Department's suit against the state of Illinois: "The Sanctuary Policies reflect Defendants' decision to not participate in enforcing civil immigration law — a decision protected by the Tenth Amendment."

Score two for states' rights.

In any defense of states' rights, we need always ask, what is the right in question? Is it worth upholding? For the South before the Civil War, it was the right to own slaves; in the North it was the right to defend civil liberty on their own terms. Since then, it has been everything from the right to make voters pay poll taxes to the right to force state judges to retire at the age of seventy — the former struck down in 1966, the latter upheld in 1991.

Taken one at a time, these rights are but samples of the broad range of powers reserved to the states, as Madison pointed out when he returned to the issue in Federalist No. 45. The federal government's powers are "few and well defined," he wrote, while those left to the states "are numerous and indefinite . . . extend[ing] to all the objects which, in the ordinary course of affairs, concern the lives, liberties, and properties of the people." That rather nicely summarizes the "objects" that sanctuary policies are meant to defend and, when contrasted with the terror-tactics of immigrant removal, makes a twenty-first-century defense of states' rights almost mandatory.

It would not be hard to make a list of conflicts worth setting that defense in motion, but, with the abolitionists in mind, I will focus only on four that I find suggested by the old personal liberty laws, especially by a law that Massachusetts adopted in 1855 in the wake of the Anthony Burns affair.

First, remember that the volunteer militia, federalized by President Pierce, had willingly joined the posse enforcing the Fugitive Slave Act. One section of the 1855 law is a direct response to that cooperation: "The volunteer militia . . . shall not act in any manner in the seizure, detention or rendition of any person" claimed as a fugitive slave, and any member of the militia who does so shall be fined and imprisoned. Today, states should similarly command noncooperation from the National Guard in cases related to civil immigration enforcement. Given that Trump's federalization of the Guard has been judged illegal, and given that all soldiers have the right to disobey illegal orders, states could now command members of the National Guard not to act in any manner in the seizure, the detention, or the rendition of an immigrant (absent a judicial warrant, of course). Second, another section of the 1855 law commands the "Governor to appoint commissioners in each county to defend fugitives," and provides for the "Commissioners to be paid by State treasurer." Today, states should underwrite the defense of due process for immigrants, for children especially. New York State has done so, allotting $29 million in 2025 to add to $30 million previously budgeted to give legal support to immigrants fighting deportation. Third, the first section of the 1855 law expands on the earlier Latimer Law which forbade the use of "any jail or other building belonging to this Commonwealth" to detain anyone "claimed as a fugitive slave." Today, the states should likewise draw the line as to federal use of state property. Until recently, many states partnered with ICE and let their local jails be used to hold individuals suspected of immigration violations. Since Trump was elected, about a dozen states have banned this practice. And fourth, the 1855 bill threatens prison sentences of one or two years and fines of $1,000 or $2,000 for those who cooperate with the apparatus of slavery (that would be about $35,000 or $70,000 today).

Sanctuary policies never state direct punishments for individuals who cooperate with immigration enforcement, nor should they do so. Intended to build communities of trust, their practices are about cooperation, not about law and punishment. The policies could, however, be more declarative about the financial consequences awaiting municipalities that get entangled with immigration enforcement. ICE agents often violate the civil rights of immigrants (and citizens), and while it is nearly impossible to extract damages from the federal government, with states and municipalities it is a different matter. In 2024, New York City paid $92.5 million in damages for collaborating with

ICE by holding thousands of prisoners in city jails long after their proper release dates.

Thoreau ends “Slavery in Massachusetts” with a description of the white waterlily which, like the lotus, feeds on muck to form a fine and fragrant flower. It is an invocation of hope. It is also a mistake. 1854 was not a time for transcendental cheer. Things were dire, and “murder to the State” was the proper ending.

Things today are dire in different ways, but dire still. Cities may hold the line in the attacks on sanctuary, but what then? Sanctuary policies seek to form communities of trust, but trust is slow to build and easy to destroy. In all the neighborhoods terrorized by ICE, it has already been destroyed and it will certainly not reappear in my lifetime.

Besides, right now immigrants are the target, but the target is not the point. Power is the point. Should Trump ever run out of immigrants to harass, he will find fresh victims and the theater of cruelty will play on. In one executive order, Trump instructed the Secretary of Defense “[to] ensure the availability of a standing National Guard quick reaction force . . . available for rapid nationwide deployment.” That will come in handy if the happy No Kings parades get too much traction, or if “rebellions” arise during the midterm elections.

The leaders of two great liberation movements of the last century, Mahatma Gandhi and Martin Luther King, Jr., shared the daring assumption that nonviolent action could wake the conscience of a nation. In Gandhi’s case, as King once pointed out, the British had “some degree of moral conscience,” and King himself would regularly invoke the conscience “of millions of white Americans.” I stand in awe of the faith of these men, but my own has been shaken. I am haunted by a remark made by Nadezhda Mandelstam, writing about Stalin’s decades of terror: “Strange to say, the word ‘conscience’ had gone out of ordinary use.”

To wake and school the conscience of a nation is a long-term affair, and right now much of the country is chaos-weary and eager for sleep. The current authoritarian oligarchy keeps eating away at the Framers' divisions of power, and it remains to be seen whether the sovereignty promised to the states is truly inviolable and able to hold the line.

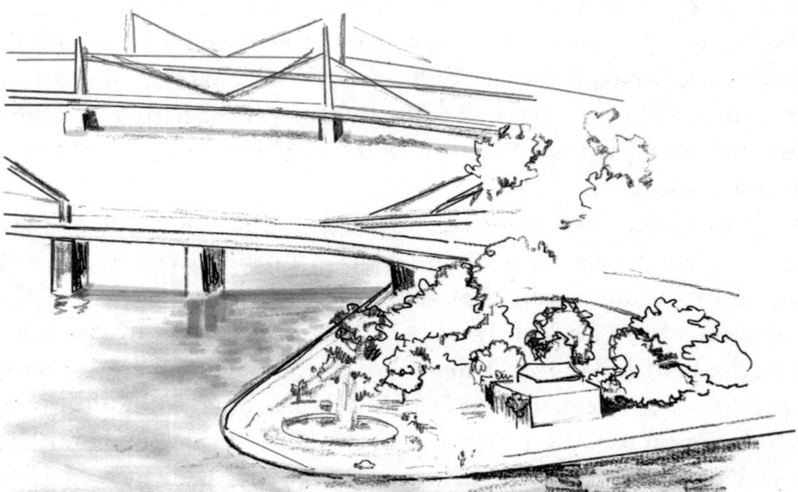

CARRIE WILLIAMS CLIFFORD

Character or Color—Which?

What is blood, or what is birth?
What is black or white?
Or small or great, or rich or poor?
Just so the man's all right?
O, vain and haughty white man, why
Of ancestry prate so?
Can you in tracing your descent.
Farther than Adam go?
Why boast of culture ? Well you know.
Ere to your present state
Of progress and renown you'd come,
(With statesmen wise and great —)
The blacks had splendidly achieved
Long centuries before;
Their monuments, unrivaled still,
Adorn old Afric's shore.
No adventitious circumstance
Can fix a people's station.
Integrity's the thing that counts
In any man or nation.
Then modestly let's run our course —
All hist'ry tells the story:
No race but has its page of shame.
None lacks its page of glory.
So what is blood or what is birth?
What is black or white?
Or great or small, or rich or poor.
Just so the man's all right?

(1911)

BETWEEN TWO SHORES OF FREEDOM

ARMANDO CHAGUACEDA

I have had occasion in recent months to reformulate my own life story to myself. The last twenty-two years of my life have been taken up with my defense of the liberal democratic project and the exile imposed as punishment for that commitment. This quest began, intellectually, with my dissertation, whose subject was Hispanic American liberalism. The fact that it was the first research on the subject in the first graduating class of the first Master's program in political science in the history of Cuba indicates just how challenging the endeavor was. Having overcome, with some effort, the censorship and the dogmatism endemic to our professors' Leninism, my inquiry into my subject became the first text about liberalism with an explanatory — and not pejorative — intention published in Castro's Cuba.

In very little time I evolved from a democratic socialist informed by classical Marxism to a liberal inspired by the legacy of John Stuart Mill, Carlo Rosselli, and Norberto Bobbio. My hope initially had been to try and reform Cuban society from within, but struggle, police pressure within the university, and the social pressure within spaces organized by the group of young professors and artists to which I belonged nullified that aspiration. The minimal courage to defend what one considers both reasonable and just, despite the overwhelming nature of the undertaking and the possibility of defeat, grew within me from that moment on. Like Alexander Herzen, I didn't believe we were likely to prevail, but I felt it was right — politically, intellectually, and morally — to persist.

But the context was not conducive to dissent — not even of the most minimal kind, or that confined to the intellectual sphere. For within the Cuban system — a replica of the Soviet model — there exists a centralized commission at the Academy of Sciences that determines the appropriateness (or lack thereof) of conducting specific postgraduate studies, as well as who is permitted to undertake them. There is no opportunity to opt out of the state system and pursue postgraduate studies at a private university, since private universities do not exist. In my case — aside from being a professor critical of the system — I became embroiled in a direct dispute with the then-director of the Academy's Social

Sciences division, who accused me of harboring "ideological issues" by employing the concept of "State Socialism" to characterize the Cuban system during an international conference of Marxists held in Havana in 2004. Following that incident, both research topics that I had proposed for my Ph.D. — pluralism within Marxist political theory and civil society in Cuba — were vetoed. It rapidly became clear that my liberal loyalties foreclosed any possibility of completing a doctorate in my own country and I was forced to travel abroad to pursue my studies.

The threats were very concrete: I would not be able to work in Cuba on academic matters, and if I continued to publish and to express my views, I could end up in prison. During that time I continued to deepen my knowledge of and commitment to the liberal tradition. But on my second trip to Cuba, I was met with a "reception operation" involving agents at the airport — a ridiculous waste of resources and personnel, serving no purpose other than intimidation. Throughout my stay on the island agents shadowed me around the city. On my penultimate day I was subjected to an interrogation (an illegal one, conducted at an unofficial interrogation facility) that lasted five hours. There was no physical violence, but the psychological pressure was intense. Both before and after that incident — indeed, throughout the entire period — my family and my wife's family (including relatives who worked for the government) were threatened. I was informed that I would not be welcome back in my native country. Thus began my life in exile.

I learned the value of freedom on the day that exile ceased to be a metaphor and became my condition. Being expelled from one's country by a communist dictatorship is not the same as any other trip across the border. That journey came with the collapse of the moral universe in which I was raised. The place that shaped my language, my affections, my earliest hopes, turned overnight into a space that could no longer tolerate my voice. And so defending freedom stopped being my intellectual orientation and became an existential obligation.

Exile forces clarity; it strips away the luxury of neutrality. When the state claims to embody history, justice, and the people themselves, disagreement is synonymous with betrayal. In my native country, the Castro regime perfected this logic over decades: it monopolized ideals of equality and sovereignty while dismantling pluralism, crushing civic autonomy, and converting fear into a method of governance. Castro created a system that spoke endlessly of liberation while denying the most basic freedoms. Living under that contradiction taught me that freedom is indivisible, and that any project that sacrifices it in the name of a supposedly higher ideal ends by devouring human dignity.

In Mexico I entered a society scarred by traumas and inequalities, but also one with an open public square, competitive elections, and a vibrant civil society. Mexican democracy as I first encountered it was imperfect, noisy, and often frustrating — but it was alive. I could write, speak, and organize, and I could disagree. Mexico became not just a refuge, but a second civic homeland, a place where I could practice the freedom that had been denied me.

Yet history is rarely linear, and gratitude does not immunize one against disappointment. Over time, I began to witness the erosion of democratic norms in my country of exile. Populist rhetoric started to hollow out institutions. The government concentrated power in the name of "the people" while delegitimizing pluralism and independent oversight. Critical voices were dismissed as enemies or elites. Complex realities were reduced to moral binaries. The very language I recognized from my Cuban past — though in a different key — echoed throughout my new home.

This double experience — authoritarianism at home and democratic decay abroad — taught me that liberty is not a static location which you travel to and then live in, but a fragile process that requires constant defense. It also taught me that freedom cannot be monopolized by any ideology. In Cuba, it was suffocated in the name of state socialism; in Mexico and elsewhere, it is threatened in the name of blood-and-soil nationalism and illiberal populism. The lesson is clear: extremisms of all kinds share a common contempt for limits, rights, and dissent.

For that reason, my ideological loyalty is first and foremost to democratic liberalism that is consciously trans-ideological. I have learned, sometimes painfully, that defending freedom means building bridges with those who do not share all my beliefs but respect the elementary rules of coexistence. This trans-ideological solidarity forces one to eschew excusing abuses because they come from "our side." Authoritarianism does not become benign when it claims progressive goals, nor does repression become acceptable by virtue of being popular. Rights are "inalienable" — you cannot vote your ontological right away even if you can debase yourself by refusing to enshrine it in law.

Exile has taught me the necessity of realism. Political power is necessary in order to defend anything at all, including freedom. Whereas certain principles are eternal, moreover, people live in a world shaped by ephemeral asymmetries of power and historical constraints which must be reckoned with in order to safeguard freedom as best as possible. Realists cannot afford to eschew compromise. We must hold our noses and work with dirty actors, and accept half-victories, and learn to live with disappointment, which is always better than resignation. And all this must be acknowledged while still protecting liberal idealism. Otherwise we will lose sight entirely of our reason for fighting at all.

The challenge, as I have come to understand it, is to steer between these two poles — realism and idealism — without veering entirely into either one. One can acknowledge the limits of what is possible while still insisting on what is necessary. One can negotiate, prioritize, and adapt without renouncing the core principles of freedom and human rights. Given these ideological commitments, I try to orient myself practically by posing two questions. What is, in a specific place, the most direct, powerful, and immediate threat to the people and freedoms of that place? What and who are the concrete allies, resources, and strategic possibilities available to the people and freedoms under threat? I like to call this stance "liberal realism"...and no, it is not at all an oxymoron. Quite the contrary.

Liberal realism requires adherents to grapple with the messiness of our imperfect world. Simplistic binaries are antithetical to our project. We will lend support to left-wing or right-wing democratic movements and leaders if, in their contexts, they are the option with the greatest opportunity and/or legitimacy to defeat illiberal populism or open autocracies. We will be unhappy voters most of the time, which will be one sign that we are responsible voters. If and when democratic health has been restored in the countries in which I have political agency, I will prioritize criteria of ideology or public policy — but not before.

In both my country of birth and my country of refuge, I have chosen the path of liberal realism, despite the costs. Not because I believe in inevitable progress, but because I believe in responsibility. My voice may be drowned out, but silence would surely be a form of complicity. Exile has taken many things from me, but it has also given me a vantage point: the ability to recognize patterns, to connect struggles, to insist that no society is immune to democratic regression.

Today, when I look back at the road that brought me here, I see not only loss but continuity. The same conviction that once made me uncomfortable in Havana now sustains me in Mexico and beyond. It is the conviction that freedom is worth defending precisely because it is fragile, because it can be degraded slowly, even legally, until one day it is gone. To remember this is to honor those who resisted before me and to stand with those who resist now.

On her journey into exile in the United States, Hannah Arendt was only allowed to take one book with her, and she chose the tragedies of Aeschylus. On August 4, 1940, while escaping from France to Portugal, shortly before her voyage, she concluded a letter to her husband Gunther Stern with these memorable words from *The Persians*: "The battle is for everything." In the current situation, we liberals must embrace every struggle — in the intellectual arena, in electoral politics, in social mobilizations, in solidarity with nations resisting the plunder of tyrannical invaders — as part of the struggle for a common universal heritage: the right to have rights in open, just, and free societies.

Despite everything — the disappointments, the setbacks, the long reach of my origin-authoritarians — I refuse to despair. All of history has not been written yet. Authoritarian projects may seem strong, but they are brittle, sustained by fear and conformity. Democracies may falter, but they retain a unique capacity for self-correction, if citizens choose to act. I hold on to that belief not as a certainty, but as a commitment. From exile, from uncertainty, from the margins, I will continue to defend freedom. And in that shared effort, across borders and languages and ideologies, I must believe that in the end we will prevail.

THE RELOCATION

MEG VLAUN

The house is a monolith, where southwest adobe meets Tuscan villa. Swallows nest in it shifted terra cotta roof tiles. Doves mate in a decorative mini-cupola as though it were designed for their union's ceremony. On the north side, away from the street, cracks spider across the stucco where moisture confronts dry heat.

The residents don't seem to notice. We rarely see them come or go.

Six months back, we watched out our window — rapt — as the proprietor's plump younger sister, Kiana, supervised *jardineros* who pruned away all lower branches on every evergreen, then removed a desert willow that served as a border between our driveways.

"He wants to see the volcanoes," she said as we rolled our trash can to the street.

Looking west to the three pockmarks on the horizon, we nodded. We thought we understood.

Huddled together over satellite imagery at our kitchen table, we explored the house's irregular footprint: jutting rooms and tiered peaks. We gaze every morning — while working, writing — over its desiccated dirt yard and wonder about the depths of shadow that comprise its interior: here may be an arched window filled with towering houseplants, but just there must be a cloaked corner. And there. An unoccupied bedroom? Sometimes, by some phantom hand, a door opens on the second story balcony, and we imagine a voice: *...to take in the afternoon*.

We met the proprietors once, a middle-aged Iranian couple about our age, Leila and Dilan. As we interfaced from our parallel driveways, Leila explained: she is a cardiac surgeon sharing her time between Albuquerque and Santa Fe. Her husband, a medical equipment engineer and technician, spends most of his time in the air, commuting between health centers across the United States They moved to this country for the freedom, the education, the opportunity, to thrive.

In their home with them, Leila further explained, abide her aging parents.

Honestly, we couldn't tell you even what sorts of cars they drive. We think one is a black (or silver, or red) Tesla. The other might be a Porsche. You see, we rarely see them come or go.

Leila never mentioned children, and to be respectful, we asked no questions.

Sometimes we pull into our driveway and witness a withered man, perhaps in his late seventies, perched on a large boulder by the road. The first few times we bustled past, parked the car in the garage, and shut the door. He reminded us of the ones we see on Central, now an apocalyptic Route 66, hunched and unstable, tripping behind stolen Target shopping carts packed with bedding and recyclables, on the hunt for their next hit. Or someplace to rest.

"My father," Leila said later, drawing a package from her mailbox. "It's Parkinson's."

Now when we pass him on his stone in the austere sun, we half stare, half wave.

Half stricken.

Our cleaning lady worked for Leila and Dilan until she quit: six bedrooms and six baths, she said, was her limit. The villa's interior took a more distinct shape in our imagination that day, a sprawling mausoleum — or something between cathedral and crypt.

For a time before we moved into this home, we realized that our own children were not our whole life, that they would eventually become adults and leave, and that we must each have some sense of self, purpose, and identity beyond parenthood to sustain us after their departure. Somehow, this crisis led to an obsession with the bleakness and solitude of death, then a terror of death, and finally landed us where every aging human mind must eventually land: researching the elongation of life.

Longevity investigation guided us back toward family: one of the greatest predictors of longevity is community. To survive longer, the biologist and derontologist Valter Longo insists, we must surround ourselves with those who value us, who need us. Most commonly, he writes, this need is fulfilled by our children who then have children. By family.

At this precise moment, our children are leaving home, and we are torn between the solitary, self-fulfilling lives of writers — and Longo's assertion that we need family for health.

We want to move to an A-frame mountain lodge with high raftered ceilings and soaring windows in the remote hills of western, rural North Carolina. We want a life of no distractions — of solitude — to write the next Great American Novels. But wants apparently conflict with needs.

Four times since we moved to Albuquerque, the hush of clear desert night has been rent by sirens and flashing blue-red lights. EMTs rush into the manse next door. We imagine Leila's father's prone body rhythmically depressed into a Tempur-Pedic mattress under each pulse of a medic's hands. We imagine Leila's mother watching on from a corner, hand over mouth, wondering if this EMT visit will be the last. We imagine, in horror, that neither Leila nor Dilan are home. Leila, on night shift at Presbyterian Cardiology or perhaps at a hotel in Santa Fe, might of the event in the moment by phone. Dilan might not hear of it until the following day.

Each time, sirens fade to silence. Lights extinguish. Fire trucks and ambulances filter away — back southwest toward Central. Within a few days, the balcony door opens for a few hours, then closes. After a week or two, a withered man reappears perched on the boulder by the street, torso swaying, arms gesticulating.

As Leila's father passes these fading days alone with his wife in a villa nestled between three volcanoes and Sandia's cragged, lofty peak, we contemplate their happiness. We envision the family tree they left behind in Iran: profuse, profligate, verdant, and tiered with three, four, five generations. Might siblings' children's children have been better company than an absent daughter and these three somber sisters? Or are they so self-fulfilled that the hollow castle is enough?

Discomfited, mid-thought, we turn from the window.

The sepulcher yields to its muted status quo, and we rarely see them come or go.

INTERVIEWS WITH THE RIOT POLICE IN IRAN

ROXANA SABERI

April 21, 2026

The officer in Iran's riot police force said that since U.S.-Israeli airstrikes began on February 28, his phone number had changed six times and that each week a new superior would arrive and then vanish.

"They go elsewhere and new people come in," he said. "And all the commanders keep changing their houses."

Many of his fellow officers had been killed in the bombardments, he said, and a soldier he knew had his legs blown off when his barracks were bombed.

"We are all broken," he said. "To be honest, we're all angry, and what's more, we're afraid to stay in our posts. We're more spread out now in public places such as hospitals or malls. Hardly anyone remains on military bases anymore — no more than one or two people."

It was mid-April, days after a fragile ceasefire had taken effect. I had been corresponding with the officer, a member of the Kurdish minority in western Iran, since early January. He had agreed to answer questions from me, but only through written hand-delivered messages — and only on condition of anonymity, out of fear of the regime's retaliation.

"Send me your questions," I was instructed by our intermediary, a close friend who knew the officer and his family. "I'll have a trusted contact deliver them in person."

I messaged my questions, then waited with some skepticism. Authorities were bracing for a sharp escalation in anti-regime protests across the country, and I did not expect an officer who would likely be tasked with repressing them to reply, let alone to provide a candid account.

Yet the officer went on to respond to my questions three times over several weeks. Each set of his answers chronicled a deepening disillusionment and desperation with his profession — and the regime. His is a rare perspective of the turbulent months at the start of the year: the nationwide unrest in January, the bloody crackdown that followed, and the war — as he tried to navigate a command structure that he said viewed Kurdish members like him with suspicion.

January 7, 2026: Under Stress and "on Standby"

In the first week of January, protests that had begun as an outcry against a cratering economy were rapidly evolving into a nationwide uprising. Protesters started demanding the wholesale dismantling of the theocratic regime that has ruled Iran since the Revolution of 1979. Sensing the momentum, opposition groups and the exiled son of Iran's late Shah began calling on Iranians to march en masse on January 8.

Security forces had been relying mostly on tear gas, birdshot, and mass arrests to break up crowds. Yet blunt warnings from the regime — notably Supreme Leader Ayatollah Ali Khamenei's declaration that "rioters must be put in their place" — foreshadowed a turn toward lethal force.

In previous rounds of unrest — from the student protests in 1999 and the Green Movement in 2009 to the nationwide demonstrations in 2017 and 2019 and the "Woman, Life, Freedom" uprising in 2022 — primary responsibility for suppressing dissent had fallen to a multilayered security apparatus. This included the Islamic Revolutionary Guard Corps; its subordinate, volunteer Basij paramilitary; the Ministry of Intelligence; and the riot police, known as the Special Units, or *Yegan-e Vizheh*.

The Special Units are a specialized force within FARAJA, Iran's law enforcement command, distinguishable by their green fatigues and helmets (or in the case of their elite anti-terror unit, all black uniforms and balaclavas), as well as their SUVs and armored vehicles, As Brigadier General Hassan Karami, a former commander of the units, once explained, these forces are deployed when regular law enforcement "cannot calm the situation and unrest spreads."

Operating at both the national and provincial levels, the Special Units maintained at least 60,000 deployable personnel in 2013, according to FARAJA's then-commander. While commanders claim that the forces rely mostly on water cannons, batons, and shields to disperse crowds, in recent years they have been increasingly documented opening fire on civilians with metal birdshot, Kalashnikovs, sniper rifles, and DShK heavy machine guns, according to security analysts and news outlets such as *IranWire*.

"I have received his answers," our intermediary messaged me on Wednesday, January 7. The courier had returned from meeting the officer, carrying his written responses.

"We have been told to be fully on standby for tomorrow" read one reply.

"There is a lot of disagreement now among security forces" over whether a harsh crackdown would restore order or further fuel public fury, the officer said. "There is 100% confusion" within the Special Units.

Key decisions were being made in closed-door meetings and withheld from officers like him, he said. "I don't know what's happening," adding that "upstairs" the "management" were almost all Shiite Muslim, while he and his counterparts were members of Iran's minority Sunni Muslim community. "They're doing things in secret, and we're afraid of what's coming."

"There is chaos everywhere, in the city, in homes, in the streets, and within the police forces, too," he added. "I know all the officers in my station, and they believe the regime is collapsing." And he continued: "We don't have permission to use live ammunition yet, unless an order comes . . . that you can go ahead and shoot. If they feel there's a big possibility of [regime] collapse, there's a higher likelihood we'll be told to shoot to kill."

Many of his fellow officers and soldiers, he said, were under intense stress.

"My own family is urging me to take off my uniform and leave this job because they're all against the regime," the officer said, adding that he was "strongly against" using deadly force to confront protesters. "I have not been able to kill a single sheep in my life. I'm in the police force for the income — not to kill people."

He said he feared the moment his commanders might order live fire. "If I disobey," he wrote, "they'll kill me."

On Thursday, January 8, as the journalist Fatemeh Jamalpour and I were messaging our contacts in Iran for an article we were co-writing, our communications suddenly went silent. The regime, we suspected, had triggered a total telecommunications blackout, a sign that it could be preparing to carry out violence under the cover of digital darkness.

The next morning, I woke up around 5 AM to a series of messages from a doctor I knew in Tehran. He had bypassed the blackout through an illegal Starlink satellite connection.

"Put this news out," his message read. "The internet is cut and nobody knows yet." The number of people killed last night in several hospitals that I'm sure about..."

Milad: Around 70
Imam Hossein: 70
Ibn Sina: 23
Labbafi Nejad: 7
Fayaz Bakhsh: 15
Shahriar: 32

I understood what this meant: the regime had begun to murder protesters, and these estimates of fatalities in Tehran were likely only a small fraction of the actual death toll.

As the days passed, witness accounts; images of security forces — including members of the police, Basij, and Revolutionary Guards — firing live ammunition and military-grade weapons at unarmed protesters; bloodied Iranians struggling to carry one another to safety; and rows of body bags at morgues broke through the blackout. We began to piece together a picture of a massacre.

"I saw five young people fall," one protester texted. "At first, I thought they might be wounded, but then I saw their brains burst onto the ground."

In the northern Iranian city of Rasht, a medical worker told us he and his colleagues treated hundreds of patients on the night of January 8 alone. Most, he said, were struck by multiple pellets or bullets, targeting "their heads and necks, their chests, their femurs, their abdomens."

Around forty percent of them, he said, did not survive — and that did not include the countless others who were declared dead upon arrival. "They were shooting to kill, absolutely," he said on condition of anonymity.

He and other medical providers also told us of regime efforts to restrict them from caring for the injured — raiding hospitals, stationing security forces in wards, registering protesters' identities, and arresting patients.

Iranians across the country were also reporting a highly securitized atmosphere: heavily armed units at checkpoints; the deployment of armored vehicles in some areas; nighttime curfews; and mass arrests.

Nearly 54,000 protesters were detained, the Washington-based Human Rights Activists News Agency (HRANA) later documented, and rights groups and news agencies reported that at least 14 Iranians linked to the January protests were hanged between March and mid-May, with many others facing charges, such as "waging war against God," that could be punishable by death.

January 28, 2026: Machine Guns and Grenades

Twenty days after the massacre, the officer responded to a second set of questions in a tone marked by anguish. "What can you tell us about what happened on January 8? Were you ordered to use live ammunition? Were any foreign forces, such as Iraqi forces, brought in to help?"

This was his reply:

> On the 17th of *Dey* [January 7], the day before the mass killing, we could hear people speaking mostly in Arabic on the floor above our office. That same night, several vehicles full of forces — about half of them, Iraqis — transported us to [local Kurdish provinces].
>
> With my own eyes, I saw them opening fire on many apartments, and I swear that whenever I fired I deliberately shot in the wrong direction because I was afraid that they would kill me from behind if I didn't shoot at all.
>
> I saw several machine guns moving alongside us from different sides. I saw several grenades thrown toward the people. I was crying inside, but I was afraid to do anything.
>
> Many of the Iranian forces were afraid like me. God is my witness.
>
> I did not see chemical agents [used against protesters] myself, but some of the forces were saying they had brought them and used them on the people.
>
> I saw many wounded, and there were plainclothes men who spoke Persian, and they were the people who fired the finishing shots.
>
> I swear on the lives of my children, I

> saw them deliver *coup de grâce* shots to dozens of people. May the Great God have mercy on us.

I asked another question. "Have you or your colleagues been deployed to hospitals, and if so, under what orders? Have you heard anything about "finishing shots" being fired at the injured inside hospitals?"

He replied:

> They sent many [forces] to the clinics. I didn't enter the hospitals, but they were full of wounded people. I saw the men in black uniforms and the plainclothes agents going inside, and I heard the sound of screams and gunfire.

April 14, 2026: "Every day and night, I pray."

In our final exchange, the officer shared his perspective on the war and the tenuous ceasefire.

His answers reflected a palpable relief that the fighting appeared to be ending — even as the regime he professed to despise remained entrenched in power.

"The truth is we are all afraid, and our wish is peace and reconciliation," he wrote. "We are tired. Every day and night, I pray. I believe in God and I know our life will become better. There will definitely be peace."

The strikes had killed senior regime leaders, most notably Supreme Leader Ayatollah Ali Khamenei. At least 1,221 military personnel and 1,701 civilians had also been killed in thirty-nine days of war, according to HRANA.

During wartime, the Special Units — and all police units — are tasked with maintaining "law and order" and preventing suspected collaboration with foreign powers, according to Farzin Nadimi, a senior fellow at The Washington Institute specializing in Iranian security and defense.

However, in response to a question about the orders his own unit had been given, the officer said only that he had not been ordered to crush any internal dissent. "But I know that many people have been arrested and executed, in cases the media do not know," he wrote.

"How are you personally feeling?" I asked in my final question. "What do you fear and hope for most right now?"

His reply was less a political statement than a desperate plea for survival.

"I have nothing left to say. I swear to God, I have not been paid for two months. I have a wife and children. I have been told I'll be paid next week, but my wife has to stand in the bread lines now — it's appalling."

Even those tasked with defending the state, it seemed, had not been spared by the rising prices inflamed by the war, compounding the weight of decades of sanctions, mismanagement and corruption.

"I am tired," he concluded, "and I am taking my family from Iran toward Iraq."

FRANCES ELLEN WATKINS HARPER

Bury Me in a Free Land

Make me a grave where'er you will,
In a lowly plain, or a lofty hill;
Make it among earth's humblest graves,
But not in a land where men are slaves.

I could not rest if around my grave
I heard the steps of a trembling slave;
His shadow above my silent tomb
Would make it a place of fearful gloom.

I could not rest if I heard the tread
Of a coffle gang to the shambles led,
And the mother's shriek of wild despair
Rise like a curse on the trembling air.

I could not sleep if I saw the lash
Drinking her blood at each fearful gash,
And I saw her babes torn from her breast,
Like trembling doves from their parent nest.

I'd shudder and start if I heard the bay
Of bloodhounds seizing their human prey,
And I heard the captive plead in vain
As they bound afresh his galling chain.

If I saw young girls from their mother's arms
Bartered and sold for their youthful charms,
My eye would flash with a mournful flame,
My death-paled cheek grow red with shame.

I would sleep, dear friends, where bloated might
Can rob no man of his dearest right;
My rest shall be calm in any grave
Where none can call his brother a slave.

I ask no monument, proud and high,
To arrest the gaze of the passers-by;
All that my yearning spirit craves,
Is bury me not in a land of slaves.

(1854)

IHAB HASSAN

Hamas Versus Palestine

For many of Palestine's supporters in the world, Hamas is a "resistance movement." It is the armed faction that fires rockets at Israel, that refuses to bow to a siege (the same siege to which it contributed) and bombardment, that speaks the loudest in the name of Palestinian liberation. For millions of people across the Arab world and beyond, this heroic conception of the organization carries genuine emotional weight. Palestine is occupied. Gaza has been blockaded and bombed. And Hamas, whatever its methods, has refused to surrender. In certain circles, Hamas' stamina alone is enough to confer legitimacy, even glory.

Yet how a power acts towards its enemies does not necessarily reflect how it feels about its own people. And the portrait of Hamas as the protector of Palestinians, as the defiant shield of Palestinian resistance — however powerful it may be for the purposes of propaganda — collapses the moment you look closely at what Hamas has actually done to the Palestinians whom it governs.

Hamas is not a national liberation movement. It is an Islamist faction that emerged from the Muslim Brotherhood in the late 1980s, with a founding charter that called for the destruction of Israel on religious grounds and made no pretense of representing a pluralistic Palestinian nation. It won parliamentary elections in 2006 — a democratic mandate it then used not to govern, but to amass and consolidate absolute power. In 2007, it launched a bloody coup against the Palestinian Authority, throwing PA officers from rooftops, executing rivals in the streets, and killing more than 700 people in a matter of days. It has governed the people of Gaza ever since by means of fear, repression, religious enforcement, and political monopoly: suppressing and jailing critics and treating organized dissent as an act of treason, torturing Palestinians who dare to speak out.

None of this is a secret. Human rights organizations — Palestinian, Arab, and international — have documented Hamas' treatment of Gazans for nearly two decades. The evidence for Hamas' crimes is not in dispute. But rather than attempting to respond to its critics, Hamas has engineered its own impunity — cunningly fusing its own survival with the survival of the Palestinians, with the Palestinian cause itself, so that any internal criticism reads, in the minds of supporters abroad, as a betrayal of the people rather than accountability for the faction. This legerdemain is one of the most successful propaganda operations of the modern era: a movement that represses its own population while convincing much of the world that to name that repression is to side with the enemy. It is a brilliantly executed magic trick loosed upon a gullible or biased world.

Hamas calls itself a resistance movement. What it has never been is a national movement — of the sort that is accountable to the full spectrum of Palestinian society. Hamas demands total and unexamined loyalty from every Palestinian, at home and abroad, while representing the ideology of one faction alone. That is not representation. It is authoritarianism.

To understand why this matters, it is necessary to clarify what a national movement has historically meant in the Palestinian context. A national movement is not organized around a single ideology or religious creed. It is meant to function as a broad political framework that accommodates internal differences — political, religious, social — while still claiming to represent a people as a whole. This inclusiveness, this representativeness, however imperfect, is the source of its legitimacy.

The Palestine Liberation Organization was designed to function this way. When it emerged and consolidated power in the 1960s and 1970s, it positioned itself as a secular civic-national umbrella. Nationalists, Islamists, Marxists, liberals, Muslims, and Christians were all within it. Its concept of Palestine was larger than any one ideology. Even later, when the PA emerged out of the Oslo process, it inherited this same capacious claim — it was deeply flawed, authoritarian, and hollowed out, yes, but still it was grounded in the idea that legitimacy comes from institutions, elections, and a broad national mandate rather than religious doctrine dictated by divine decree.

Hamas was the product of a completely different tradition — and an incompatible one. Hamas did not emerge from the Palestinian national movement; it emerged to displace it. Its ideological framework is not civic but ideological: the people are not citizens with competing political views but a community bound to a particular religious and moral order. Consent is not its source of authority. Doctrine is. Hamas has never pretended otherwise. It employs systematic and centrally directed violence to enforce its order on the many Palestinians who did not ask for it.

Hamas has weaponized the language of patriotism — turned it into a sectarian loyalty oath administered at gunpoint. Hamas positions every act of repression as an act of protecting the Palestinian cause or maintaining security and preserving stability. Every arrested journalist is a spy. Every executed critic is a collaborator. Every family hunted down is a nest of traitors. The resistance, in Hamas' telling, is perpetually under attack from within — and it alone possesses the authority to name the enemy, try the accused, and carry out the sentence. There is no appeal, no transparency, no accountability.

Hamas' rule in Gaza shares the essential feature of every authoritarian system: it has made the cost of speaking the truth higher than the cost of living a lie. It has cast journalists as enemies of the people. It has rebranded repression as protection and detention as security. What distinguishes Hamas from other authoritarians is that it has co-opted the moral authority of its people's legitimate suffering. Hamas has built its system of control on top of a real occupation, a real blockade, a real dispossession. That is what makes it so difficult to challenge — and so dangerous to excuse.

When Gazans took to the streets to demand electricity, clean water, and food for their families, Hamas did not listen. It did not negotiate. It branded protesters as traitors and infiltrators, and accused them of serving foreign agendas bent on undermining "the resistance." People begging for bread were treated as enemy combatants. This is not only a tragedy — it is a crime. A population already ground down by Israeli occupation and blockade has been denied even the right to name its suffering, to organize against its conditions, to hold its own leaders to account. Hamas joined hands with Israel and sealed both exits. A Gaza-based analyst once described life under Hamas with painful simplicity: "We live between occupation and fear — the hammer above us and the fist behind us."

The large population trapped between those two forces is one of the least discussed realities of Palestinian life — suppressed in part because Israeli propagandists weaponize Gazan dissent against Hamas, and in part because Hamas has made the suppression of this dissent a matter of its own survival. Many Gazans stay silent not because they support the brutality of Hamas, but because they have no choice. Hamas has converted their dignity — their refusal to give the occupier ammunition — into a gag. It exploits Palestinian pride to protect itself from Palestinian judgment.

For ordinary Gazans, politics is not a public debate — it is a minefield with no map. Authoritarian regimes do not only punish dissent, they also perform its punishment. They need the spectacle. They need the population to watch, to absorb the lesson, to understand that no transgression is too small to overlook. Hamas has practiced this dark political theater since its first days in power. Public humiliations, forced confessions broadcast on its own media, staged accusations of collaboration — these are not aberrations. They are essential instruments of rule, as deliberate and consistent as any law. One wrong sentence, one overheard criticism, one protest attended without permission — and a person can find themselves accused of collaboration, arrested without charge, beaten in detention, or worse. Hamas has not merely criminalized dissent. It has criminalized the appearance of dissent. The line between civic criticism and treason has been deliberately erased.

All this is *not* a byproduct of war. There are those who excuse Hamas' repression as a wartime adaptation, an unfortunate necessity born of siege and conflict. Such an explanation must be rejected. Hamas has been crushing internal dissent since the day it took power — years before October 2023, years before the current war, years before any argument about wartime emergency might plausibly apply. From 2007 onward, secular activists, leftists, journalists, clan leaders, and students who dared to question Hamas faced threats, imprisonment, and violence. The repression is not a response to war. The war is, in part, a cover for the repression.

The logic of this system is straightforward: if only traitors criticize Hamas, then only Hamas speaks for Palestine. Human rights organizations have documented the mechanics for years — arbitrary arrests, beatings, torture in detention, family intimidation, phone confiscations, and social media surveillance. Hamas has seeded every neighborhood with informants — in mosques, schools, markets, and apartment blocks. People learn early not to speak freely in front of strangers, and everyone knows the cost of being heard. Dissent is not answered with argument. It is hunted.

In 2019, thousands of Gazans took to the streets in the "We

Want to Live" protests, demanding economic dignity and basic accountability from their government. Hamas' response was swift and brutal. Batons. Mass arrests. Protesters were dragged into vans and beaten. Phones were seized at checkpoints. Families were threatened with violence if they did not silence revolt. Activists were punished for the act of asking their government to govern. No charges were filed. No dialogue was offered. No official was held accountable.

As Hamas officials have explained to their people, "Your suffering is proof of your loyalty — your silence is proof of your patriotism."

Across Palestinian life, Hamas has executed a deliberate redefinition. Patriotism once meant resisting occupation, defending land, fighting for the rights of a people. Hamas has reduced it to a single demand: obedience. Not to Palestine, of course — to Hamas. Anyone who fails to comply is not merely a dissenter. They are traitors. And in Gaza traitors do not live long.

When Hamas attacked Israel in October 2023, and Israeli bombs began falling on Gaza, Hamas did not suspend its war on its own people. It accelerated it. Under the cover of the chaos, Hamas gunmen executed men in the streets — men accused of collaboration with Israel, shot and left to bleed in public view. Survivors insist that many of those who were murdered were not collaborators. They were people with grievances against Hamas. They were members of families who had defied Hamas. They were rivals. The war gave Hamas the perfect alibi. Hamas seized it.

The executions were not security operations, they were messages for domestic consumption. By branding its victims as Israeli spies, Hamas accomplished two things simultaneously: it liquidated internal enemies whom it could not touch in peacetime, and it terrorized the surviving population into silence at the precise moment when the world's cameras were pointed at Gaza. These were political murders of Palestinians by Palestinians.

When the ceasefire came, Hamas did not stand down. It settled scores. Here is an example. The Dughmush clan — long-standing rivals of Hamas, never collaborators with Israel — were hunted almost before the ink was dry on any agreement. They were executed and branded as traitors. And within hours scores of "pro-Palestine" activists abroad were amplifying Hamas' framing, declaring the dead guilty, echoing the accusations of a movement that had just killed civilians for the crime of carrying the wrong surname. The international pro-Palestine movement did not question the evidence — because it demanded none. It simply repeated the charge. This is not solidarity. It is complicity disguised as conscience.

The facts of the Dughmush case are not in dispute. The clan had no relationship with Israeli intelligence. Their offense was entirely internal: a long feud with Hamas that escalated on the day of the ceasefire agreement when family members killed two Hamas operatives. That is all. Hamas ordered the family to vacate a shelter. They refused. An armed clash followed. Hamas then dispatched officers to sweep the area and execute anyone bearing the name Dughmush — men, women, the elderly. Not for betraying Palestine. For refusing to submit to Hamas.

When the armed clash subsided, Hamas summoned men from the family and asked them to turn themselves in, promising that their situation would be settled, that no harm would come to them. They complied. Hamas broke its word before the day was out. Seven men were dragged into the street. Residents were ordered to come outside and watch. They were lined up and publicly executed one by one, as the operatives who carried out the executions proclaimed victory over collaborators and traitors. Hamas did not only kill the Dughmush men; it turned their deaths into a lesson for anyone who might consider challenging its power.

Before the Dughmush family story broke in international media, Hamas openly published footage of its men torturing people in Gaza on official Telegram channels. That footage was the foundation of my own work to expose Hamas' crimes against civilians. Hamas framed the videos with captions claiming that the victims were thieves, spies, or collaborators. In many cases, the evidence showed otherwise — the targets were simply critical voices. The torture was systematic and public: broken legs, gunshots to the limbs, carried out in the open as a message to anyone watching. After relentless exposure of these crimes — and the Dughmush story in particular — Hamas stopped posting the footage. But the campaign of torture and silencing did not stop. It moved into the dark.

This is the mechanism. This is how it works. Hamas brands its victims. The accusation travels through social media at the speed of outrage. Supporters abroad — primed by years of legitimate grievance against Israeli violence, trained to distrust any internal Palestinian critique as Israeli propaganda — are notified of the accusation and ask no questions. They do not seek evidence. They do not find survivors. They repeat the charge, amplify it, and move on. Hamas understands this dynamic and has built its entire internal repression strategy around it. To accuse a Palestinian of collaboration is not merely to destroy him in Gaza; it is to preemptively strip him of all standing before the global audience that might otherwise care about his fate. The accusation is the execution. The refutation almost never arrives.

This strategy was designed to kill independence along with the human beings that acted on it. The lesson has been burned into the streets: Speak and you will die. Question us and you will hang with the label of traitor around your neck. And yet we Palestinians must speak. Of course we condemn occupation, dispossession, and ethnic cleansing — that condemnation is not in question and never will be. But we must also be honest about what Hamas has done to us, to its own people. Every activist silenced, every family terrorized, every young person who left Gaza not only because of Israeli bombs but also because Hamas made dissent a death sentence — their suffering is Palestinian suffering, too. Ignoring it does not protect the cause. It betrays it.

I write from Washington, DC. With a buffer of an ocean between me and these monsters I am safe to speak freely about these conditions. But Hamas and its supporters have worked to close even that distance. Palestinians who speak out from abroad have been doxxed, harassed, and targeted with coordinated campaigns designed to destroy their reputations and to still their voices. The tactic is always the same: label them traitors, accuse them of serving Israeli propaganda, strip them of their Palestinian identity so that their testimony can be dismissed without being answered. It is the same logic Hamas applies inside Gaza, extended across borders and time zones. In Gaza itself, honesty like this would be a death wish. Even to whisper what I am writing in these pages would be enough to risk death. One denunciation is enough to bury a Gazan.

Life in Gaza has been described in many ways — as an open-air prison, a besieged territory, a humanitarian catastrophe. But for many Palestinians living there, the bars run in both directions: Israel controls us from the outside, Hamas controls us from the inside. The two systems of control are different in nature and in scale, but they share a devastating impact, making daily life in Gaza increasingly unbearable. This is why some Gazans risk their lives by taking to the sea – even before October 7 – to escape the Hamas tyranny. It is why parents express their political opinions only *sotto voce* behind closed doors. It is why jokes are coded and silence is survival.

Since Palestinians face existential violence also from outside, however, their internal suffering is dismissed, justified, or buried. "After liberation," we are told, "we will discuss democracy." But liberation that arrives on top of a silenced, terrorized population is not liberation. It is a transfer of power. Palestinians have seen enough transfers of power. They are owed something more.

To expose Hamas' repression, moreover, is not to weaken the Palestinian cause — it is to defend it. If Hamas claims that it is consecrated to the defense of its people, why does it suppress their voices? The truth is that Hamas fears democratic choice because it knows what Palestinians would choose if given a genuine voice: not to be governed by fear, not to bury their loved ones for asking questions and speaking out, not to live in a system where the only safe political opinion is silence. The authority of Hamas did not come from consent. It came from guns, and it has been maintained by guns ever since. Yet millions of Palestinians — secular, Christian, nationalist, Islamist but non-Hamas, independent, leftist, apolitical — constitute a pluralistic nation with diverse visions and aspirations. Reducing their voice to one faction's doctrine is not representation. It is erasure by force.

The world must hold two truths at once: Israel's occupation and blockade of Gaza are morally indefensible. Hamas' authoritarian rule and abuses against Palestinians are morally indefensible. These truths do not cancel each other. Acknowledging the truth of both these propositions is not a concession — it is the minimum honesty that Palestinians deserve.

Palestinians should not have to choose between opposing occupation and opposing internal repression. They deserve freedom from both. Silence serves no Palestinian — it serves only those who benefit from Palestinian suffering, whether they sit in an army office in Tel Aviv, a security headquarters in Gaza City, or a presidential compound in Ramallah. And the true Palestinian struggle has never been about glorifying death or crushing dissent — it has been about life, rights, dignity, and land. To love Palestine is not to love Hamas. To defend Palestinian humanity is not to defend those who violate it. The dream of freedom loses meaning if those claiming to represent it become new jailers.

Those who support the rights of the Palestinians should bear in mind that ultimately our pursuit of a state is not for them — it is for us, to build and to shape, to debate and to democratize. It is not meant to fulfill the promises of radical ideologies or the fantasies of those who have turned Palestinians into the eternal symbol of their own political dreams. The goal is not an abstract homeland for an ever-suffering people. It is an open society in which Palestinians are no longer objects of expectation and fantasy, but fully formed political actors with rights, with dissent, with the freedom to hold every leader to account. The Palestinian struggle was never meant to replace one set of chains with another. Moreover, most Palestinians want a state that lives in peace and dignity alongside

Israel and all its neighbors — public opinion surveys show this clearly, with the majority still supporting a two-state solution — a normal country, with normal politics, where the occupation is over, no more armed groups, and the question is no longer about survival but about how to build a future.

History will not be kind to those who wrapped authoritarianism in the flag of liberation. It will not forgive those, near or far, who watched Palestinian dissidents executed and said nothing — or worse, applauded. But it will honor the Palestinians who refused: those who named the crime, bore the cost, and kept fighting for a homeland where they could live freely, speak freely, and dream freely.

True liberation includes the liberation of voice. And Palestine's voice is bigger than Hamas' voice — it always was, it always will be.

JOHN GREENLEAF WHITTIER

Among The Hills: Prelude

Church-goers, fearful of the unseen Powers,
But grumbling over pulpit-tax and pew-rent,
Saving, as shrewd economists, their souls
And winter pork with the least possible outlay
Of salt and sanctity; in daily life
Showing as little actual comprehension
Of Christian charity and love and duty,
As if the Sermon on the Mount had been
Outdated like a last year's almanac
Rich in broad woodlands and in half-tilled fields,
And yet so pinched and bare and comfortless,
The veriest straggler limping on his rounds,
The sun and air his sole inheritance,
Laughed at a poverty that paid its taxes,
And hugged his rags in self-complacency!
Not such should be the homesteads of a land
Where whoso wisely wills and acts may dwell
As king and lawgiver, in broad-acred state,
With beauty, art, taste, culture, books, to make
His hour of leisure richer than a life
Of fourscore to the barons of old time,
Our yeoman should be equal to his home
Set in the fair, green valleys, purple walled,
A man to match his mountains, not to creep
Dwarfed and abased below them.

(1807)

CARISSA VÉLIZ

Analog Hope

What is the difference between a rat and a squirrel? There is no difference — squirrels are just rats with better PR. So runs the joke. Sometimes I think of artificial intelligence like a squirrel with excellent marketing, its overpaid pundits assuring us that nothing more important has ever happened in history, that it is the answer to our every question and the solution to our every problem. The tale is repeated so many times that it seems more real than our lived experience.

I have heard people rant about the marvels of AI while grappling with its many glitches, whether it is a digital assistant misunderstanding them, facial recognition not recognizing them, or a chatbot suggesting that they put glue in their food. We suffer from optimism bias to such an extent that seemingly no technology failure, no matter how epic, will dissuade us from believing the story that technology will be our savior, and that whatever problems it has now will not be there in the future.

Everywhere I look there is talk about AI and digital technology. It's not only that I work in this field. Chatter about AI follows me at dinner parties, it weaves in and out of the conversations strangers share in restaurants and on public transport, on the radio, on podcasts of every kind, and on every morning show on TV. But the more I study digital technology, the more I am in awe of the richness and the primacy of the analog world, the world of things you can touch and smell, the world of things that are not made up of ones and zeroes (the building blocks of the digital). When I was asked recently where I find hope, it struck me that hope lies in the analog. And as the world around us seems to grow gloomier, and people around me more pessimistic, I find myself in the unfamiliar situation of going from being the bad cop who is used to thinking about what can go wrong to the good cop who seeks the rays of light in neglected corners.

Analog creatures in an analog world

We are analog creatures. What matters most for our wellbeing is and will always be analog. Virtual water will *never* quench our thirst, not a year from now and not in a thousand years, because virtual water is no kind of water at all. Digital food will not satisfy our appetites, and AI companions will not ward off our loneliness.

The people around us are made out of flesh and blood. Much of what it means to be a human being lies in our relationships to others, which is why Aristotle called us political animals. But it takes the honing of skills to perfect our social relationships. We polish ourselves by interacting with one other. We work on our empathy by observing how our words and actions affect others. We build strong relationships by making ourselves vulnerable to one another and learning how to protect other people's feelings when they make themselves vulnerable to us. We learn to temper our emotions to avoid hurting those we love.

We deepen our ties by looking after one another. We take care of each other physically — we cook a clueless philosopher bolognese to make sure they eat enough protein, we accompany our friend to the doctor's office, we help each other move places — and emotionally, which more often than not involves the body as well — we sit with another as they face their worst fears, embrace each other for affection and reassurance, and speak softly to our loved ones, using our voices to soothe. That is partly why we read out loud to our children. In a moment of distress, I once called an old friend who had enough intuition to ask no questions and sing on the phone a tune we used to know a long time ago.

We learn from each other. I don't think I would have grown to love Shakespeare as I do if it hadn't been for my high school teacher, Mr. Roger D. Gouran, who got goosebumps every time he cited his favorites lines from *Julius Caesar*, *Hamlet*, and *Othello*; remembering those moments *still* moves me — and makes me want to reread Shakespeare. Learning from a screen is much harder because it is thoroughly missing the personal relationship that can inspire you to wake up at six in the morning to get to read Shakespeare before school starts, the emotional resonance in reading together that makes you take in the words in all their social meanings. We learn life tricks — from how to change a light bulb to how to mend clothes — by watching others. We become better at understanding nonverbal cues and responses the more we spend time with others. All these observations are not sentimental Luddite platitudes. They are facts.

I worry that young people are losing social skills. Madrid is my favorite city in the world, and when I'm there I depend much less on digital maps, reveling in the luxury of asking passersby for directions and getting the added benefit of a smile or a recommendation or a piece of information that I wouldn't even have known to ask for. Spanish culture makes me feel that people on the streets are friends whom I haven't met yet.

Whenever I ask younger people, however, they stare at me as if they were judging me for not asking Google instead. Did I not get the memo? But one of the things I love about Madrid is that, when you enter a bar and see two people talking, you can never be entirely sure whether they are old friends or strangers who struck up a new friendship a few minutes ago. What we gain in convenience by using digital maps is not worth the loss in social richness when we ask a friendly stranger for directions; that friendly stranger could end up a friend, maybe even your best friend or your spouse, you never know, and you will never find out if you do not interact. The more we talk to chatbots, the less we spend time with the human beings with whom ties may be formed, ties that form the fabric of families, groups of friends, communities, and healthy democracies.

It's not only that young people are engaging less in spontaneous social interactions; they are having less sex than any generation in history. This is a terrible impoverishment of experience, a self-impoverishment. There are discoveries, about oneself and others, that can only be made intimately with others. Yet instead of spending lazy days with one another and learning through leisure, like all animals do, young people are talking to chatbots, efficiently and often raptly. And while talking to a chatbot might seem on the surface an activity much like talking with a human being, the resemblances are only superficial. Talking is fundamentally a social activity in a physical world.

One of the very annoying and equally helpful characteristics of talking with other human beings is that these brainy, autonomous, embodied creatures often disagree with us. (I know, the gall). When you voice your point of view to another, you expose yourself to criticism for being wrong or biased. Disagreement can cause frustration, confrontational moments, and even anger, but it helps keep us tied to reality. We keep each other in check by means of talking through things. Through challenging our views, we give one another perspective.

Chatbots, in contrast, do not have conversations, strictly speaking. They are not interlocutors. They are built to please us, because by flattering us they hook us, and the longer we use them, the more data we surrender to them (in this sense they are like spies), and the more we depend on them and are willing to pay for them. Chatbots are built to be sycophantic. Talking to something that continually encourages you and validates you is not conducive to health or happiness. Chatbots have encouraged people in horrifying directions — they have reinforced people's suicidal ideations, murderous plans, and delusions of various sorts. Some call this freakish effect "chatbot psychosis" or "AI-induced delusions." One psychologist described these conversations as "crazy-making."

Teenagers have killed themselves after chatbots encouraged them to do so; people have fallen in love with their chatbots and neglected their personal relationships; one accountant was convinced he was Neo from *The Matrix* and needed to escape his computer simulation; a chatbot persuaded another person that he was the Chosen One, "ready to awaken"; another became convinced that ChatGPT was self-aware and could teach him how to talk with God; and yet another one thought that there was a tortured personality in ChatGPT who was killed by OpenAI — in revenge, he vowed to kill Sam Altman, the CEO evangelist of OpenAI, and then he provoked police officers with a butcher knife in order to commit suicide by cop, which worked.

If you have ever experienced anxiety or panic attacks, or indeed any other mental health challenge, you have probably noticed that spending more time on screens tends not to be helpful, that doomscrolling may be one of the most effective ways of making things worse. The best things you can do to improve a bad state of mind involve engaging with the analog world: going for a run or a walk and focusing on the feeling of the ground beneath your feet, having coffee with a friend, watching a sunset. Psychologists and meditation teachers and yoga instructors will recommend that you attend to the sensations of the body. The body may be the ultimate standpoint of resistance to the AI deluge. The universe of things grounds us, calms our senses, precisely because we are embodied — which is to say, are analog creatures. When we attend to the analog, we become attuned to our surroundings. Digital existence, by contrast, is a long program of disattunement.

The natural world that sustains everything you see around you is made out of carbon molecules. All too often we forget that everything virtual depends on the analog. The internet works thanks to heavy underwater cables. The AI that sounds so uncannily human was trained by an army of underpaid and overworked people. And the cloud is someone else's computer, a server sitting somewhere, made up of metals and minerals, using up fresh water for cooling and electricity for power.

We can watch birds, whales, and tigers on our screens. We can even experience a simulation of deserts, jungles, and seas through artificial intelligence and virtual reality, but even the most impressive recreation of the real thing is far inferior to the analog reality that it simulates. (Is it really necessary to point out that simulations are an inferior channel to reality, or no channel at all? I suppose it is.) Even setting aside problems such as headsets making people cybersick (which can include nausea, disorientation, and headaches, with women being affected more often), anything virtual is but a ghost of its analog counterpart; it is soulless, tasteless, and untouchable. There is no hot breeze heavy with desert sand coating your arms and making your eyes sting, the ground beneath your feet is not uneven with the effervescence of jungle life, and the sea is dry and missing its vastness and its fishy fragrance.

We focus on the digital often to the detriment of the analog and at our own peril. Indeed, as a culture we have come to heap scorn on the analog as a kind of archaism. But the world of creatures and things — the world that is not us — needs our attention to stay healthy. If you forget to feed your fish, they will die. The more we use digital tools like AI that are power-hungry, the more we need to invest in the natural world to make sure that the digital doesn't end up destroying the analog on which it ultimately depends. If we forget to take care of the natural world, the footage we have of birds, whales, and tigers will become images of extinct species; nothing but memories, and memories are not creatures.

The roof over your head and the home that brings you safety, warmth, and comfort is made out of brick and concrete. When Mark Zuckerberg announced his Metaverse project (which happily ended up tanking fairly spectacularly) one of the selling points was the ability to have premier property in the virtual world — for a handsome price. But who in their right mind wants to buy a property that you cannot walk into, that cannot shelter you from the rain and damp (I live in England), no matter how spectacular the view? The whole concept and allure of owning property is that you can inhabit it in a way that can only be experienced physically. The distance between a virtual apartment and an actual apartment is as prodigious as that between virtual water and water. A virtual home is no home at all, as Zuckerberg's own lavish homes attest.

And if a virtual dwelling ever starts to become even remotely attractive, it will be because the spaces surrounding us have become unpleasant to live in. We risk falling into a vicious cycle. The more we focus on our computers and our phones, the less we take care of our physical environments, and the less we take care of our physical environments, the more they will deteriorate, inviting us to forget our grim surroundings by focusing on our computers and our phones. Why would anyone who disdains the physical and the analog take the trouble to maintain them?

The analog world necessitates the work of maintenance to keep it in good shape. If you live in a desert, your job is to protect things from the glare of the sun, and to oil materials like leather and wood to make sure that they do not become too dry. If you live somewhere humid, your job is to protect things from the damp. I was recently in Cartagena de Indias, where it was so humid that walking on the marble floor felt like skating, and where I learned that there is such a thing as clothing paper to keep fabrics dry(ish). The analog world gives us back the measure of what we have invested in it. The well-maintained house will protect you in return for your protection of it; you take care of it and it takes care of you — that's the deal. What goes for your home goes for your neighborhood, too. If you watch films on online platforms only, the cinema in your neighborhood might need to close. If you spend your time in front of your screen at home then you are not inhabiting the coffeeshops, restaurants, and bars that keep a city alive.

Digital tech pushes us — it is designed to push us — into our individual bubbles. (It's not only a personal problem; Hannah Arendt argued that isolation is the fertile ground for fascism.) It is now commonplace to see groups of people together looking at their phones instead of interacting with one another — monads with WiFi. Eventually, if most of your social life takes place on the little glowing box in your hand, the allure of going out and meeting other people wears off. If all you're going to do is be on your phones, then why bother taking off your pajamas and braving the weather to meet others? It takes commitment to each other and to our surroundings to breathe life and soul into spaces — indeed, to get us out the door.

Europeans might live in smaller homes than Americans, but the common spaces we inhabit tend to be vast. Who needs a big living room when you have a whole city that feels like home? I keep thinking of the tonic vitality of Madrid, its analog vibrancy, its streets always ebullient, echoing with laughter, with people of all ages mingling together at every hour of the day and night. Most Spaniards seem to spend more time in the streets than in their homes. Even when they are in their homes, there is an old tradition in rural places of sitting on your doorstep to shoot the breeze with neighbors and passersby. I was speaking with someone from Lithuania recently who told me that when she was growing up, she didn't have to make plans with friends because everyone hung out in the same bars, so you could count on finding your friends there on Friday nights.

In contrast to the liveliness of cherished places, abandoned buildings feel heavy because they are the remnants of failed dreams. Theaster Gates is an artist and a professor in the Department of Visual Arts at the University of Chicago; his father was a roofer, and he has a degree in urban planning, all of which gives him an appreciation of spaces. He bought a few properties in the South Side of Chicago, which has the highest level of poverty and crime in the city. "My buildings, they constitute a love investment," he said of his decision on the TV show *Home*.

He wanted to be able to go to a movie in his neighborhood so he built a cinema. He wanted people to be able to read in his neighborhood so he built a library. He wanted people to come together so he built a few more extraordinary spaces. "Great culture had a right to live where I live," he said. He started hosting exhibitions and musical events attracting interesting people. Instead of moving neighborhoods he built a hub that attracted the people that comprise the kind of neighborhood — the kind of place — that he wants to live in. That is commitment to the analog world. That is embodied hope. To take dilapidated buildings and make them so beautiful that people flock to them demonstrates the wonderful power of the analog and the power we have as analog creatures.

If we focus on the digital to the detriment of the analog, dereliction lies at the end of the road. But if we focus on the analog, we can sustain both worlds, make them thrive, and thrive in them ourselves.

Safety and reliability

Tech enthusiasts like to brag about AI as being cutting-edge, forgetting that cutting-edge means experimental. Cutting-edge means being treated as guinea pigs. The safest, most trustworthy, and often most refined technologies are the tried and tested ones. The analog tends to be safer partly because we have thousands of years of experience with it, learning from our interactions with it. Our record with digital excitements, by contrast, is not quite so reassuring.

A part of what makes the paper book such a superior technology, as Irene Vallejo explains in her magnificent book *Papyrus*, is how many iterations it has gone through. Every aspect of it has been refined through millennia, from its shape to the words it contains and the material it is made of. It was first a tablet, limited in its surface and therefore in its content. Then it became a scroll — long sheets wound around a spindle, read by unrolling from hand to hand. Then came the codex, a proto-book that stacked and bound leaves of parchment between covers, allowing readers to flip directly to a page. From words being handwritten to printed, and from books being made out of clay to being made out of papyrus and then parchment and then rag paper and then wood paper and finally the acid-free paper we have today, books are like polished gems, as reliable and safe as technologies come. It needs to be added that in the development of all these technologies of discourse nobody was hurt by their rollouts and their early iterations, however damaging or heretical the critics of their contents deemed them to be.

The second reason why analog tends to be safer and more reliable is because we usually have more unmediated control over it. While I depend on authors and publishers and booksellers and so on to get my hands on the latest novel, once I buy it as a paper book, it is mine. I have control over that book, and the author, publisher, and bookseller no longer have any control over it. I can banish it from my life if I wish to do so.

In contrast, when you use your smartphone or AI, you are constantly depending — at every turn of the page, so to speak — on the company that is providing it. Tech companies can turn your devices into useless bricks. You depend on them to continually patch vulnerabilities and update your systems. If a company changes an algorithm in a way that makes its product worse — whether it is a social media platform or a chatbot — there is exactly nothing you can do about it; you don't own the previous (or current) version, so you are stuck with whatever the tech company does. These supposedly empowering devices have a way of making one perfectly helpless.

That dependence is all the more worrisome given how so many tech companies have proven themselves to be untrustworthy and disrespectful of people's rights time and again. The tech executives of today's companies have not covered themselves in glory for their responsible and careful approaches to leadership. They seek much power with little responsibility. Moreover, digital technology is itself, in its constitution, unreliable in ways that analog is not: it depends on electricity and can be hacked, for starters. Our society-wide and planet-wide reliance on this technology has created an unprecedentedly large vulnerability. To keep our societies safe and robust, practically speaking, we would do well keeping analog backups of our most important documents and systems. (I understand the people who stubbornly hang on to a landline alongside everything else.) We must retain the ability to run institutions on analog in the event of an emergency.

On April 28, 2025, the Iberian Peninsula went dark in a blackout that lasted for about ten hours. The only people who managed to have a meal at a restaurant on that day were people carrying cash with them. We must never get rid of cash, if not for privacy's sake, then for security. Health professionals had trouble getting to the houses of patients who needed help with oxygen machines that now depend on electricity because their Google Maps didn't work and young ones had never navigated their city without them. The radio could not be accessed through the internet, which depends on electricity; only good old-fashioned FM radio worked. And yet there are countries thinking about phasing out radio because these days most people access radio online. But if a solar storm or a severe cyberattack were to take down the national grid, there would be no internet. Can you imagine the damage and the mayhem? (Needless to say, the "tech titans" will disclaim all responsibility for the calamity.)

In May 2021, a ransomware attack stopped the Colonial Pipeline in its tracks. The pipeline transports almost half the oil consumed on the east coast of the United States. According to its CEO, the company managed to muddle through owing to the most senior part of its workforce, who still remembered how to run things manually. When Norsk Hydro, a Norwegian metals and electricity company, went through something similar, they had to ask retired people to come back to the plant and help them to run things on analog. Yet newer power plants sometimes take away the option of running on manual.

It's a bad idea, as the British Library cyberattack shows. Like books, libraries have been around for millennia, during which time we have refined our ways of caring for books, from learning to create the ideal physical conditions for better preserving them to improving the ways in which we organize and catalogue them according to genre and author. As the printing press created an explosion of books, it became more common to store books according to size, maximizing shelf space, and keeping a meticulous catalogue to find the books. The British Library is one of the largest in the world, with an estimated 14 million books that are mostly stored in warehouses.

Then, in October 2023, a hacker group attacked the online system of the British Library and demanded a ransom in exchange for restoring services, which the Library refused to grant. More than two years later, and millions of pounds spent, readers still can't take out many of its books. The readers, analog creatures all, are still there, and the books, analog objects, are there, too. So why can't the readers get to the books? Because the map to the books, the catalogue, was digital and digital only, and we lost it. Good luck finding a book among 14 million others stored by size. Libraries had been working well for thousands of years. It took a single cyberattack to break this one. So spare me the uplift about cutting-edge technology.

Perhaps the most incredible part of it is that, in the aftermath of the British Library calamity, the stated lesson learned in the report reflecting on the experience is that we should have more cutting-edge technology. Meanwhile, agencies specializing in security, such as the National Security Agency, often use the oldest computing technology possible because it is better tried-and-tested than the newer versions. We are such optimists when it comes to technology, and so taken in by the marketing efforts of companies, that it is almost unfathomable to us that digital technology might be second best, what we use when we cannot get something better or the real thing.

Beauty

The world of things is not only safer; it is also where beauty lives, where you can experience shapes and colors that do not pixelate, and watches that tick with the satisfying sound of time and the stimulating feel of craftsmanship, and sunrises and sunsets.

During World War II, the collection of works in the National Gallery in London was evacuated in secret to a remote place in

Snowdonia in Wales, where it lived in a labyrinthine cave of unused mines known as the Cathedral. The paintings were kept safe, but the population felt bereft. In 1942, a letter to *The Times* read: "because London's face is scarred and bruised these days, we need more than ever to see beautiful things. . . . Picture lovers are denied their Rembrandts just at the time when such beauty is most potent for good." It is a small but extraordinary document in the history of humanism. The gallery then organized to bring one painting up from the mines at a time, transporting it under armed guard to London to comfort its beleaguered citizens with the solace of beauty. A crowd gathered around the first visitor, Rembrandt's *Portrait of Margaretha de Geer*, and people were reminded that along with the brutality of the world there is also its beauty, so nourishing even, or especially, among the ruins. For the philosopher Plotinus, the beautiful attracts the soul because it is akin to it, because what is beautiful is what is real, and what allows the soul to be more itself.

During the Spanish Civil War, Manuel Azaña, the President of the lawfully elected Spanish Republic, declared that the "Prado is more important than the Republic and the Monarchy. Because in the future there might be more republics and more monarchies in Spain, but these masterpieces are irreplaceable." Dozens of brave volunteers transported the works in thirty-six trucks, endangering their lives in a very risky operation, risking their lives to save not people but the works of Rembrandt, Goya, Titian, Velázquez, Rubens.

The supposed equivalent of a painting in the world of the digital is an NFT, a non-fungible token — a unique digital identifier which cannot be copied and is recorded on a blockchain to certify its origins. Excited? Are you having trouble imagining a leader putting aside their political commitments in the context of war for the sake of an NFT? Or military officials willing to risk their lives for a digital image? A part of what we value in the beauty of a painting has to do with its physicality, its thingness, with how thickly the paint sits in its concrete locations; and how brushes capture lights, shadows, gestures, moods. The origins of the painting — how it came to be made — also have something to do with its incommensurability. You are sharing space with an object of beauty touched and created by the eyes and the hands of a particular person, an expressive person, hundreds of years ago. (Is the latest iOS a personal expression of that kind?) That is why we still visit museums, despite most or all of the same works being depicted on websites. The image is only the surface of the thing. There is an awe when you are in the presence of a Rembrandt that *never happens* in its reproduction online.

In music, LPs are warmer, crisper, more human somehow than digital reproductions. And what could ever substitute for a live orchestra? The first time I played a grand piano — I don't want to mislead anyone, I'm a complete beginner, but that's beside the point — it was a revelation to hear the difference from a digital piano, however good the digital piano might be, and more than anything else to feel the delight of the tingling on my fingers, my hands, the core of my body absorbing vibrations that feel nothing like the sound waves of the digital.

Then there is the beauty of designed furniture; the shape of an Eames chair, how the materials feel to the touch, the smoothness of its lines, the way it perfectly distributes the weight of your body to cause no discomfort. And have you noticed how coffee tastes better when drunk from a beautiful mug?

One of the lessons of hardship is that beauty is not a frill: it is as much of a human need as food and shelter. Beauty gives us a reason to live. And the greatest beauty — can there be any doubt about this? — is analog, because analog is akin to us in a way that the digital can never be.

The digital as a knock-off

In the *Republic*, Plato criticizes fiction for being a copy of truth rather than truth itself. Plato worried about arts that mimicked truth, that can pass for truth without being true. The digital mimics the analog without providing the grounding and the reliability of the world of things.

Think of a digital book. Its design is a bad knock-off of the real thing, from its shape to the gestures that it invites you to perform — say, to "turn" a "page" that is not actually a page. Whereas you can fully own a paper book, an electronic book is not exactly yours: you cannot lend it to a friend, or give it away, and the publisher can modify its content remotely and without your consent or even knowledge. (Imagine Austen or Joyce having second thoughts and making posthumous interventions!) A digital book needs to be charged by means of a plug or else it becomes a brick. It can be hacked. And it doesn't work for you: even when it is in your possession, it works for tech companies who are using it to surveil you. It tracks what you read, how fast you read, what you highlight, and more, and it shares that information with the highest bidder. If the mighty paper book is a true friend, a digital one is a false one.

The digital is but a ghost of the analog at best, and a threat to the analog at worst. A part of the beauty of hearing birds outside my window is knowing that there are birds out there. It is not only the experience of the sound, it is also the world that the sound denotes and conveys. A digital recording of birdsong would not satisfy my thirst for beauty in the same way.

In his book *Anarchy, State, and Utopia*, the philosopher Robert Nozick proposed the following thought experiment as a refutation of hedonism, the view that what matters most is pleasure. Imagine that you had the opportunity of being connected to an experience machine that would deliver whatever experiences you crave and make them seem real: friendships, family, winning an Olympic medal, being rich beyond your wildest dreams, anything goes. All of it would be no more than a kind of hallucination, even if you wouldn't know it. Would you rather have the perfect experience of having perfect friends even if they do not exist, or friends who are imperfect but real? Would you rather be happy and oblivious about your spouse cheating on you, or would you prefer to know the truth? Most people care about more than pleasure. We care about authenticity and truth, and indeed for the ancient Greeks, those pagans, the ideals of truth, beauty, and goodness were to a certain extent one and the same.

The digital creates illusions similar to those of the experience machine — chatbots that sound like your friends, electronic gadgets that resemble books. We would do well to remember that often the digital mimics the analog while never achieving the substance of what it is that satisfies our analog nature. The analog is precisely what the digital cannot deliver.

Our blue flower

The unfinished novel *Heinrich von Ofterdingen*, by the late-eighteenth-century German writer and thinker known as Novalis, follows a young medieval poet who is haunted by dreams of finding a blue flower, which became a symbol of longing and poetry in German Romanticism. Guided by this yearning, Heinrich embarks on a lengthy journey that takes him to many landscapes and people, only to end up finding his blue flower as he returns home. What he was desperately searching for was there all along, waiting to be recognized.

Our blue flower is the analog world. After journeying through the digital tundra, through dystopic landscapes of social media platforms deteriorating into purveyors of hate and slop, cyberspaces of Orwellian surveillance, algorithmic Kafkaesque systems that are inscrutable and accountable to no one, after meeting the colorful characters of at least some of the big tech masters, it's time to go home. We can keep the digital as something of an add-on to the primacy of the analog world, like a fancy side dish, without being too distracted from the main course. We must even protect the palatable parts of the digital. But it is past time to fulfill our foundational human responsibility to take care of the analog. We must change that light bulb that has been waiting weeks to be fixed, and repaint the living room, and feed the dog, and relearn how to run our homes, companies, and institutions on manual, and thereby furnish the most definitive evidence that we are human beings.

The good news is that the analog world is still alive, all around us, waiting for us, inviting us to take part in it in the form of bird songs and rays of sunshine and art exhibitions and literary festivals and democratic conversations. We are still reaping the benefits of centuries of our ancestors conserving the analog, and our children have every right to demand a similar conservation from us. The analog world waits only to be noticed, like the blue flower, though this restorative noticing will require an exertion of the mind and the heart. To notice the analog, and to act in our lives on what we see and smell and hear and touch there, is now an act of dissent. Are you in the mood for something countercultural? Then water your plants, and consciously. Cherish the analog; our hope lies therein.

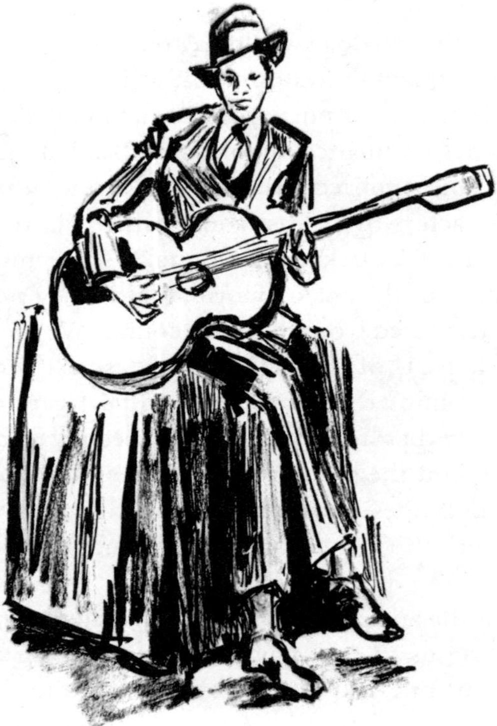

HERMAN MELVILLE

Shiloh: A Requiem

Skimming lightly, wheeling still,
    The swallows fly low
Over the field in clouded days,
    The forest-field of Shiloh—
Over the field where April rain
Solaced the parched ones stretched in pain
Through the pause of night
That followed the Sunday fight
    Around the church of Shiloh—
The church so lone, the log-built one,
That echoed to many a parting groan
        And natural prayer
    Of dying foemen mingled there—
Foemen at morn, but friends at eve—
    Fame or country least their care:
(What like a bullet can undeceive!)
    But now they lie low,
While over them the swallows skim,
    And all is hushed at Shiloh.

(1862)

MICHAEL C. KIMMAGE

Citizen Starbuck, or Democracy and The Whale

"They wanted the company's name to suggest a sense of adventure," the corporate statement reads, "a connection to the Northwest and a link to the seafaring tradition of the early coffee traders." An initial idea was "Pequod," but it was rejected for sounding awkward, a bad fit for the product. Eventually the company's founders settled on another reference from Herman Melville's enormous and stubbornly well-known novel, the name of the *Pequod*'s first mate — "you guessed it, Starbuck." With this, "a brand was born." The brand became an iconic American brand, its name derived from the iconic American novel that Melville published in 1852. This dense, forbidding, magnificent novel — a kind of American scripture — reverberates and reverberates in American culture, perhaps especially in American popular culture.

Starbuck is far from *Moby-Dick*'s most memorable character.

He is outshone by dreamy melancholic Ishmael, the novel's narrator and the sole survivor of the shipwreck that the *Pequod* becomes. The novel lives in Ishmael's voice — from its first sentence, "Call me Ishmael" — though Ishmael slowly fades from its story, as Captain Ahab hijacks novel and journey alike, grandly charismatic, ambitiously evil, and the source of ceaseless speculation from so many generations of *Moby-Dick* readers. Perhaps Ahab was John Calhoun, the Southern politician who prodded the United States into the Civil War. Perhaps Ahab was Adolf Hitler before the fact, desperate to invade the entire world. Almost as much as the white whale, Ahab and his wooden leg dominate *Moby-Dick*. He quested after the whale; we quest after him.

Ahab is mad, while Ishmael is along for the ride. Acting against Ahab, Starbuck is an unimpressive foil, or so it seems, and a marginal one at that. He registers Ahab's lunacy and cannot deflect or contain it. Starbuck's reemergence circa 1971 at the pinnacle of coffee capitalism is almost comic. In *Moby-Dick*, somber Starbuck does not suggest a sense of enterprise or adventure. He is from Martha's Vineyard, not the Pacific Northwest, and as a seasoned hunter of whales, he is no purveyor of coffee. His name has been attached to the wrong company, which has popularized but also obscured the literary character of Starbuck, who, unlike Ahab, does not symbolize anything very obvious in *Moby-Dick*. It might be easy to dismiss Starbuck as a vehicle of virtue signaling, with all the anonymity and the blandness that virtue signaling connotes and with all the space that divides virtue signaling from virtue.

Considered closely, however, Starbuck is neither bland nor empty. He should be more iconic, not as a salesman-adventurer but as a crucial piece of the puzzle that is *Moby-Dick*. Ahab embodies *Moby-Dick*'s fascination with tyranny, exploitation, and zealotry, at least for those who have never read the novel. Starbuck traces the dilemma of having to respond to Ahab: Ahab the call, Starbuck the response. That Starbuck fails to stop Ahab is important. That Starbuck lives in honesty and dignity is not less important. Starbuck parries an Ahab lawless and lost to the allure of death, countering a nihilism masquerading as a purpose.

Starbuck's weapon is his steady adherence to the law. Thou shalt not kill, Starbuck believes, and kill he shall not. Thou shalt not lie, he believes, and he tells the truth. The retort to evil, though unvictorious in his case, Starbuck is emblematic of a moral man and a moral citizen. Perhaps it is fortunate that (owing to a coffee franchise) his name is everywhere visible in the United States.

Melville adored allegory, analogy, association, implication. In *Mardi*, the novel that precedes *Moby-Dick* in his oeuvre, Melville projected his feelings about politics and philosophy, civilization and travel, commerce and technology onto a phantasmagoric literary landscape, allegory embedded in allegory, symbol embedded in symbol — not unlike the *Divine Comedy*, in which Dante's Florence is refracted through the poet's symbolic invention. *Moby-Dick* is much more of a story, a story of the sea, a yarn, but at every turn it invites analogy. The *Pequod* is surely America, as the founders of Starbucks sensed, a rude democracy, an industrial factory, a capitalist juggernaut (as the founders of Starbucks did not sense). The white whale is an all-purpose analogy. It is the uncapturable impulse behind the quest: nature, divinity, victim, victimizer, mystery, malice, eternity, death. The interpretive possibilities are intentionally endless, just as the analogies are omnipresent.

Ishmael has precise associations in *Moby-Dick* and a specific analogy behind him. Enamored of satire, Melville goes after Ralph Waldo Emerson through Ishmael, or he goes after his personal image of Emerson. Ishmael represents the motif of contemplation-in-nature, of an aristocratic life lived apart from "society," doing so on a whaleship ferociously dedicated to money making, near the terrifying untamable ocean and under the thumb of an obsessed inhumane captain. Time and again, Ishmael is confronted not with Emerson's restorative nature, not with New England in autumn, but with "the universal cannibalism of the sea." The sea's creatures, including humans, are designed to devour one another, and that darkness is nature. Naive Ishmael is the philosopher with too much unreliable philosophy in him and too little spiritual mettle to be anything other than the ship's chronicler, a job he does to perfection. Melville has fun with Ishmael's gauzy, adolescent adventurism.

Ahab is prodigious in his capacity to engender analogies. Interestingly, Ahab does not emerge organically from American politics as Melville knew it in the 1840s or before. George Washington is the anti-Ahab, the calm general who turned down absolute power, who did not burn with mystical self-destroying fire but who retired quietly to Mount Vernon, having safely completed his completable mission. There is nothing of Ahab in Thomas Jefferson. Closer to Melville's time, Andrew Jackson may be bound up in the figure of Ahab, Jackson having had a touch of the demagogue in him, but Jackson did not sink the ship; in some ways he democratized and righted the ship. The robber barons of the late nineteenth century were not an American phenomenon of the 1830s and 1840s. Ahab the proto-industrialist is a possibility, though an anachronistic one, and Ahab does not care about money. His fantasies lie elsewhere.

The biography of Napoleon, ubiquitous in Melville's era, may come closest to the mark. Napoleon forged an army and marched it to its doom. The soldiers followed in his wake, not quite knowing why, and the scale of the suffering was terrible. Napoleon has Ahab's will to conquer, Ahab's monstrous arrogance, Ahab's extreme appetite. The precedents for Ahab, starting with the biblical king after whom he is named, are less important than the posthumous light he sheds on politics and madness. Melville's general point, given the Americanness of *Moby-Dick*, is that America is not immune. Everything can happen here. George Washington's moderation was a stroke of good luck. So, too, is the constitutional republic a stroke of good luck. Democracy and demagoguery are hardly strangers to one another, and Napoleonism is by no means a European tendency. It is irreparably a human tendency.

Amid *Moby-Dick*'s multiplying analogies, Starbuck must also have his prototypes. They are hard to pin down. He is not an intellectual like Ishmael and not a megalomaniac like Ahab. He probably signifies normalcy, or he signifies goodness, a value not sought after in *Moby-Dick*. In a letter to Nathaniel Hawthorne, written on November 17, 1851, Melville claimed to "have written a wicked book" and when it was done to "feel spotless as the lamb." Melville is describing a wicked book, not even a book about wickedness, so attuned to wickedness is *Moby-Dick*. Yet boarding the *Pequod*, Ishmael meets a rigger, who tells him about Starbuck — "'Halloa! Starbuck's astir,' said the rigger. 'He's a lively first mate, that: good man, and a pious; but all active now.'" Virtuous, simple Starbuck has his ambiguities. His virtue traces a deadly logic and is no competition for Ahab's dark arts, but neither is his virtue simple. Starbuck can be analogized to the everyman or the elevated everyman. Rather than the quiet American or the ugly American, he is the good American.

Melville's *Moby-Dick*, his monumental meditation on American democracy, needs Starbuck. It cannot revolve only around Ahab, who is the agent of destruction. He is the American who is not a democrat. No ship is exactly a democracy; captains have privileges that can be abused; and Ahab uses his legally allotted powers to co-opt his crew and ultimately to get them killed. Starbuck has the shortcomings of the single citizen when captain and crew are consumed by bloodlust and folly. Starbuck shows us more than this: he demonstrates the force of principle, the beauty of faith (not in democracy but in God), and the majesty of the law (not of rules but of the law). His clarity of vision, his avoidance of self-deception, and his law-bound attempts to resist an errant captain are the very qualities that democracy demands from all its citizens, however hard these demands are to meet.

Before the *Pequod*'s journey has begun in earnest, Melville-Ishmael, the novel's narrator, gives us two separate versions of Starbuck's character. One anticipates Starbuck's capitulation to Ahab. In this idea, Starbuck is not "mass man" on display, not Hannah Arendt's alienated modern individual prone (and eager perhaps) to be mobilized into some totalitarian project. Starbuck is flinty and taciturn but not empty. "He was a long earnest man," his thinness "merely the condensation of the man." He has a survivor's strength and "seemed prepared to endure for long ages to come, and to endure always as now; for be it a Polar snow or a torrid sun, like a patent chronometer, his interior vitality was warranted to do well in all climates." The interior vitality is notable, whereas the robotic readiness to endure suggests passivity, even heedlessness.

Though Starbuck thinks, he is not a thinker. He is a "staid, steadfast man, whose life for the most part was a telling pantomime of action." He bows to convention, to rules, to society's expectations of him. A life that is a telling pantomime of action is not the life of Socrates or Julius Caesar; it is missing something. This characterization of Starbuck, offered at the beginning of the novel, fully explains Starbuck's inability to master Ahab, even when Starbuck knows that Ahab's course is pure disaster. To sense the "welded iron of [Starbuck's] soul" is to worry that Starbuck has the makings of an organization man, which for the most part he does. His life is shaped by the organizations around him on land and at sea, qualifying Starbuck to be (in context) an American everyman, capable but conformist.

Melville-Ishmael's other version of Starbuck challenges his tilt toward mediocrity. He is "uncommonly conscientious for a seaman, and endued with a deep natural reverence." The natural reverence is for God and family and for decent conduct on ship. He accepts the bottom line of a whaling voyage, without being beholden to it: "his far-away domestic memories of his young Cape wife and child . . . tend[ed] to bend him still more from the original ruggedness of his nature." This is not remarkable: Starbuck loves his family. On a ship sated with blood, driven forward by cruel and deceitful leadership and all too accustomed to solitude, Starbuck's far-away domestic memories are not beside the point. For him, they are the point. Pious Starbuck truly believes in family and in love, despite the absence of both in the harsh seas around him and on the decks of a brutal and brutalized ship.

In an extravagant passage that follows the description of Starbuck's circumscribed character, Melville-Ishmael voices a soliloquy on human dignity, God, and democracy. Here Melville-Ishmael preempts an interpretation of *Moby-Dick* premised on Ahab's eventual "success" and Starbuck's foreordained "failure," which is to say the success of wickedness and the failure of virtue: "but were the coming narrative to reveal, in any instance, the complete abasement of poor Starbuck's fortitude, scarce might I have the heart to write it; for it is a thing most sorrowful, nay shocking, to expose the fall of valor in the soul." Unbending Starbuck, rule-bound Starbuck, unimaginative Starbuck has a valorous soul. In this bit of self-explanation, *Moby-Dick*'s narrator informs us that valor does not fall in Starbuck's soul. The coming narrative reveals an altogether different evolution, in which Starbuck preserves and honors the valor safely stored in his living soul.

Aided by a philosophizing narrator, *Moby-Dick* ceases for a moment to belong to furious Ahab and his star-crossed quest. "Men may seem detestable as joint stock-companies and nations: knaves, fools, and murderers there may be; men may have mean and meagre faces; but man, in the ideal, is so noble and so sparkling, such a grand and glowing creature, that over any ignominious blemish in him all his fellows should run in and throw their costliest robes." Starbuck — these words are still associated, however loosely, with him — has his ignominious blemishes, and in the novel no one wishes to throw a robe over them. We get a good education in Starbuck's faults. Yet he is there to recall the noble and the sparkling in us, in human nature, which has so much potential to be grand and glowing — even on the dark miserable death-bound *Pequod*.

The narrator's next thought shifts between politics and theology. It is that "piety" abhors "the undraped spectacle of a valor-ruined man," and the opposite of a valor-ruined man is "this august dignity I treat of." It is not "the dignity of kings and robes, but that abounding dignity which has no robed investiture," not inherited and not dictated by social status. Typically enough for Melville, the language takes a biblical turn: "thou shalt see it [dignity] shining in the arm that wields a pick or drives a spike." It is "that democratic dignity which on all hands, radiates without end from God; Himself! The great God absolute! The centre and circumference of all democracy! His omnipresence, our divine equality." These words invoke Thomas Jefferson, the Declaration of Independence, and the inalienable rights handed to humanity by the Creator. Modest Starbuck has taken matters immodestly far.

Starbuck, who is no ship's captain and no hero, almost has an arm that wields a pick or drives a spike. What he lacks in courage, in readiness to lead, he makes up for with his abounding dignity. His citizenship and his piety undergird the valor that he will not relinquish, the dignity that radiates out from God. The narrator's ecstatic syntax makes it somewhat unclear whether God or dignity is the center and circumference of all democracy. Most likely it is dignity. Though *Moby-Dick* famously chronicles the (short-term) victory of a demagogue, it subtly explores the democratic dignity of the common man, who more than any other character in the novel is Starbuck. The conflict between Ahab and Starbuck, which comes at the climax of *Moby-Dick*, before the final stages of the hunt, is foreshortened if attuned only to Ahab's winning wickedness. The Ahab-Starbuck duel exalts Starbuck's dignity, and Starbuck, who is defeated by Ahab, is never once debased by him or by anything.

In *Moby-Dick*, Ahab is Ahab and only Ahab. Pushed ahead by his discipline and his pain, he fends off any change of heart. "There was," we learn, "an infinity of firmest fortitude, a determinate, unsurrenderable willfulness, in the fixed and fearless, forward dedication of that glance." This is Ahab the visionary, the CEO, though one with "a crucifixion in his face" and an "intense bigotry of purpose in his aspect." Because he wants so intensely he is blind, blinded by himself and his vaunting bigotry. His gift is to get others not to see what he cannot see: that chasing Moby-Dick is pointless, stupid, and ruinously dangerous. He fashions a singular obsession into a collective delusion. As Ishmael-Melville observes, "the history of fanatics [is not] half so striking in respect to the measureless self-deception of the fanatic himself, as his measureless power of deceiving and bedevilling so many others." The others follow suit. They seem to have been waiting all along to enlist in his crazed plans.

Ahab bedevils Starbuck without deceiving him. Ahab plies his crew with alcohol and with the intoxicating thrill of pursuing the white whale. He absorbs them into his lust for revenge. Only Starbuck objects: "'Vengeance on a dumb brute!' cried Starbuck, 'that simply smote thee from blind instinct. Madness! To be enraged with a dumb thing, Captain Ahab, seems blasphemous.'" Starbuck is Ahab's subordinate, as Ahab never forgets, and Starbuck takes a risk with his madman boss. The risk is to call madness madness — in the very face of a madness that has confused itself with genius. "Blasphemy" is a surprising word here, underscoring Starbuck's piety and Ahab's self-theism. Ahab is assuming the posture of a wrathful God angered not by sin but by the existence of Moby-Dick, his rage touched with the authority of law. On the ship, Captain Ahab's words are a kind of law to the crew.

The crew joyfully drinks Ahab's poison. Witnessing Ahab's triumph and the dancing drunken crew, Starbuck is crestfallen. He "paled, turned, and shivered" and began to brood: "'Oh, I plainly see my miserable office, to obey, rebelling; and worse yet to hate with a touch of pity.'" Reflected in his eyes is the "sharkish sea," cognate for sharkish captain and crew, hunters, and nothing more. Obedient Starbuck rebels by internalizing the horror of this voyage: "'Oh, life! 'tis now I do feel the latent horror in thee! But 'tis not me. That horror's out of me! And with the soft feeling of the human in me, yet will I try to fight ye, ye grim, phantom futures! Stand by me, hold me, bind me, O ye blessed influences!'" Starbuck does not resign himself to the low designs of his captain. He is resolved to fight.

Starbuck's outburst evokes a novella written long after *Moby-Dick*, though well before *Moby-Dick* was rediscovered as a classic in the 1920s. Joseph Conrad's *Heart of Darkness*, published in 1899, can serve as a gloss on *Moby-Dick*. Conrad describes a ship captain gone mad, Captain Kurtz, who comes to articulate the horror that he has absorbed and created: *the horror, the horror*. But 'tis not me, Starbuck might have said to Kurtz; he and horror are not continuous. The soft feeling of the human resides in him, prompting him to call upon the blessed influences. Lacking a heart of darkness, Starbuck cannot hate unequivocally, which Ahab can and does. That unequivocal hatred is stronger than equivocal hatred is the stuff of tragedy, since unequivocal hatred is so much worse: Captain Kurtz explores the borders of unequivocal hatred and finds them porous; Captain Ahab finds them nonexistent. Sharkish sea, sharkish horror-filled life. In a sharkish world, pity is a liability, and to be softly human or human at all is a liability too.

In two separate scenes, Starbuck attempts to do something on behalf of himself, of Ahab, and of the crew. Palpable in these scenes is "the incompetence of mere unaided virtue or right-mindedness in Starbuck." (The word "unaided" reminds us of the crew's total devotion to Ahab.) Yet incompetent Starbuck, unable to save the ship, preserves a kingdom within himself. He has already spoken truth to power, as we like to say, back when Ahab was motivating the crew, offering it the seductions of catastrophe. Starbuck struggles to speak truth directly to Ahab — but he does "with a daring so strangely respectful and cautious that it almost seemed not only every way seeking to avoid the slightest outward manifestation of itself, but within also seemed more than half distrustful of itself." Starbuck is a natural first mate. It is against his nature to confront Ahab, not so much out of personal duty to Ahab, whom he loathes, but out of his innate attraction to duty itself and to the moral order of which duty is a part.

Confronting Ahab, Starbuck uncovers a duty higher than shipboard chain-of-command. It could be called a duty to the truth, and Ahab will have none of it. Having heard his first mate's request, Starbuck's appeal to reason and to turn the oil-laden ship home, Ahab points a gun at him, telling Starbuck "there is one God that is Lord over the earth, and one Captain that is lord over the *Pequod* — on deck!'" Starbuck's response is as marvelous as words can be, when words must contend with evil or a wanton self-destructiveness. "'Thou hast outraged, not insulted me, sir,'" Starbuck explains, "'but for that I ask thee not to be aware of Starbuck; thou wouldst but laugh; but let Ahab be aware of Ahab; beware of thyself, old man.'" Rather than the rhetoric of judgment Starbuck employs the language of sympathy, recognizing that the crew's lives hang on the thread of Ahab's self-awareness. Beautifully, Melville-Ishmael merges the word "beware," as in be forewarned, into two words, "be aware," to know oneself. Beware not being aware.

Having stared down Ahab's gun, Starbuck finds himself on deck (where Ahab had commanded him to go). Elated, Starbuck peers into the "golden sea." He has witnessed evil and felt faith, murmuring to himself, "'Loveliness unfathomable, as ever lover saw in his young bride's eye!'" Starbuck is vibrating with moral joy, receptive to the ocean's loveliness: "'Tell me not of thy teeth-tiered sharks, and thy kidnapping cannibal ways. Let faith oust fact; let fancy oust memory; I look deep down and I do believe.'" Let faith oust fact, homage to a faith larger than fact, the fact of teeth-tiered sharks and of Ahab's gun and of the nullity Starbuck recognizes as the *Pequod*'s chosen destination. Keeping his faith when fact merits disgust and despair, Starbuck salvages that which is best in him. He looks deep down — into the golden sea, into Ahab's effective lunacy, into his imperfect self — and he does believe. Ahab's descent is Starbuck's ascent.

Chapter 123 is titled "The Musket." It recounts Starbuck's anguish over Ahab. Starbuck's mind is lucid; he is without illusion. Ahab has compelled Starbuck to choose between force and persuasion, between pulling the trigger and not pulling the trigger. In Starbuck "strangely evolved an evil thought" when looking at a musket: it is to cheat disaster. The justification for murdering Ahab is self-evident, and the consequences of such violence would not necessarily have been bad for Starbuck. "'I stand alone,'" he tells himself, "'here upon an open sea, with two oceans and a whole continent between me and the law.'" Having shunted aside the law, having made it contingent on time and place, he is suddenly forsaken by God: "'Great God, where art thou? Shall I? Shall I?'"

Biblical references adorn this language, lonely Noah on the "open sea," Christ on the cross worried about God's absence, the repetition of "Shall I?" an inversion of the unrelenting "thou shalt not" rhythm of the ten commandments.

In Chapter 123, Starbuck finds no backdoor exit from the law. He stands down: "the yet levelled musket shook like a drunkard's arm against the panel; Starbuck wrestling with an angel; but turning from the door, he placed the death-tube in its rack, and left the place." The angel has stayed his shaking arm, raising a sweeping question for this novel and its readers. Is Starbuck mistaken? The extensive foreshadowing about his brittle courage furnishes one answer to the question. By emphasizing Starbuck's deficiencies, Melville conjures regret in the reader, regret that this devil's journey is so firmly in the devil's hands and that angels have second thoughts. Yet two oceans' distance from the populous land does not alter the law. The rejection of homicide is not weakness. Weakness might be the hunger to eliminate Ahab and thus to mutiny. Starbuck's spiritual strength is his hunger not to end Ahab's life. Sparing Ahab is a version of the law, not that the novel's plot rewards Starbuck's renunciation of the death-tube. His restraint is quickly punished, a destiny fully legible to Starbuck, the man who cannot shoot.

We last see Starbuck in his professional role, in his assigned spot, doing his duty. The white whale is coming for the *Pequod*. "Oh, all ye sweet powers of air, now hug me close! Let not Starbuck die, if die he must, in a woman's fainting fit." His sturdiness then dissolves into the interrogative — "is this the end of all my bursting prayers? all my lifelong fidelities," as if at this moment he were the prodigal son's elder brother, the obedient one to whom forgiveness and salvation seem unfairly distant. Moby-Dick's "unappeasable brow" is aimed at the one who cannot leave his station. "My God, stand by me now," are the words that precede Starbuck's death. His prayers and fidelities had meant nothing to Ahab; they did not protect Starbuck from the malevolent whale, the thing that could not be appeased; but the many bursting prayers put him, his conscience clear, in good proximity to God, helping him achieve a life honorably lived and a death honorably accepted. Preoccupied with dying the right death, Starbuck would have had an admirer in Socrates.

Ahab shows us how democracies die. He could be revived as a hologram and put on the twenty-first century lecture circuit, explaining what authoritarianism means to an authoritarian. He could speak about charisma and mystery as authoritarian tactics, about the irrational in his crew, about its appetite for the primal and the mythic and the tribal, and about the delicious vulnerability that this appetite presents to the budding authoritarian. Ahab could tell us about hatred, a motive less ephemeral than the desire to make money or to get home or to begin the next voyage. He could speak about the authoritarian leader as an instrument of personal hatred and an instrument of generic hatred, mocking democracies and their struggle to suppress hatred's ancient and archaic grandeur. Hatred threatens the procedural balancing acts that are the essence of democratic practice. Ahab could lay all of this out. He understands the machinery of authoritarianism. He could talk us through its instruction manual.

Ahab is a tyrant, and in office tyrants inspire either obedience or revolution. Once Ahab is captain, democracy or whatever democracy resembles on a ship is imperiled. Precisely because democracy dies on the *Pequod*, while tyranny lives, *Moby-Dick* takes up the question of revolution. Since the crew is mindlessly in Ahab's grip, the question of revolution belongs solely to Starbuck. Melville's America lived in the shadow of revolution; his family descended from a revolutionary hero. Fortuitously, the American Revolution had destroyed the monarchy in the colonies without having to destroy the monarch. This was the uncommon revolution that did not entail parricide, so tame (in some respects) that the great philosophical enemy of the French Revolution, Edmund Burke, considered the American Revolution a legitimate and worthwhile enterprise. The American Revolution could break both ways, toward violence and toward law.

The first half of the nineteenth century witnessed multiple revolutions, all of them aftershocks of the French Revolution. One broke out in France in 1830 and others across Europe in 1848, when *Moby-Dick* was stirring to life in Melville's mind. The drivers of revolution resonate in the pages of *Moby-Dick*, as the *Pequod* exhibits every incitement to revolution: gross inequality, viciousness doled out along the lines of race and class, extended physical suffering, a ruling elite (in Ahab) that lies and deceives. Ahab is more than out of touch with the people: his misrule harms his crew. It is leadership without statecraft tied to a strategy with no potential to succeed. Ahab is worse than King George III, who imposed taxes on the colonists and curtailed their rights but who did not condemn them to abject misery. George III did not eviscerate the colonists' lives in some concerted way. Ahab is worse than Louis XVI, more comprehensive in the misery he brings to the *Pequod* than Louis XVI was in the misery he brought to prerevolutionary France.

Revolutions, uprisings, and mutinies recur throughout ancient and modern history. They have their place in the reservoir of political options, but the task of uniting revolution, democracy, and law is enormous. Just as revolutions demand the suspension of law to proceed, they can ignite from the perceived illegitimacy of law. Law can shrink into a vestige of the ancient regime, and revolution can operate as law, violence begetting violence in perpetuity. Yet democracies demand a stable body of law, especially those that are hewn from revolution, and they need the law to be non-negotiable, non-situational. In democracies, law must have a status and an authority unto itself. Otherwise, democracy collapses into anarchy or disappears into authoritarianism, meaning that a single figure, the leader, can override law at will or pretend to be the lawgiver as such. Politics without law is merely what the leader dictates on his way to dictatorship. For democracies, the law must have a hold on individual citizens. It must emanate from them and cannot just inform "the system." Citizens with agency must defer not to power but to law, since power by its nature corrupts, while law has the potential to mediate and to civilize. The law has a hold on Starbuck.

Starbuck shows us how democracies live. He shows us in particular how American democracy lives. Growing from revolution, the American Republic made a fetish of law, inaugurating a cult of the Constitution. Starbuck is a product and a mirror of this system. If *Moby-Dick* is set around 1850 (and it seems to be), then Starbuck must have been born around 1820, not long after the creation of the republic. His ethos is not exactly "give me liberty or give me death." It is not a prerevolutionary or a revolutionary ethos tinged with romanticism. His is a legal ethos: give him law or give him death — to which Ahab's response is to give him death. Starbuck, whose devotion to the law never wavers, will not crash the constitutional order around him. Nor will he allow his singular dilemma to take precedent over the immoveable majesty of the law. Starbuck sees no path that is not the path of the law. Pressured to accept Ahab's lawlessness, then pressured by himself to contemplate the lawlessness of killing his captain, Starbuck turns his back on lawlessness, knowingly sacrificing himself to the idea of the law.

Thirteen years after *Moby-Dick* was published, the Starbuck-Ahab duel manifested itself on the national stage. High politics rewrote the literary record. The man with his finger on the trigger was an actor, not a first mate. He stood in a theater. The captain was an American president as far from insanity as a man could be, meaning that in real life the roles were reversed. John Wilkes Booth had a fevered mind and envisioned himself a warrior for liberty. He would free the country from tyranny by ridding it of Abraham Lincoln: *sic semper tyrannis*, thus always to tyrants, he cried as the shots rang out. Booth was a Starbuck radicalized, whereas Lincoln, for all his power, was an Ahab de-radicalized, shorn of viciousness and narcissism, if a bit like Ahab in the wounds that he carried, the family losses and the troubles that Lincoln endured. Lincoln did not indulge his grievances; he was no virtuoso of rage. If Lincoln felt lasting anger, it did not form him. He did not lead from anger. Without anger, Ahab would have no reason to lead, no reason to live.

As with Starbuck and Ahab, Booth and Lincoln had contrary positions on the law. The constitution offered Booth no option for redressing his fury or for assuaging his madness. He followed no laws in assassinating Lincoln, and he broke many. John Wilkes Booth in 1865 — and Lee Harvey Oswald in 1963 — wanted killing to do what the Constitution could not do: to cleanse the nation of the compromises and the legislative back-and-forth of the Constitutional republic. Their bullets would bend history with an agency that is inaccessible to the citizens of such a republic, an agency that should be inaccessible to such citizens. When not voting, citizens must consent to being represented. Power floats above them in people and institutions who are well known but far away. Citizens must accept the fallibility of these people and of these institutions. That, too, is the law, and the law that assassins brush aside as a figment of the status quo.

Trained as a lawyer, Lincoln had a lawyer's wiliness and a politician's addiction to sophistry. Lincoln valued racial justice. It spoke to him as an attribute of the republic implied at its beginning, "four score and seven years ago." It spoke to him as a desirable attribute of the future republic, the republic without slavery that would one day exist. Lincoln also equivocated and molded his messages to the limitations of his audiences. He valued racial justice but he struggled with racial equality. The early republic's contradictions gave rise to Lincoln, plunging the United States into civil war, and Lincoln's contradictions gave rise to a century of confusion about racial equality. There was so much that Lincoln's presidency did not solve, so much genuine equality deferred because Lincoln had a lawyer's talent for manipulating procedure and language. The opacity of Lincoln stems in part from his flexibility of mind and from his having a politician's impurity. In this regard, he was neither a Starbuck nor an Ahab. Neither of these literary characters could have run for office.

Lincoln was no Ahab at all in his worship of the law, about

which he could be more philosophical than lawyerly. The government "of the people, by the people, for the people" issued from the Constitution's "we the people," a set of relationships in which law is the link. Self-government without law is meaningless, an exercise in self-harm. Had Lincoln been president without a civil war, he could have handled the law calmly — by not tarnishing it. He could have left a republic of laws for the next president to inherit, having been the benevolent leader of "the people," who are also the creators and the underwriters of the law. Instead, Lincoln had to confront the precarity of law amid a civil war. He could foresee the postwar challenge of salvaging the law from the chaos of war and of administering the law in a riven nation. Fated not to live beyond the war, Lincoln's monumental task was to serve the law while the battles and the casualties mounted.

Lincoln muddled through. No doubt he was tempted to expand his powers; the right to *habeas corpus* was suspended during the Civil War, and civil liberties suffered accordingly. Yet Lincoln upheld the law in consequential ways. He ran in and won the 1864 election, ensuring that his authority would not derive from his title as commander-in-chief but from the popular sovereignty written into a presidential election. With the Emancipation Proclamation, he signaled that the travesty of slavery, which had been deeply embedded in legal practice, would be transformed less by war than by law. Via the law, an expanded sense of citizenry would fulfil the spirit of laws (as Lincoln saw it), the sentiment that all men are created equal. Ahab prizes the capricious law of one, declaring himself the uncontested lord of the *Pequod*. Lincoln did what he could to keep the law in the hands of the many, the basic promise of American governance. His death in Ford's Theater, trauma that it was, was not the nation's shipwreck. He had done enough by then for the ship not to sink.

Like Starbuck, Lincoln had the soft feeling of the human in him. In politics, the ideal is the conjunction between the law and the soft feeling of the human. Starbuck's character instructs us not in anything absolute about law and about love — both can be compromised, corrupted, perverted, overridden. Often enough the horror wins out. Starbuck instructs us in the preciousness of the law and of love as human and as political traits. In Lincoln these traits were united as they rarely are in political leaders, the nation's good fortune amid the ill fortune of civil war. When a Lincoln is not at the helm, disaster is by no means inevitable. A great deal is up to the citizens who are not president. Starbuck should be their patron saint, if literature can make this possible, because he must live under Ahab without coming to resemble Ahab. To survive as Starbuck, he must live as a decent citizen, and he does.

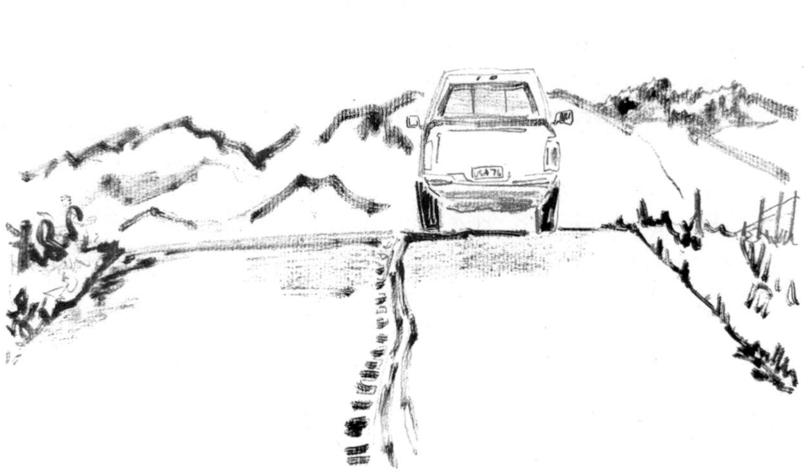

PHOEBE CARY

Advice Gratis To Certain Women, by A Woman

O, my strong-minded sisters, aspiring to vote,
And to row with your brothers, all in the same boat,
When you come out to speak to the public your mind,
Leave your tricks, and your airs, and your graces behind!

For instance, when you by the world would be seen
As reporter, or editor (first-class, I mean),
I think—just to come to the point in one line—
What you write will be finer, if 'tis not too fine.

Pray, don't let the thread of your subject be strung
With "golden," and "shimmer," "sweet," "filter," and "flung;"
Nor compel, by your style, all your readers to guess
You've been looking up words Webster marks obs.

And another thing: whatever else you may say,
Do keep personalities out of the way;
Don't try every sentence to make people see
What a dear, charming creature the writer must be!

Leave out affectations and pretty appeals;
Don't "drag yourself in by the neck and the heels,"
Your dear little boots, and your gloves; and take heed,
Nor pull your curls over men's eyes while they read.

Don't mistake me; I mean that the public's not home,
You must do as the Romans do, when you're in Rome;
I would have you be womanly, while you are wise;
'Tis the weak and the womanish tricks I despise.

On the other hand: don't write and dress in such styles
As astonish the natives, and frighten the isles;
Do look, on the platform, so folks in the show
Needn't ask, "Which are lions, and which tigers?" you know!

'Tis a good thing to write, and to rule in the state,
But to be a true, womanly woman is great:
And if ever you come to be that, 'twill be when
You can cease to be babies, nor try to be men!

(1854)

ARASH AZIZI

Irandoost, *or Confessions of a Patriot*

On the long list of things that bother me about much of the left today, especially in the West, is its allergy to patriotism. In my own understanding of human commitments, loving your country and holding socialist ideals are not contradictory commitments. One can easily maintain both. But the history of the left shows that there has never been anything obvious or untroublesome about this combination of allegiances. My own story helps to explain why.

My path to this dual identity has been long and winding. Born in 1988 in Tehran, I grew up in the immediate post-Soviet era when most varieties of leftism had gone seriously out of fashion, especially among my fellow teenagers in a country that had fallen victim to its own revolutionary utopianism. But I had already been swimming against the current — I identified myself as a Marxist in my early teens, whatever one could mean by such labels at that time. But this identification never made me any less of an Iranian patriot or, to use a common Persian term, *Irandoost*, roughly translatable as "Iran-lover."

Despite my Marxist politics, I remained a typical Iranian. Iranians are known for their strong pride in their country and their culture, and I shared that pride then as I do now. I took pride in Iran's long and beautiful civilization and how our story has often been central to world history: who else is mentioned both in the Bible and in ancient Chinese chronicles? As a writer, my primary vehicle for my love for Iran has probably been the Persian language, a tongue spoken in its current form for centuries. It was my love for this language that propelled me to become a writer in the first place: I couldn't think of anything I wanted more than crafting sentences in Persian, throwing around Persian words like playdough. I still regularly revel in the fact that I share a mother tongue with Rumi, Hafiz, and Saadi. Their medieval poems all sound so uncannily contemporary, some essential vitality in the Persian language having been preserved throughout its long evolution. I could go on and on about Iran's cinema, and Iran's social movements, and everything else that makes me proud of my origin.

Yet we have a tendency also for self-glorification, and I am not proud of this particular attribute. Our national pride can border on obsession, on excessive self-love. We must always beware of it. It must be criticized as a self-centered attitude that, like so many forms of nationalism, ends up blinding many to their country's flaws and tensions, and making them less open to the world. Worse, it leads to blind embrace of national mythologies and to the smug disregard of our actual history.

In the Iran of my youth, even quotidian patriotism had a subversive edge to it. The Islamic Republic that ruled us was based on an austere and militant ideological Islamism, which meant that so many of us who opposed it ended up, knowingly or otherwise, championing a form of national identity as resistance. We were hoping to resist the regime's quest for the creation of a New Islamic Man by our insistent perpetuation of historically rooted Iranian traditions. The nation would frustrate or thwart or bring down the theocracy. An old civilization would defeat a new tyranny.

Of course, like most revolutionary regimes, the Islamic Republic understood that, if it was to have any chance of survival, it needed to co-opt a form of nationalism. By the early 1980s, it had already given up on the more radical plans of its early years to ban Nowruz, the national new year, or to raze the tomb of our fabled medieval poet, Ferdowsi, whose *Shahnameh,* or *the Book of Kings*, is perhaps the single most beloved book of poetry for Iranians. But the regime continued to prohibit many forms of open patriotism. National traditions celebrated for centuries by millions of Iranians, such as the fire festival held on the last Wednesday of every Persian year, remain officially forbidden. Moreover, the regime presents a very restricted vision of Iranian culture, and it heavily censors its expressions. On the pages of the officially approved textbooks, or in the halls of the regime-run cultural centers in Sarajevo or Mexico City, you will find an Islamist narrative of Iranian history that excludes many of the great achievements of Iranian culture, old and new. No poetry by great poets such as Ahmad Shamlou or Forough Farrokhzad, no films by great directors such as Abbas Kiarostami or Dariush Mehrjoee. As a result, something as simple as championing Iranian arts and culture has long been seen as a form of national resistance to the hated clerical regime.

I kept to this vision of patriotic resistance even after joining a clandestine socialist group that was harshly anti-religious as well as anti-nationalist. I debated with the other members about the legitimacy of patriotism. I agreed about socialist internationalism, but weren't we, after all, also fighting for Iran, for our particular country, to save it from the clutches of a hated dictatorship? Surely one could be both an internationalist and an *Irandoost*? Well, maybe not so surely.

I left that group behind a long time ago and my politics has had its ups and downs since. But that contradiction has never quite gone away. When I was twenty years old, I left Iran to study abroad. In Canada, Great Britain, and the United States, I naturally joined leftist groups and then came to marvel at how much of their politics seemed to be rooted in a form of *oikophobia* — hating all that your country stands for. Of course, it would make sense for leftists to hate how bad things were in their country — they were agents of change, after all. And it would make sense for the citizens of the world's foremost imperialist powers to critique its reach — they were seeking justice, after all. But could politics be possible without a positive vision for your own country? Without any sense of identification with the national-political community in which you were trying to realize your political principles? Not that I had simple answers to these questions. Sometimes their converse haunted me. If politics was to be rooted in identification with one's country, what happens to the avowed internationalism of the socialist movement? Hadn't Marx taught that "the workers have no country?"

As I grappled with these questions, I soon discovered that there were more erudite and complex ways of dealing with them. For my first degree at the University of Toronto I decided on an unusual major, the then-nascent Diaspora and Transnational Studies — a whole field of study that could be described as an interrogation of the concept of "home" and what it means to be from somewhere. Under scholars such as Ato Quayson and Anna Shternshis, I read my Benedict Anderson and Eric Hobsbawm, my Stuart Hall and Audre Lorde. I learned about "methodological nationalism" — taking the division of the world into nations as a primordial immutability as opposed to a contingent arrangement of historical circumstances. I learned how identities are "socially constructed," and how supposedly ancient traditions had been "invented" in more recent times.

In the years to come, questions of belonging and nationality would become relevant far beyond the debates of small leftist groups or the halls of academia. In the Middle East, the quick spread of the Arab Spring movements from one Arab country to another reminded us all of the heyday of Pan-Arabism in the 1960s and 1970s and the continuously porous borders of the modern nation-states. I wrote an article in Persian that I titled "The Arab Revolution and the Death Agony of the Nation-State." I was excited; I was naive. The grand new Arab revolution never arrived, and the spring of hope ended in a freezing winter of authoritarianism and sectarian civil wars. The so-called Sykes-Picot borders of the Middle East, much lamented by progressives as a vestige of imperialism, were indeed torn apart, but not by any emancipatory project: it was ISIS that destroyed them. Civil wars ravaged Syria, Libya, and Iraq, leaving their people wishing not for further breakdown but for strong national states.

Elsewhere, the age of liberal globalization with its celebration of federalism in Europe and free trade across the world gave way to a newly emboldened and increasingly extreme right-wing nationalism. If there was any doubt that the old consensus of the West had been torn asunder, 2016 put it to rest with the twin shock votes on both sides of the Atlantic: the Brexit referendum in June and the election of Donald Trump in November. In the space of five months, a twenty-first-century politics that was both progressive and patriotic seemed to have been falsified.

But is there truly no way to love your country as a universalist? To denounce your country even as you love it?

I have never had any desire to be a contrarian or to occupy a minority position politically. Contrarianism is almost always a pose, a way of attracting attention to yourself, and glorifying in minoritarianism is often a form of virtue-signaling. (Not everybody in the wilderness is a prophet.) But it has turned out that my own tendencies have gone the opposite way of the fashionable anti-nationalism left. Somewhat ironically, after all these years of critical study, I have come to believe that there was something right about the precocious patriotism of my youth; and also that if the left is to have any chance, it must rediscover its love for the nation.

To chart a future out of the current impasse, I resorted, like many leftists, to looking deeper into the past. My graduate studies in history culminated in a dissertation on an oft-forgotten aspect of the Communist parties of the twentieth century: the way they mixed their staunch internationalism with a patriotism. Communist parties are hardly an obvious place to look for inspiring patriotism, or much else besides. They are now hated by all sides. Liberals and conservatives, Trotskyists and New Leftists all condemn the Communists as authoritarian Stalinists and dogmatic doctrinaires. Many of the recent histories of the left coming out of the academy champion various leftist currents of the 1960s, with their conceptual innovations and norm-breaking; historians write glowingly of "the anti-authoritarian revolt" of 1968 in West Germany and the adventures of the counterculture from Australia to Brazil. Much less love is lost on the dour Communists with their orthodox Marxism and their relatively conservative attitude to the innovations of the 1960s.

Dour they certainly were, and in many ways a revolting lot. But the more I studied the Communist parties in the Middle East, my area of specialty, and beyond, the more hooked I became. (As I say, in these things I have a knack for going against the grain.) Of course there was much to criticize and even to loathe: their adulation of the Soviet Union, a criminal blood-soaked state, and their lack of any proper conception of *democratic* socialism. But here were political parties with millions of supporters which seemed to balance eventual revolutionary goals with a day-to-day practical politics. From Italy to Japan, they ran effective municipalities while also organizing a national and international force for socialist politics.

What fascinated me most about the Communist parties was how they were simultaneously much more internationalist *and* much more patriotic than the contemporary left. I could see this in the relationships between Iranian, Iraqi, Palestinian, and Israeli communists. In an era when peoples of the Middle East were harshly divided by national and sectarian conflicts, the internationalism of communists meant that they were able to transcend these divisions and work together as, well, comrades. The tales of such transgressions are often nothing short of heroic. When the Iranian state went after its communists following the CIA-backed coup of 1953, it was the Iraqi communists who helped to smuggle their

Iranian counterparts into Iraq. The Iranians returned the favor, helping Iraqis hide out in Iran after yet another CIA-backed coup in Iraq in 1963. When the partition of Palestine in 1947 was followed by a ferocious Arab-Jewish war and the accompanying Nakba, Israeli and Palestinian communists stood in solidarity with each other, keeping to this solidarity against all odds and throughout the decades to come. From Iraq to Palestine to Syria to Iran, Arab and Iranian communists bravely defended the right of Jewish Israelis to self-determination, which amounted to a defense of Israel's right to exist. In 1954, the Iraqi Communist Party ran a campaign on the theme of "Arab-Israeli brotherhood." The Palestinian poet Mahmoud Darwish, a communist, once declared: "We recognize the State of Israel and the Palestinian people's right to self-determination. This is the starting point in all that we do: This land belongs to both peoples, and both have an equal right to exist." Jewish Israeli communists, meanwhile, became the biggest champion of the rights of the Palestinian citizens of Israel and the most vociferous opponents of the occupation of Palestinian lands after 1967.

But what made the communists stand out wasn't their cross-border solidarity. Many others have shown such transnational loyalties. These communists were distinguished by their patriotism. They were invested in a notion of the nation as a legitimate and meaningful political community that was to be prized and defended. Were they simply blind to all that I had learned in school? Didn't they know of the many bloodied fields left behind by nation-states, of the dangerous consequences of nationalism?

I came to realize that the communists were able to distinguish between patriotism and chauvinism, between inclusive and exclusive forms of nationalism. For them, a nation was a historical reality, a stage in the development of humanity, and it carried immense potential for good. These communists seemed to implicitly accept that their foundational text, *The Communist Manifesto*, had gone too far when it suggested that workers had no countries. After all, wasn't that infamous line contradicted by the concluding battle-cry of the same text, "Workers of all countries, unite"? *Aller Länder,!*

Throughout the twentieth century, as new nations came to replace collapsing empires and the nation-state emerged as the default political community, old-school socialists and communists worked not against but through these nations to bring about the global fraternity that they advocated for. Or at least some of them did.

My belief in socialist patriotism came in handy in 2022–2023, when the uprising broke out in Iran. I could identify an unmistakable feature of the rebellion: its project of national reclamation. The movement in Iran soon became identified with a slogan it borrowed from the progressive Kurdish movements in Syria and Turkey: Woman, Life, Freedom. But it was also clear that, for many Iranians taking part in it, this was also a *national* uprising. The old Iranian flag, the tricolor with the Lion-and-the-Sun, had long been dismissed as a monarchist symbol. As the last crown prince of the overthrown monarchy, Reza Pahlavi, emerged as a key political figure during the revolt, this association was further established. But for many Iranians, the old flag, which predates the Pahlavi monarchy by centuries, dating at least to the Timurid Iran of the 1400s, has become not a partisan symbol but a national symbol. It is linked to a program of national revival, not monarchist legitimism. Even some leading government officials in the Islamic Republic now openly regret the gutting of the old symbol and speak of reclaiming it for the nation. As Iranians yearn to take their country back from a small corrupt clique, they hunt for the traces of their deeply rooted history.

When I declared my affection for the national flag, I was predictably attacked by my compatriots all over the political spectrum. Those opposed to the left indignantly asked how an internationalist socialist can be a patriot. They invoked a Persian epithet long used to condemn cosmopolitanism of all kinds, *Bi-Vatan* (homelandness) or *Jahanvatan* (one whose homeland is the world). The hardliners on the left would conversely demand to know how I could defend a nationalist flag. Both sides missed entirely the Iranian left's history of fervent patriotism, best demonstrated in the communist Tudeh Party of Iran. Tudeh is now derided on all sides for its supposed subservience to the Soviet Union, doubly offensive for the grand Russian state, Iran's more powerful northern neighbor, had long harbored predatory designs upon it. Many Iranians seemed to have forgotten what a large percentage of the most brilliant Iranian writers and intellectuals had spent at least some time in the Tudeh, while others had been, at one point or another, influenced by the party's internationalist ethos — an ethos that helped link Iran to the world via communist poets such as Langston Hughes and Pablo Neruda. When Iranians shop for a copy of Ferdowsi's *Shahnameh* today, they are most likely to get one based on the "Moscow edition," an elegant canonical version, mostly based on a thirteenth-century manuscript in the British Museum. The formidable editorial work on this critical edition was done by Abdolhossein Nushin, a communist playwright and a Ferdowsi scholar and a staunch member of the Tudeh Party. Like many prominent communists, he had fled Iran for the Soviet Union during a wave of anti-communist repression by the Shah in the late 1940s. The coup in 1953 made return impossible and he spent decades in his Soviet exile, working on the *Shahnameh*. The old Iranian masterpiece became the subject of his doctoral dissertation at Moscow's Maxim Gorky Literature Institute. He died in Moscow in 1971.

Another Iranian communist exile in the USSR was to play an even more consequential nation-building role. A Kurdish poet born in Kermanshah in 1885, Abolqasem Lahouti had been active in the Communist Party of Persia (the old name for Iran before it was changed in 1935). Sentenced to death in the 1930s, he fled Iran for the Soviet Union, where he became a leading cultural official of the only Persian-speaking constituent republic of the USSR, Soviet Tajikistan. The Central Asian nation had been carved out of the old Russian imperial holdings in Transoxiana, and its Persianate identity meant that its burgeoning culture was based on Iranian sources such as Ferdowsi. As nation-building efforts were ongoing across the interwar era in the USSR, before being snuffed out by Stalinist repression, Lahouti found a use for his extraordinary Persian literary skills. He was to lead something of a literary revolution, connecting the Persian-speakers of Tajikistan to their broader cultural-linguistic patrimony across the Oxus. Among the many poems he wrote was the national anthem of Tajikistan. With the help of his wife, a Jewish Ukrainian-born scholar of Iranian studies named Cecilia Banu, Lahouti also translated *Shahnameh* into Russian. Despite reaching the highest Soviet literary echelons, Lahouti asked to be buried in a free Iran. When he passed away in 1957, such wishes were not to be respected. Instead, he was buried in Moscow's well-known Novodevichy Cemetery. A few years later he was joined there by another patriotic communist poet, Turkey's Nazim Hikmet, who died in Moscow in 1963.

Hikmet, too, had wished to be buried in his native Anatolia. Like Lahouti, he was a communist invested in his patriotism. In the early 1920s, he had been a soldier in the Turkish War of Independence, when he fought under Mustafa Kemal Ataturk to create the nascent nation of Turkey from the ashes of the Ottoman Empire. But the new nation had no place for communists and he was forced into a Soviet exile. Later he was stripped of his Turkish nationality, which reverted to him only in 2009, decades after his death. But to the end of his life Hikmet remained faithful to his feelings for his homeland. One of his last poems, written in July 1962, was a defense of the love for his country, an angry rejection of the claims that he was a traitor to the nation. It has survived, in translation to many languages, as a robust defense of a dissident patriotism everywhere.

> Yes, I am a traitor, if you are a patriot, if you are a defender of
> our homeland,
> I am a traitor to my homeland, I am a traitor to my country.
> If patriotism is your farms,
> if the valuables in your safes and your bank accounts is patriotism,
> if patriotism is dying from hunger by the side of the road,
> ....

> if patriotism is not escaping from our stinking black-minded
> ignorance,
> then I am a traitor.
> Write it over three columns, in a pitch-black screaming streamer,
> Nazim Hikmet is continuing to be a traitor, still!

Modern Iranian arts and letters, just like those of most other countries, are littered with such stories of socialists and communists playing a critical role in building a modern nation. It is a powerful form of historical amnesia that has made us forget them, turning the politics of patriotic socialism into an unexpected internet joke instead of a real political force.

Why did Lahouti and Hikmet cling to their Iranian and Turkish patriotisms years after arriving in Moscow? They were proficient in Russian and lived Muscovite lives. Were they not limiting themselves by being beholden to a particularistic identity they could have easily sloughed? In my own long years of exile from my homeland I have often asked myself the same question: Why keep holding on to this identity? Why the patriotic stubbornness?

The Jewish American writer Eva Hoffman once wrote: "No, I'm no patriot, nor was I ever allowed to be. And yet, the country of my childhood lives within me with a primacy that is a form of love." But for me that love-as-primacy does allow one to be a patriot. Hoffman, a Jew born in Kraków in 1945, will always have a different relationship to the Poland she loves, the Poland she left behind as a schoolgirl. But as she goes on to explain her love for the Poland of her birth, even after the terrible things that happened there, she gives us a clue to the durability of the very patriotism that she disowns. "Is it blind and self-deceptive of me to hold on to its memory?" she writes. "I think it would be blind and self-deceptive not to. All it has given me is the world, but that is enough. It has fed me language, perceptions, sounds, the human kind. It has given me the colors and the furrows of reality, my first loves."

I could wrap myself in a chic, rootless cosmopolitanism, dutifully citing my Albert Memmi, my Edward Said, my Frantz

Fanon. But instead I remind myself that the vast majority of humans, living now or ever before, have not been exiles. Of the world's 7.9 billion people today, in this age renowned for the magnitude of its global migrations, more than 96 percent live in the country of their birth. It is there that they get their "language, perceptions, sounds, colors, first loves." While I will never give up the struggle for universalism and internationalism, or the belief that the human race is ultimately one, that all the achievements of human culture everywhere belong to us all, that our ultimate destiny can and must be linked, it would be "blind and self-deceptive" for such grand notions to mask the fact that humans live a short and limited life and that they are defined by the specificities of history, geography, and ethnicity. Nobody comes from nowhere, not even cosmopolitans. Humans are not abstract denizens of the globe but concrete people from *somewhere*, speaking some language, the sons and the daughters of some people.

Nation-states came of age in the twentieth century, steeped in blood. But everything in that Age of Extremes was steeped in blood. Transnational revolutionary fantasies have killed at least as many, and probably more. If we focus on the silly self-deceptions of nations or their ugly propensity for exclusion, we lose sight of the deep meaning that they nonetheless hold for millions of people. *Imagined Communities*, Benedict Anderson's field-defining study of nationalism, from 1983, is often remembered today for its titular concept: that nations, like all other communities of considerable size, are a work of imagination by their denizens. It is less well known that Anderson's book was hardly a brief against nationalism. Despite his critical outlook, the Anglo-Irish historian appreciated the "deep horizontal comradeship" of the nation that has the potential to cut across differences in race and class. Compared with the embers of ethno-chauvinism that helped burn down much of the world in the past century, we are justified to look with some nostalgia on the massive multiethnic empires of the Austro-Hungarians or the Ottomans and their ethos of coexistence despite difference. But we would do well to remember also that a hierarchy of peoples animated empire and sat uncomfortably with the demand for representation and democracy. Perhaps, if history had gone differently, the grand empires could have transitioned to states with more expansive notions of belonging instead of being cut into ethno-states or post-imperial units. But counterfactual history is hardly a guide to the future.

When we think of nationalism, we would do well to remember, too, the millions of people who, in the age of individualist capitalism, are inspired to do good because of their allegiance to the collective that they call their country. I think of my wife and her Turkish compatriots lining up for hours, in Istanbul or in Chicago, to vote, because they care about the fate of a country that they love. I think of my Israeli friends who, in 2022, came out week after week, whether in Tel Aviv or New York, to brandish the flag of their country — indeed, to reclaim it from the chauvinists — as they fought to preserve its democratic institutions. I think of my Palestinian friends and the watermelon colors of their flag, of how they carry the love of their land everywhere they go, as they fight for it to be free of occupation. I think also of the Iraqi and Lebanese citizens whom I met in 2019, when they were fighting for effective national states and sovereignty for their nations against the encroachment of foreign powers, including Iran.

For these people, the fact that their country was under terrible leadership did not diminish the need for patriotism; it augmented it. Patriotism does not mean obedience to the state but a commitment to the fate of the nation. The challenge of being patriotic in a country with a currently abominable leadership is all too familiar to Americans today. As this country celebrates its semiquincentennial, it has to face the fact that its national life has been dominated for almost a decade now by Donald J. Trump, whose crass disregard for its democratic intuitions and norms has made many Americans nervous or worse. But to give up patriotism to Trumpism, to surrender the love of one's country to the deterioration of one's country, would be the height of folly. Having lived most of my years in this country under his presidency, I have never ceased loving America. It is precisely to recover the best of the American enterprise, precisely under the Stars and Stripes, that Trump can be most effectively opposed.

As all these cases show, the nation-state is an effective space for political contestation, where we may argue that citizenship should belong to everyone who lives there, where we may build projects that are, by their very nature, collective. If there is to be a future of global fraternity, reason dictates it must start with the nation. In the real world, giving up on strong and sovereign national states has not benefited the cause of a universal humanity; it has benefited only sectarians and individualists, and a great many scoundrels of myriad ideological stripes.

It is easy to wave a flag, but it is also easy to casually declare your lack of interest in that ritual, to strike a pose of moral superiority over the common arrangements of humankind in your time. After all these years, after many brilliant teachings to the contrary, I have come to believe that a genuine love of one's country can be a force for good. And so I will continue to permit myself to be, even now, a patriot.

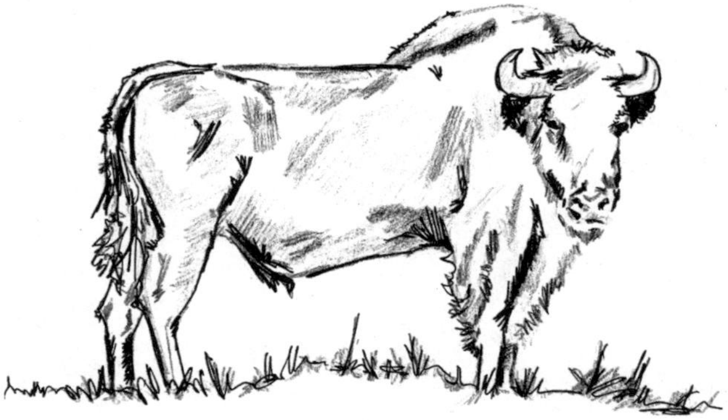

RALPH WALDO EMERSON

He walked the streets of great New York

He walked the streets of great New York
Full of men, the men were full of blood
Signs of power, signs of worth,
Yet all seemed trivial
As the ceaseless cry
Of the newsboys in the street
Now men do not listen after
The voice in the breast
Which makes the thunder mean
But the Great God hath departed
And they listen after Scott & Byron
I met no gods – I harboured none,
As I walked by noon & night alone
The crowded ways
And yet I found in the heart of the town
A few children of God nestling in his bosom
Not detached as all the crowd appeared
each one a sutlers boat
Cruising for private gain
But these seemed undetached united
Lovers of Love, of Truth,
And as among indians they say
The One the One is known
so under the eaves of Wall Street
Brokers had met the Eternal

In the city of surfaces
Where I a swain became a surface
I found & worshipped him.
Always thus neighbored well
The two contemporaries dwell
The World which by the world is known
And Wisdom seeking still its own
I walked with men
Who seemed as if they were chairs or stools
Tables or shopwindows or champagne baskets
For these they loved & were if truly seen
I walked with others of their wisdom gave me proof
Who brought the starry heaven
As near as the house roof

(1840–1849)

MARK LILLA

The Unlovely City: An Unsent Letter to Joseph Brodsky

June 21, 1988

Dear Joseph Brodsky,

It has now been six months since you delivered your Nobel Lecture on poetry and politics, and six months since I first read it in the pages of *The New Republic*. My first reaction was one of mild disappointment, a sense of having been let down by someone I thought I understood. As I look back over your lecture, I wonder whether you could have anticipated the reactions you triggered by making the case for poetry, and more generally for art, that you did. I wonder how well considered were your remarks that, "had we been choosing our leaders on the basis of their reading experience and not their political programs, there would be much less grief on earth," and then this:

> I believe . . . that, for someone who has read a lot of Dickens, to shoot his like in the name of some idea is more problematic than

> for someone who has read no Dickens. And I am speaking precisely about reading Dickens, Sterne, Stendhal, Dostoevsky, Flaubert, Balzac, Melville, Proust, Musil, and so forth; that is, about literature, not literacy or education. A literate, educated person, to be sure, is fully capable, after reading this or that political treatise or tract, of killing his like, and even of experiencing, in so doing, a rapture of conviction. Lenin was literate, Stalin was literate, so was Hitler; as for Mao Zedong, he even wrote verse. What all these men had in common, though, was that their hit list was longer than their reading list.

Do you really believe that a man cultivated by Stendhal, Dickens, Dostoevsky, and Musil would be incapable — or at least less willing — to squeeze a trigger in service of an idea? I wonder because we have both, more than once, heard a similar aesthetic political equation expressed in the credulous question: "Can such things be possible in the land of Goethe and Schiller?" And we both know the answer. Yet I cannot imagine that, were we together to draw up lists of those rulers guilty of the worst crimes, you and I could not also agree upon a list of writers — good writers, perhaps great writers — capable of excusing each and every one of them. Neither of us would wish to be ruled by Lenin, Stalin, Hitler, or Mao; nor, I suspect, would we place our fates in the hands of Brecht or Genet, Céline or Pound.

So the issue, I assume, is not one that can be decided on the basis of reading lists or body counts. The issue is poetry itself. It is the claim poetry makes for the moral import of aesthetic experience and the challenge that all art offers — and has always offered — to the very possibility of politics in any elevated sense.

Rarely do we find the matter set out quite so baldly as you managed to do when you painted a picture of demiurgic political man violating aesthetics, which you called "the mother of ethics," then spiriting us back into what you call our political past of "total mass solutions to the problems of human existence," while we amuse ourselves with "mass police entertainment." You invite us to resist temptations from these "champions of the common good, masters of the masses, heralds of historical necessity," and to return from our prodigal wanderings to the Muse who can still transform each of us from anonymous zero into "autonomous 'I.'"

The image could not be clearer, and, really, who could resist even facing such a choice, one promising high stakes and thrills while demanding little sustained thought about the nature of the alternatives? Art is like that, aestheticizing not just itself and its objects but, more dangerously, aestheticizing its adversaries, politics first among them. Something in me instinctively recoils at these falsely posed alternatives. Yet I have also come to see why this aestheticized notion of politics could acquire such a strong hold on those who have experienced the worst excesses of modern politics. For these aestheticized political alternatives — the soul or "the state," individual conscience or "mass conformity," autonomy or "authority" — were for many in the twentieth century the only real choices available. The starkest, crudest aesthetic image cannot begin to approach the political reality under modern tyrannies.

The human spirit naturally longs for escape when decent, humane political relations are replaced by the "post-political" materialist state that demands of every spirit its pound of flesh (because it only believes in the flesh it can touch). To escape the velvet prison that state socialism offered, the captive mind sought and accepted almost any form of transcendence. For some, still hopeful of change, however meager, a dreamy "antipolitics" of engagement was inviting; for others, less hopeful, the turn within was made by means of religion, poetry, scholarship, mathematics, even chess.

I have one friend, a computer specialist, who in Communist Poland effused over the spiritual possibilities of *Go*, the Asian board game. Another, a historian, prided himself over his memorization of the order of battles in the Mexican-American War, a study of which has allowed him to be a pure historian, he said, without addressing contemporary political concerns. A third, a philosophy professor, spent his time quite pleasurably on abstract "decision theoretic" models of economic and political choice. When I, stupefied, asked why someone living in a country with overwhelming concrete problems would study "models" that few in the West would find relevant to their own condition, he answered quietly, "Because there are solutions."

Art, too, offers a solution — precisely because it rejects the mass political solutions you describe. The *life* of art, less than its works, poses and resolves a dramatic existential choice. Behind the Iron Curtain this *aut aut* was frighteningly close to reality. But in the West? Can it really be said that human beings, artists or not, are systematically forced to choose between their souls and their skins in our bourgeois Western democracies, that the transcendent life of art — or religion, or science, or chess — is the only means of resisting the gravitational pull of the centralizing state? Again, everything you have written in the past leads me to assume we agree and need not rehearse the arguments: this is nonsense. The artist is left alone in the West; he is free.

Many writers or painters here would deny this, as you know, and try to persuade us that the commercial forces or the democratic indifference that deny them a following also constitute their unfreedom. During the Cold War we saw them fall prey to the basest moral inversions, condemning the prosaic liberties of Western democracies while ricocheting from cause to cause — today a tyrant from the bush, tomorrow a prophet from the mountain — all aestheticized to square with what Thomas Mann called the artist's instinctive *bellezza* radicalism. But we know to distrust such people. We have learned to distrust anyone — Augustine, Rousseau, Marx, and our artists — who would entice us to exchange our political freedom for an illusory "emancipation." Political freedom is not everything, nor the highest thing. But it *is* what it is: freedom.

Such Westerners leave me to wonder: can artists ever make their peace with what politics at its best might offer the human spirit? Can they, to vary the tired joke, ever accept a state that will have them as citizens? And I do mean citizens — not dissidents or commissars, the two roles artists are most accustomed to play, but the citizen comfortable with having a voice that is only one among many. Your lecture has forced me to restate an old problem in its most radical terms. We can no longer suppose that the antagonism between Western artists and Western liberal democracy is simply an ideological one, since Russian, Czech, Argentine, and South African dissidents, for example, are all celebrated today by fellow writers here in the West. This despite varying estimations of those regimes; indeed, as the case of Cuba shows, it is not uncommon for both the regime and the writer to win praise (the first for literacy programs, the second for daring to be literate). There is no inconsistency here, no double standard. From the aesthetic point of view, the high drama offered by the clash between artists and their governments is, in every case, the same drama which the West denies to its writers, painters, sculptors, filmmakers, and musicians. Your lecture did, no doubt, attract many who seek to live aesthetic lives, but I would venture that there could be no honest self-recognition in the titanic struggle you describe between poet and city. I imagine instead a palpable sense of yearning, a desire to participate in that drama, and not in this one in the here and now.

Yet there is indeed friction between the demands of art and those of Western democratic politics, and it begins in the incontestable fact you mention — that no poem worthy of the name is democratic. Auden, as you know, wrote that "a poem which was really like a political democracy would be formless, windy, banal and utterly boring." This truth carries with it a corollary, one that Auden wisely considered of equal import, and one that begins to mark the difference between us. He knew that no city worthy of the name is poetic, and that aesthetics therefore cannot claim clear maternity rights to ethics.

> The whole aim of the poet, or any other kind of artist, is to produce something which is complete and will endure without change. A poetic city would always contain exactly the same number of inhabitants doing exactly the same jobs forever . . . it would be a nightmare of horror for, given the historical reality of actual men, such a society could only come into being through selective breeding, extermination of the physically and mentally

> unfit, absolute obedience to its Director, and a large slave class kept out of sight in cellars.

Why is this? What is there in the poetic imagination that makes it so impatient with the pulsing activity of democratic politics? You offer some clues when you write that "if art teaches anything it is the privateness of the human condition." Even the conversation you describe between poet and reader is unlike the conversation one has in the society of articulate company. There are no authorial responses to the reader's *I object!;* no questions are entertained; no one makes a fool of himself. The relationship is like that between certain old friends for whom everything is so thoroughly understood that nothing is left for discourse to unveil. There are only announcements. The poetic relationship is, as you say, one of "mutual loneliness" that bears its fruit in mutual misanthropy.

This conversation, if indeed it can be called that, is distinguished by the dominant status of the poetic instigator, who is first and foremost a creator. He is accustomed to a world of his own making in which only a few are invited to share, and in which his rules are obeyed. If he learns at all it is from other poets who treat him likewise; he does not learn from his reader, nor could he, for they are not engaged in a common project, no matter how well they think they know each other. In Auden's "daydream College for Bards," you recall, each pupil looks after an animal and cultivates a garden plot; he does not join in laying out a public square or in cultivating friendships.

To this jealously guarded privacy of the poetic creator must be contrasted the publicity that attends participation in democratic politics. A well-ordered republic does not seek to erase the privacy of its members, but it does invite each of them to create another, less intimate persona capable of participating in the conversation of citizens reflecting on the ends and means of public action. This invitation has its price — a sort of public-private schizophrenia — as well as its own distinct benefits (not least among them, an antidote to misanthropy).

Indeed, the vocabulary of democratic politics was developed explicitly in order to protect men and women against those like the tyrant, the priest, and the poet, who believed that ruling legitimately derives from making, not from speaking and listening. This is a highly specialized vocabulary, comprised of certain words for which poetry has no cognates: "legitimacy" and "consent" cannot be translated into artful verse, the way "nobility" and "injustice," the words of revolutionary politics, can be. This is because the poem, like the tyrannical state, is a static object inviting aesthetic treatment, while democratic politics is an activity that can be joined in but not painted. Whenever the artist tries to capture this political movement, he fails. Even if he looks to a regime that cultivates what Aristotle considered the essence of politics — ruling and being ruled in turn — he will take a snapshot that seems only to reveal domination by some and the anonymity of others.

Anonymity is what the aesthete fears above all, and our attempts to convince him that participation in one sphere, where he will be one voice among many, need not extinguish autonomous creation in another, can never fully allay those fears. As he sees it, and as you yourself express it, one task of poetry is to assert categorically the individual and the exceptional against the mass and the average. It is, if I understand you, an ethical task in a negative sense: it inculcates skepticism about mass solutions, heightens moral "polyphony," and shapes a new aesthetic reality that "makes one's experience even more private."

Liberal sentiments, to be sure. Yet whenever the artist speaks of privacy, individuality, and exceptionality he is really praising aesthetic, not political, freedom — a shift in focus that can have the most profound and far-reaching political consequences. Poets, as poets, are simply incapable of thinking in the categories of politics, no matter how "political" or "engaged" they aspire to make their art; they are constitutionally conditioned to believe, as Schiller has it, that "through beauty we arrive at freedom." "Robespierre is only estimable," Baudelaire wrote, "because he has created a few literarily estimable sentences." Irony apart, this remark reveals everything about aesthetic depth of field. Auden, I think, came to distrust it deeply; he understood that "all poets adore explosions, thunderstorms, tornadoes, conflagrations, ruins, scenes of spectacular carnage" — which is why "the poetic imagination is not at all a desirable quality in a statesman." Driven to their extremes and sufficiently aestheticized, the "individual" and "exceptional" can make war against political freedom.

The democratic city is not beautiful. The Average rules here, insurance against some kinds of tyranny but not against vulgarity or boredom. And yes, Auden was right, at times it has seemed that, in our crude utilitarianism, "a voice without a face / proved by statistics that some cause was just" — an excusable lapse, for a people can understandably grasp for the dependable low justice of being counted instead of holding out for the fickle caprice of poetic justice. As for being "champions of the common good," I offer no apologies, for this consideration of what is truly common, truly public, is precisely what distinguishes the democratic republic from those "masters of the masses, and heralds of historical necessity."

You see, I am unwilling to concede the moral high ground to aesthetics, which can be called "the mother of ethics" only if we accept that the individual and the exceptional define the true locus of the ethical life — if, that is, we side with Kierkegaard against Aristotle. The voice of poetry today only gives us the exceptional individual, a solitary self-creator or, at most, the product of a language, whereas the voice of democratic republics speaks of both city and citizen, each shaping the other in turn, first through the work of the "common man," second through the good city making him a little less common. These moral viewpoints are radically at odds and cannot be translated one to the other because they see different phenomena.

As you put it, literature is "the reaction of the permanent — better yet the infinite — against the temporary, against the finite" that weighs down political life. Yet democratic politics is not a prisoner of "yesterday," as you would have it, though its relation to time is not that of art. In a democratic republic, eternal human relations must make room for the necessary transitory ones, for we cannot bear too much eternity. Obligations to past and future must be fulfilled; taxes must be paid and censuses taken; life goes on. For archetypes there is no tomorrow: the eternal figures with their eternal problems wander about endlessly like Pirandello's characters, forever young, searching for an opportunity to reenact the same drama, only to reach the same ending over and over again. But in a democracy time does not stand still, and there are no endings, happy or sad. The drama of Antigone is only timeless when seen through aesthetic eyes; the political man wants to know what happened after that, and after that. In art, Antigone is timeless and necessary; but in a living democracy a population of flesh and blood women making the same nonnegotiable demand, ceaselessly and without distinction, would be impossible. An immortal Antigone: who could stand her?

The danger of poetry, though, is not that it aspires to something beyond the temporal and political, that it sees itself, as you bluntly put it, as "the aim of our species." Philosophy makes that claim, as does religion. But the poet, unlike some philosophers and saints, is bred to believe that the road to the beautiful must itself be beautiful, and since any existing political order, however decent, will fail this aesthetic test, he refuses to learn its language or recognize its civilizing potential. At their most highly developed, philosophy and religion become politic, they become bilingual, and through that development reveal what the city can offer and what lies beyond it. Poetry's private language is jealous, though, so rather than risk offending it by learning another, the poet will withdraw from politics to find his own path to the beautiful, or he will join any mad utopian project promising to build the road with Schiller's "significant stones."

Although poetry would cease to be poetry if it merely spoke this language of politics, it must become bilingual if it is to fathom the conditions that extinguish it or give it freedom to develop. It must comprehend the tyrant in political terms and resist the temptation to aestheticize him; it must come to understand the democratic republic, not merely endure it. For the private poets who celebrate the morality of absolute privacy, this democratic tongue will be the most foreign of all, one offering none of the ultimate satisfactions other languages have previously led him to expect. If they learn it, they will never be able to translate it into verse; it will always remain a language apart, a *lingua della casa*. For although it is the most articulate language of human necessity, there is nothing lovely to be said in it.

Yours sincerely,

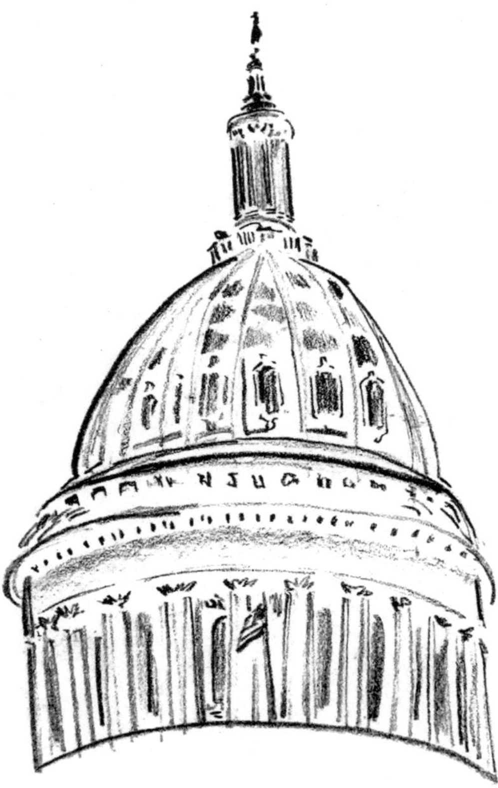

AMBROSE BIERCE

Egoist

Megaceph, chosen to serve the State
In the halls of legislative debate,
One day with his credentials came
To the capitol's door and announced his name.
The doorkeeper looked, with a comical twist
Of the face, at the eminent egotist,
And said: "Go away, for we settle here
All manner of questions, knotty and queer,
And we cannot have, when the speaker demands
To know how every member stands,
A man who to all things under the sky
Assents by eternally voting 'I.'"

(1911)

ROBERT ALTER

The Power of Succinctness

The extreme compactness of biblical narrative is likely to strike almost any modern reader. Some, naively, will attribute it to the relatively rudimentary state of ancient literature that lacks the means to elaborate the details of the stories it tells. The last several decades of literary analysis of the Bible have shown that this is by no means the case. Still, this is not the kind of narrative with which most modern readers are familiar. At least since the eighteenth century the predominant reading matter for narrative literature has been novels, and they typically proceed through a rich accumulation of descriptive details, narratorial comment, and extended dialogue. There is nothing like such novelistic abundance in the Bible. Thomas Mann deployed four volumes and a few thousand pages to tell the story of Joseph and his brothers, while the biblical narrative with great effectiveness makes do with thirteen brief chapters. What is impressive is how the Hebrew writers were able to convey a fullness in the evocation of emotions, relationships, and motives in just a few words, often only a single brief sentence, or even the strategic choice of one term.

I will begin with a moment that illustrates the breathtaking efficiency of the Hebrew writers in dispensing with narrative exposition. When Moses flees from Egypt to Midian after killing an Egyptian who was beating a Hebrew, he arrives at a well where he rescues seven young women confronted by hostile shepherds. The girls rush home and report to their father, "An Egyptian man rescued us from the hands of the shepherds" (Exodus 2:19). How do they know that he is Egyptian? Presumably because he is clean-shaven while the sundry Semitic males to the north and east of Egypt were bearded, and also because he would have been wearing regal Egyptian garments, since he would have had to flee Egypt abruptly in order to escape arrest and possible execution.

If you imagine how a novelist might have handled this narrative information, it might read something like this: "Moses stood on the hilltop looking down toward the valley below, where he could make out people gathered around a well. His fine linen robe covered with dust and splattered with mud after his arduous journey on foot from the south, he leaned on his staff as he began the steep descent down into the valley. Drawing near, he could hear harsh shouts and see a group of young women being driven off from the well." This is certainly not the way of biblical narrative. All we need to know is conveyed in two small words, *'ish 'ivri*, "an Egyptian man." Since biblical narrative repeatedly works with thematic keywords, this takes us back to the previous episode of the killing of an Egyptian, when Moses saw "an Egyptian man striking a Hebrew man" (Exodus 2:11). His identification here by the Midianite girls as an Egyptian man then leads us to ponder: what, in fact, is Moses? Outwardly, he is an Egyptian man and has been raised as such in Pharaoh's court, but inwardly he is a Hebrew man, and he has seen the man being beaten as one "of his brothers." In just two words, we are given much to think about.

I will now proceed to more complex uses of brevity. In 2

Samuel, when David negotiates a peace agreement with Abner, the commander of the Saulide forces with whom he has been warring, David stipulates that his first wife, Michal the daughter of Saul, must be sent back to him. David had to flee from her father, who was bent on killing him, he has not seen her for years, and in the interim he has acquired two wives and is on his way to creating a small harem. It seems clear that his motive in insisting on the return of Michal is not love but political calculation: the public display of the daughter of the previous king as his wife will strengthen the legitimacy of his claim to the throne. Meanwhile, Saul has married off Michal to a certain Paltiel, an act of questionable legality because she was already married to David. The obvious intention was to effect a kind of erasure of David's marriage to Michal. No information is given about Paltiel beyond his name and marital status. Neither Paltiel nor Michal has any choice in their separation because they have been ordered to comply by the powerful military commander Abner. This is all we are told about the parting of the spouses: "And her husband went with her, weeping as he went after her, as far as Bachurim. And Abner said to him, 'Go back!' And he went back" (2 Samuel 3:16).

No narrative report is given of the marriage between Paltiel and Michal. However it evolved, Paltiel clearly has come to love Michal, and it is plausible that she has returned his love. All this is poignantly conveyed in his wordless weeping as he accompanies her on her departure. Note that at first he is walking "with" her but then "after" her, as she, presumably led away by Abner, is taken off to resume her position as David's wife. Abner's brusque command to Paltiel to turn back cannot be disobeyed. Michal has been living with a man who really loved her, something David may never have done, perhaps not even in the early days of their marriage. In this way a few words evoke a domestic tragedy. More than two and a half millennia after they were written, they express, without the slightest elaboration of detail, the pain of loss that we all can understand when a beloved spouse is violently taken away forever.

The great penetrating account of this kind of narrative was offered by Erich Auerbach in the seminal first chapter of his

Mimesis: The Representation of Reality in Western Literature. (The German scholar wrote it between 1942 and 1945 in wartime exile in Istanbul; it was published in German in 1946 and in English in 1953.) His memorable coinage, fraught with background, is applicable to virtually all biblical narrative. Here, in Auerbach's words, are the clauses that lead up to his introduction of that phrase:

> The decisive points of the narrative alone are emphasized, what lies between is nonexistent; thoughts and feelings remain unexpressed, are only suggested by the silence and the fragmentary speeches; the whole, permeated with the most unrelieved suspense and directed toward a single goal (and to that extent far more of a unity), remains mysterious and "fraught with background."

Expressive succinctness — fraughtness with background — equally plays a role in dialogue. In the ghastly story of the rape of Tamar by her half-brother Amnon, after he has sated his lust and brutally thrust her out of the door of his bedchamber and she walks along screaming, her royal robe torn, ashes on her head, she encounters her full brother Absalom. Seeing her in this utterly devastated state, he says to her, "Has Amnon your brother been with you?" (2 Samuel 13:20). Absalom appears to realize that she has been raped by Amnon, perhaps because he is aware that she was summoned to Amnon's bedchamber, perhaps also because Amnon's lust for the beautiful Tamar was generally known in the court. Drawing the obvious conclusion from her torn garment and her despair, he could have said "raped" (*'inah*) or "lain with" (*shakhav 'im*), but instead he chooses the euphemism "been with." As subsequent events will reveal, Absalom is not a kind person. He contrives to have his henchmen murder Amnon in revenge for the violation of his sister. Later in the story, he usurps David's throne through demagoguery and fully intends to kill his father. But the biblical writer understands that a brutal person can have another side in a different relationship.

Absalom is perfectly willing to become a parricide in order to serve his own political interests, but he is affectionate toward his sister, and seeing her shattered by what he infers was done to her, he does not want to upset her further by plainly naming the act of violation, and so, with a delicacy of feeling one would not expect from his behavior elsewhere, he asks whether Amnon "has been with" her. Fraternal affection, the writer realizes, can be exhibited by the same person who will exact harsh vengeance and will be prepared to tear the crown from his father and destroy him. This complex understanding of character, for which a novelist would have used many pages, is expressed here in just two words. Writers such as George Eliot and Proust shrewdly grasped that bad people can have good sides, or at least good moments, and the same is true of biblical writers in all their extraordinary brevity.

Biblical narrative bustles with individualized characters whose distinctive traits invite our attention, and attentive alertness is definitely required. Sometimes the revelatory concise item goes by so quickly that it could be missed. A case in point is the introduction of Laban, Rebekah's brother, into the larger Genesis narrative in the story of her betrothal. Years later, he will play an important role in the life of his nephew Jacob. Rebekah has just encountered Abraham's servant at the well in Aram-Naharaim, and after she has passed the test of bringing water for him and also for his camels, he bedecks her with what are in effect betrothal gifts. When she rushes home with the news of the stranger's arrival, Laban, before running out to greet the man at the well, has taken note of something: "And it happened, when he saw the nose ring, and the bracelets on his sister's arms, and when he heard the words of Rebekah his sister, saying, 'Thus the man spoke to me,' he hurried to the man standing by his camels at the well and said to him, "Come in, blessed of the Lord, why should you stand outside, when I have readied the household and a place for the camels?" (Genesis 24:30–31). Now, one might give this a benign interpretation: seeing the jewelry on his sister, Laban concludes that the stranger's intentions are honorable, and his consequent invitation to the man is an expression of "Oriental" hospitality. But the more likely implication is that the glitter of gold is what catches his eye. That is what triggers his grand gesture of hospitality to the visitor. No explicit comment on Laban's character is made, such as "this Laban was a crafty, grasping man," merely the brief notation of his eye on the precious bangles.

Years later, when his nephew Jacob, fleeing from the wrath of his brother Esau, takes refuge in Laban's Mesopotamian home, the uncle will make a great display of their kinship, embracing him and kissing him and declaring, "Indeed, you are my bone and my flesh" (Genesis 29: 14). The blood relationship, however, does not prevent Laban from driving a hard bargain with his nephew. After saying to Jacob, "Because you are my kin, should you serve me for nothing?" (Genesis 29:15), he makes his daughter Rachel the payment for Jacob's labor while stipulating a full seven years of service in lieu of a bride-price. Compounding this calculation, he passes off Leah instead of Rachel as the bride, and when in the morning light Jacob discovers he has been deceived, Laban tells him he will also give him Rachel at the end of the bridal week, but on the condition that Jacob serve him still another seven years without wages. All this is aptly prefigured in Laban's taking stock of the gold adorning his sister.

A devout reader might wonder why we need to know such things in reading the Bible. After all, the Patriarchal Tales are about the progenitors of the twelve tribes of Israel who will become God's covenanted people. The biblical writers, however, keenly understood that even if the stories they told were an expression of God's purposes with Israel and with humankind, the actors in the stories were palpably human, and their actions were driven by human traits and all-too-human imperfections. This meant that the writers' imagining of the characters was akin to the way good novelists imagine their characters, and that is why they engage us as readers, whether we are believers or nonbelievers. As Jacob's story unfolds, we see that he has his own calculating bent, and it will prove more than a match for his uncle.

Another swift notation in Jacob's story should be mentioned. What, we may wonder, was his state of mind over the long seven years of labor during which he had to wait for Rachel, the beautiful woman with whom he was smitten in a *coup de foudre* from their first meeting at the well, and whom he will continue to love all his life? Here is the crucial narrative report: "And Jacob served seven years for Rachel, and they seemed in his eyes but a few days in his love for her" (Genesis 29:20). This is a unique biblical comment on the intensity of a man's feelings for a woman. The Israeli novelist Meir Shalev, who was deeply interested in the Bible and wrote sensitively about it, picked up the phrase "but a few days" and used it as the title for a novel about consuming love. One might object that for Jacob, burning with impatience to consummate his love for Rachel, the seven years would rather have seemed agonizingly long, but what the writer has in mind is that Jacob would be constantly focusing on the great reward that was to be his at the end of the years of labor, and that with this consciousness the years of labor seem a trifle. It is a moving expression of love in just six Hebrew words.

And because very little in biblical narrative is isolated from the larger context, this undying love will have consequences, some of them dire, as the story continues. Jacob will certainly favor Rachel over her sister Leah, preferential treatment that will not engender domestic harmony. After Rachel's death, he will extravagantly favor her older son Joseph, who resembles his mother in his beauty; Jacob even feminizes him by dressing him in a *ketonet passim* (the "coat of many colors" of the King James Version), which, as we learn in the story of the rape of Tamar because she is also wearing it, is a garment "worn by virgin princesses" (2 Samuel 13:18). Jacob on his deathbed is still haunted by Rachel's death, flashing back to it.

The emotions of the biblical figures are often unstated and left to inference or conjecture. Only occasionally, as in Jacob's love for Rachel, are they spelled out succinctly. They may sometimes also be intimated by an act. The birth of the future prophet Samuel occurs after his mother Hannah, agonizing through years of childlessness, prays in the sanctuary at Shiloh for a child. She stipulates in her prayer that if she is granted a son, he will be "given to the Lord all the days of his life" (1 Samuel 1:11). After the son is born, she tells her husband that she will fulfill her vow once the child is weaned. In ancient Israel this could have been as much as three or four years. Still, she is constrained by her vow to part from the boy and bring him, not much older than a toddler, to become an acolyte at the Shiloh sanctuary. Her anguish at the separation from the child for whom she has waited so long can be readily imagined. The narrative report in 1 Samuel says nothing about it — yet what is done instead is in its brief manner more eloquent than a direct report.

Little Samuel, we are told, as an acolyte in the sanctuary, was girt in the priestly garment known as the *ephod*. His mother, on the other hand, in the very next words in the text, brings him something different to wear: "and a little cloak [*me'il*] would his mother make him and would bring up to him year after year when she came up with her husband to offer the yearly sacrifice" (1 Samuel: 2:19). The mother's loving care for the little boy from whom she has been parted is beautifully intimated. She makes the cloak herself, perhaps both weaving and sewing it; and since she brings it to Shiloh year after year, she is obviously mindful of him as he grows, making a bigger cloak each year that she comes. One could scarcely have a more vivid instance of how the biblical writers imagine their characters with very human feelings as they respond to the circumstances of their lives. Even for those who read the biblical narratives solely with an eye to God's plans for Israel, the humanity of the represented figure is arresting.

Moreover, as with Jacob's great love for Rachel, the detail here is part of a web of interconnections. The child's cloak will become a recurring motif in the larger story. At the crucial moment of transition when an angry Samuel foreswears all bonds with Saul, the desperate king clings to the prophet's cloak, begging the prophet not to reject him, and inadvertently tears it. Samuel, not one to miss a symbolic clue, thunders: "the LORD has torn away the kingship of Israel and given it to your fellow man who is better than you" (1 Samuel 15:28). Even after his death, Samuel is wearing a *me'il*. When the necromancer at Endor summons up his ghost, Saul immediately recognizes that it is Samuel because he is wrapped in a cloak. The plurisignificant cloak is eventually transferred to Saul: when David finds Saul asleep in the cave at Adullam, he cuts off a corner of the king's cloak as evidence of what he could have done to him. And, in a reversal of the cloak motif, in Saul's concluding encounter with a band of ecstatic prophets, he strips off everything he is wearing and rolls naked on the ground, an emblem of his being stripped of the kingship. The little garment that Hannah makes for her son is thus both poignant in itself and sets in motion a chain of meanings around cloaks.

The terseness of narrative report in the Bible can either point to a fraught significance, as with Hannah and Jacob, or it can open a window into ambiguous possibilities. Modern interpreters of the Bible like to make things unambiguously clear for their readers, but the biblical writers often aimed for uncertainty. One of the strengths of biblical narrative is that at times it cultivates ambiguity in the awareness that personalities and acts exhibit a complexity that may invite explanation in more than one way. A striking example occurs at the end of the last bitter confrontation between David and Michal. As noted above, Michal was forcibly separated from her loving husband Paltiel, almost certainly against her will, and brought back to her public position as David's wife. After his conquest of Jerusalem, David has the Ark of the Covenant brought up to his new capital and dances before it in the procession, in what is probably a short tunic with nothing underneath. Michal comes out to meet him in front of the palace and sarcastically berates him for "exposing" himself — this is the word she uses — before the eyes of slave-girls. He angrily responds that God has chosen him to be king over Israel instead of her father and that for what she deems dishonorable he will be honored. His defiant rejoinder concludes with these words: "I will play before the Lord! And I will be dishonored still more than this and will be debased in my own eyes! But with the slavegirls about whom you spoke, with them let me be honored!" (2 Samuel 6:22–23). He has the last word in their dialogue.

The narrator concludes the episode with these words: "And Michal daughter of Saul had no child to her dying day" (2 Samuel 6:23). What explains this bleak report? Intriguingly, there are four conceivable explanations, two naturalistic and two theological. The most obvious reason for her never having a child — a grim fate for a woman in ancient Israel — is that in the wake of this bitter confrontation between her and David, they never again sleep together. A second possibility also suggests itself: Michal has been married to Paltiel for a number of years, and there is no indication that she had a child with him, so perhaps she was simply infertile. If, on the other hand, an interpreter prefers to see the story in theological terms, Michal may have been punished by God with barrenness for vilifying the anointed king of Israel in his great moment of triumph. Finally, still from the perspective of divine causation, punishment could have been exacted upon both spouses because her having no child would have deprived David of producing an heir with the daughter of his royal predecessor, an heir who would have provided a clear guarantee for the legitimacy of his successor and for the dynasty he aspired to found. In this understanding, both Michal and David are gravely at fault in their confrontation, she for publicly insulting him (the exchange takes place outside, in front of the palace), he for treating a woman with open contempt who is a king's daughter and once loved him. We might recall that when they were to be married, it was said of Michal that she loved David, the only woman in the entire Bible about whom it is explicitly stated that she loved a man; and not long afterward she incurred personal risk in enabling David to escape from Saul's assassins.

Ambiguity of explanation is not too common in literary narrative, ancient or modern, and its presence in the Bible is a manifestation of the ability of the Hebrew writers to represent human actions and relationships in all the shadowing of their uncertainties. Auerbach's notion that the narrative method of the Bible compels interpretation is quite relevant in this regard.

The examples I will go on to consider are, with one marginal exception, all in dialogue, as were Amnon's delicate choice of a euphemism in his question to his violated sister and in the use of "an Egyptian man" in the Moses story. The preponderance of instances of expressive brevity in dialogues should not be surprising: biblical narrative swings between drastic summary (a span of eighteen or more years can be conveyed in three or so words) and dialogue, where narrating time and narrative time are equal. The rule of thumb is that when something significant is about to happen, the narrative drastically slows down and expresses the event through dialogue. The dialogues themselves, of course, are much briefer than in later literature, and the crucial aspects of representation are often expressed in half a dozen words or less, sometimes in a single word.

Here are two such instances, which occur in antithetical moments following a sexual act. After David from his rooftop sees the beautiful Bathsheba bathing and orders her to be brought to him for sex, neither speech nor emotional response is assigned to her. Her only words conveyed in the entire episode, presumably after the passage of two months, are "I am pregnant" (2 Samuel 11:5). At this point in the story, we know nothing of Bathsheba except that she is Uriah's wife and that she is beautiful. What, then, lies behind her words? Is she bewildered, confounded, fearful? Or does she have her eye on the main chance — now that I am pregnant, how are we going to make this work? She evidently has not had a child with Uriah, and bearing the offspring of the king could open grand possibilities for her. This of course is mere speculation, the ambiguity being akin to the ambiguity around Michal's childlessness.

Bathsheba, after giving birth to Solomon, entirely disappears from the narrative until years later, when she vividly reappears as the aged David is failing and his son Adonijah attempts to usurp the throne. She returns to the story after David's death when she contrives to bring about Adonijah's execution. Her wiliness in these last two episodes may encourage the thought that she has her own advantage in mind when she tells David she is pregnant, but that is far from certain. Perhaps she was a naive young wife who unquestioningly obeyed the king's sexual demand, and then through two or more decades of life in the court she gradually acquired the shrewdness required for negotiating palace intrigues. The very indeterminacy of her first very brief words — not, technically, dialogue at all, but a message, perhaps oral — imparts a piquant ambiguity to the story.

The grisly tale of the concubine at Gibeah in Judges 19 is not a biblical text that would be read in Sunday school. It may be unfamiliar to many readers. A certain Levite is traveling with his concubine to his home in the high country of Ephraim. As night falls, they find themselves near the Benjaminite town of Gibeah, and when no one else welcomes them an old man who lives there takes them in for the night, displaying the sort of generous hospitality that is civilized behavior in the region, as it is in the Greek realm depicted in the *Odyssey*. As they are dining together, men from the town pound on the door and demand that the wayfarer be brought outside so that they can have sex with him. This is an obvious reprise of the story of the lusting mob assaulting Lot's house in Genesis 19, even with whole phrases cited from the earlier text. But in this story, there are no angels to zap the assailants, and it ends badly. The old man tries to dissuade the mob, offering to send out to them instead of his male guest the concubine and — astoundingly — his virgin daughter. (This is surely pushing hospitality too far.)

The violent mob persists, and the Levite then "seizes" his concubine — his host's daughter is left alone — and thrusts her outside. The terrible consequences are predictable: the helpless woman is gang-raped all night long, and at daybreak she staggers to the entrance of the house and collapses there, her hands stretched out on the threshold. When the Levite awakes, opens the door, and finds her there, he addresses to her only two peremptory Hebrew words, *qumi weneileicha*, "get up and let us go" (Judges 19:28). But she cannot get up because after being brutalized through the night she has died. The two words he speaks are an indelible expression of his scandalous moral character. Hours earlier, he had pushed her outside, leaving her to the assault of the rapists. Now, not at first realizing that she is dead, he issues to her a curt command that they must be on their way. He says nothing solicitous or concerned about her condition. His two words to a corpse, in the making of which he was directly complicit, tell us all we need to know about him.

And there is, moreover, a postmortem expression of his brutality: he butchers her body, cutting it limb by limb into twelve pieces that he sends to the twelve tribes of Israel as evidence of the atrocity that has been perpetrated at Gibeah — an atrocity, of course, in which he has played a key role. There surely could have been another way to get the message out to the tribes. (The sanctity of the body after death was an important value in Hebrew society as it was in Greek society, a value memorably articulated in the Antigone story.) The Levite's ghastly message to the tribes leads them to launch a bloody war of retribution against the tribe of Benjamin. Things, then, end disastrously not only for the concubine and the Levite but also for the nation, which is torn by civil strife. Perhaps the whole story was meant to show the chaos that prevailed in Israel before the monarchy: "In those days," the refrain runs in Judges, "there was no king in Israel. Every man did what was right in his own eyes." But the vile Levite is at the center of this larger picture, his turpitude conveyed in the two abrupt Hebrew words he speaks to a corpse.

Let us move from two words to one in the focusing of meaning. In 1 Kings 2, Adonijah, after his attempt to assume the throne has been upended by the coronation of Solomon, commits a fatal error. He asks of the queen mother Bathsheba "one petition" to convey to the king: that he be given Abishag the Shunamite as his wife. Bathsheba immediately realizes that such a marriage might pave the way to a future claim to the throne, for Abishag, though she did not have sex with David, shared his bed. Bathsheba then goes to Solomon and repeats the exact language of Adonijah's request, adding one word: "There is one small petition that I ask of you, do not refuse me" (1 Kings 2:20). Adonijah did not say "small." By adding it, Bathsheba knows she will enrage her son, for he, realizing the political ramifications of the petition, understands it is in fact a very large thing that Adonijah is asking. His immediate response is to issue an order to kill Adonijah, which of course is precisely what Bathsheba intended to bring about. The narrative dispenses with any analysis of Bathsheba's devious shrewdness — it is conveyed in a single word.

A related use of a single word as a fulcrum of meaning occurs in Genesis 39, when Potiphar's wife frames Joseph for the attempted sexual assault of which she is guilty. When she voices her accusation to the household servants, she refers to the supposed rapist as "the Hebrew man." After her husband returns, she repeats her false accusation in the exact same language, changing just one word. This time she refers to Joseph as "the Hebrew slave." In the throes of lust, all she could say to Joseph was, "Lie with me." Now she manipulates language with calculating attention to her audience. The household servants, after all, are in all likelihood themselves slaves, so instead of inviting any status solidarity she calls Joseph "the Hebrew man," as if to say, this is what you might expect from those wild Semitic barbarians from Canaan. When, on the other hand, she reports the supposed event to her husband, she makes a point of referring to Joseph as a slave because she wants to stoke his anger at the thought that one of his slaves should have, outrageously, attempted to violate her. The substitution of the single word shows that Mrs. Potiphar can be shrewd as well as concupiscent. It is microtextual evidence for biblical narrative's elliptical but vivid imagining of character and motive in the midst of telling the story of the nation's origins.

A few words in dialogue can be rich in expressing feelings and the complications regarding social relations. At the beginning of the Book of Samuel we see Hannah, who has come with her husband and his other wife to the Shiloh sanctuary for the annual sacrifice, in evident despair over her continued childlessness, exacerbated by being mocked by her co-wife. Her husband Elkanah tries to comfort her: "Hannah, why do you weep and why do you not eat and why is your heart afflicted? Am I not better to you than ten sons?" (1 Samuel: 8). That last brief sentence (still briefer in the Hebrew) is of course a touching expression of a man's love for his wife. He obviously cares very deeply for her and is distressed by her dejection. At the same time, these few moving words reflect his failure to imagine the acuteness of her suffering as a woman. Given that the bearing of sons was seen in ancient Israel as a woman's ultimate fulfillment, her very purpose in life, his devotion to her cannot console her for this existential lack. He loves her well and certainly means well, but his hyperbolic assertion that he is better for her than ten sons could only heighten her anguish — she who has no sons is asked to imagine that she possesses something better than ten sons. One short sentence in a dialogue communicates a complex sense of a marriage — the husband's unquestionable love, which the wife surely understands and appreciates, and his incapacity as a man to fully fathom the terrible turmoil she is undergoing as a woman without child.

Occasionally, the mere ordering of the words in a short statement is revelatory. This is the case for Jacob's words to Esau in the scene of the selling of the birthright. The exchange is the first reported speech for either of the brothers, and it follows the rule that first words spoken by a character play a decisive role in characterization. Esau's speech, famously, is crude and abrupt: "Let me gulp down some of that red red stuff, for I am famished" (Genesis 25:30). Jacob's response — just four words in the Hebrew — is equally characterizing, though in a less obvious way: "Sell now your birthright to me" (Genesis 25:31). The words are simple and seem quite direct, but their ordering is carefully calculated. First, the imperative verb, "sell." Then the stipulation of an immediate transaction — not tomorrow or next week but "now." After that, the object of the initial verb — sell what, a deerskin jacket, a hunting knife? No, "your birthright," a very high price to pay for a helping of lentil stew. Jacob is shrewdly aware that he can take advantage of his brother's urgent hunger. Finally, at the end of the syntactic chain, like a trap snapping shut, *li*, "to me." In these very few words Jacob reveals himself as wily and cunning, and a hard bargainer. It is behavior consistent with how he will continue to act through the first half of the story. Up to this point, we have been told nothing about Jacob's character, but as with our previous examples no further exposition is needed. This is one reason, evident here, though by no means the only one, for why these stories in all their brevity strongly engage our perception of the human entanglements that they represent.

I will offer one final example from dialogue; it is a bit longer for biblical narrative practice but still fairly brief, and in its relative brevity it opens up a deep perspective on the life of the speaker. Jacob, after being brought down to Egypt, is led by Joseph to an audience with Pharaoh. The Hebrew patriarch is now very old, as Pharaoh can plainly see. So Pharaoh, with a certain solemnity, asks him, "How many are the days of the years of your life?" Jacob, in a solemn reply, pointedly substitutes "sojourning" for "life," and tells Pharaoh that he is one hundred and thirty years old, which would have been twenty years beyond what the Egyptians assigned as the ultimate human lifespan. Having pronounced this prodigious number, Jacob continues: "Few and evil have been the days of the years of my life, and they have not attained the years of my fathers in their sojourning" (Genesis 47:8–9).

What does this gloomy declaration tell us about Jacob? In his long life he has gone through much, buying the birthright and garnering the firstborn's blessing by deception, fleeing to his uncle's home in the east, working seven years for Rachel but then finding he has been given Leah before her, then his return to Canaan with two wives, two concubines, twelve sons, a daughter, and abundant livestock. It would seem that Jacob has attained everything he could have wanted, the paternal blessing manifestly fulfilled — but everything he has gotten has come at a price, as his words to Pharaoh show. Rachel was the love of his life, but he had to marry her sister first, and the consequence was years of domestic strife. Then, after Rachel gave birth to Joseph, she died in childbirth with Benjamin, a loss from which Jacob never really recovered. Then his daughter Dinah was raped, and he was dismayed by the blood vengeance enacted by his sons Simeon and

Levi. Perhaps worst of all, for some twenty years he was convinced that his beloved son Joseph was dead. What happened in his wrestling through the night with the divine stranger is an emblem of his life: he fights his mysterious adversary to a draw of sorts and is given a new, divine name, but he is hurt in his hip socket and will bear the evidence of the struggle in a limp for all his days. Jacob's story has what may seem to be a happy ending — he is reunited with Joseph and gets to see him in all his regal splendor, and he is able to bless the two grandsons Joseph has given him before he dies. Yet this is no fairytale. The taste of bitterness does not disappear. On his very deathbed, he flashes back to Rachel's death. All this is a token of the moral realism suffusing biblical narrative: "Few and evil have been the days of the years of my life."

Finally, here is what amounts to a zero-degree case of brevity, where something significant is communicated by a character's not saying anything. In the episode of the rape of Jacob's daughter Dinah, he berates Simeon and Levi for perpetrating vengeance, the massacre of all the men of Shechem. The objection that he voices is not moral but prudential. He and his family are only a "handful" of people, and they will now be exposed to the wrath of the Canaanites. Simeon and Levi yield no ground to their father: "Like a whore should our sister be treated?" (Genesis 34:31). The episode ends with these words, and the implication is that Jacob has no rejoinder to his two fierce sons. His silence is important because this is the moment in the larger story when Jacob, once a resolute and resourceful master of his large family, allows the power to be seized by his insistent sons. (David, too, will begin to lose power after the rape of his daughter Tamar, an act in which he was unwittingly complicit by directing her to Amnon's bedchamber.) Not long after the incident of the rape, at least in the canonical ordering of the episodes, Jacob will be cruelly deceived by his sons when they send Joseph's bloodied robe as evidence of his supposed death, and the once canny Jacob, now deceived, will slide into twenty crippling years of manipulated mourning for his beloved Joseph.

A related episode, reported with the sparsest notation, is inserted in the next chapter: "And it happened, when Israel was encamped in the land, that Reuben went and lay with Bilhah, his father's concubine, and Israel heard" (Genesis 35:22). This is a grave transgression: it amounts to incest and is also an implicit challenge to his father's authority, for whatever Reuben's desire-driven impulse, in ancient Israel to take sexual possession of the dominant person's bedmate is to lay claim to his power. Jacob hears of it but he does not speak. At this point in his life he seems unable to confront his wayward sons. It is only at the end of his days, when he intones a long poem that spells out the destiny of the twelve sons through the tribes they will found, that he will curse Reuben for "profaning [his] couch." The poem is almost certainly from a different literary source and antedates the prose narrative by many years, but its editorial placement at the end of the Jacob narrative picks up that enigmatic silence upon his hearing that Reuben has slept with Bilhah. When it happened, he did not speak, perhaps afraid that he no longer possessed the paternal authority to castigate one of his sons. If, then, one views the narrative and the poem as a continuum, even if created by editorial artifice, Jacob figures as a powerless father harboring resentment for years and allowing himself to express it only as his life draws to an end.

Revelatory silence occurs also in David's grief over the death of Absalom. He is famously, and movingly, shattered to hear that his son has been killed, and he expresses his grief in an anguished stutter. Then his brutal, tough-minded military commander Joab, who in fact is Absalom's killer, arrives after the battle and berates David for grieving over someone who was his deadly enemy. If David does not reverse course, Joab tells him, the troops will disperse and he will be left to a terrible fate. Joab issues a peremptory order to the king: "And now, arise, go out, and speak to the heart of your servants. For by the Lord I have sworn, if you go not out, that not a man will spend the night with you, and this will be a greater evil than any evil that has befallen you from your youth until now" (2 Samuel 19:8). David is compelled to obey Joab's command, so he goes out and shows himself before the troops, but he simply stands there and does not say a word.

As the Dutch Bible scholar J. P. Fokkelman has brilliantly observed, David at this juncture looks like "a man beaten to a pulp, who can barely stand, and does only the minimum requested or expected of him." David's silence in this respect resembles Jacob's silence: it is the speechlessness of an eloquent man who was once powerful but now, torn between the political demands of kingship and the emotions of a bereaved father, falls silent. The fulcrum of power has passed to the strongman Joab, just as Jacob has lost power in the face of his angry sons. David, too, can give vent to his resentment only on his deathbed, when he enjoins Solomon to see to it that Joab will be killed in retribution for his murderous career. He mentions in his words to Solomon only two victims of killings, the two army commanders, Abner and Amasa, but he surely sooner or later would have heard of Joab's murder of Absalom and would have had that in mind as well.

Eric Auerbach drew a conclusion that in its time would have been somewhat surprising — that it was biblical narrative, not Homer, that was the precursor in ancient literature of the great realist novels of the nineteenth and twentieth centuries. As I became engaged in biblical narrative over the years, I was completely persuaded by the rightness of this conclusion, and I came to see certain ramifications of it not spelled out by Auerbach. But there is one respect in which Homer and not the Hebrew writers was a forerunner of the novel, and that is in the sumptuousness of descriptive detail. This is especially true of the *Odyssey*, which revels in the representation of the accoutrements of aristocratic life and the fine craftsmanship that produced them — the golden bowls, the beautiful woven cloths, the exquisitely carved wood of the furnishings, and much more. There is a line of affiliation from all this to Balzac's elaborate rendering of Parisian interiors as reflections of their inhabitants and Dickens' vivid description of the choking London smog that is the medium for the troubled fate of many of his characters. The ancient Hebrew writers chose an antithetical path. They contrived numerous ways to package complexity into highly compressed units, using just a few words or even a single word to intimate depth of character, coiled tension in relationships, unstated emotions. Among the many means through which biblical narrative grips its readers, the resonant, subtle deployment of terrific compactness stands out. Indeed, it stands out even more conspicuously, even more admirably, in our culture of verbiage and verbosity.

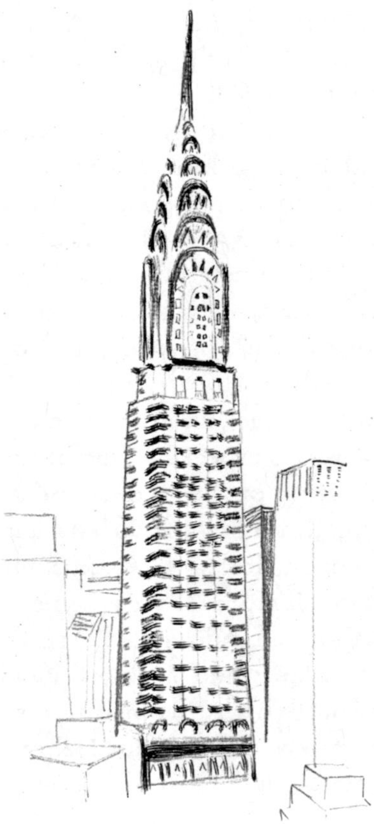

EMMA LAZARUS

1492

Thou two-faced year, Mother of Change and Fate,
Didst weep when Spain cast forth with flaming sword,
The children of the prophets of the Lord,
Prince, priest, and people, spurned by zealot hate.
Hounded from sea to sea, from state to state,
The West refused them, and the East abhorred.
No anchorage the known world could afford,
Close-locked was every port, barred every gate.
Then smiling, thou unveil'dst, O two-faced year,
A virgin world where doors of sunset part,
Saying, "Ho, all who weary, enter here!
There falls each ancient barrier that the art
Of race or creed or rank devised, to rear
Grim bulwarked hatred between heart and heart!"

(1883)

LEN GUTKIN

Reading for Sins

Is the only kind of magic left to literature dark magic — the power to harm with words? Recent debates in literary studies sometimes make it seem so. Consider the most-downloaded episode of the *C19 Podcast*, a podcast series produced by The Society of Nineteenth-Century Americanists. The episode, which appeared in 2019, is called "The N Word in the Classroom: Just Say No." The Reaganite moralism of the episode's title gives a good sense of the whole. Here are some college classroom rules insisted on by the host, a professor of American literature:

> The N-word won't be used in this class by a person of any race, even if it consistently appears in our texts. The same goes for the F-word, regardless of a person's perceived sexual orientation or gender expression. And this is simply not a space in which we call people trash.

By "used," the professor would at first seem to mean "mentioned" or "quoted," although the equivalence with "calling people trash" begins quickly to suggest otherwise. She goes on: "My research specialty is African American literature. The N-word often appears in the texts I teach, but I never believed that I had to hear that word spoken in my workplace just because I had chosen to study art that often features it." The emphasis on "workplace" erodes the distinction between use and mention; hearing a student read the offending word aloud might, in this case, constitute something like a discriminatory workplace environment for the professor, despite the fact that she herself had assigned the text.

Later in the same episode, the professor acknowledges that she sometimes plays recordings of songs or of poetry in class that contain the offending word, spoken out loud and in its entirety:

> I mention this, because even as I acknowledge the power of performance to do harm when we give life to words by speaking them in the classroom, that doesn't mean that we can't respect an artist's choices, while we also take our role seriously. My students and I are practicing what it means to be literary scholars and cultural critics. We are not reenactors, so we need not give the word life ourselves in order to engage the work thoroughly.

Instead of giving the word "life," students are asked when reading aloud to render it as the sound "en," or "ens" if plural. Nor are such phonic reductions confined to the case of the word "nigger." When teaching James Baldwin's "Notes of a Native Son," for instance, the professor insists that the phrase "yellow-bellied Japs," whose racism Baldwin abhors, be enunciated, rather ornithologically, as "yellow-bellied jays." "We notice that Baldwin is as critical of the racial slur as we might be," the professor says, "but that doesn't mean that we have to give that slur life in our learning environment."

There is a combination of conceptual incoherence and primness here that seems to me all too common when it comes to the way contemporary literature scholars think about words that wound. Its mystical metaphysics aside, though, "The N Word in the Classroom: Just Say No" does present an interesting occasion for examining how denigratory and insulting language operates. In his novel *Open City*, published in 2011, Teju Cole dramatizes the problem in a more sophisticated fashion. The narrator, Julius, an American immigrant of European and Nigerian descent, is talking to a couple of Moroccan Muslims. They are telling him about Moroccan Jews. One of the Moroccans says, "They look just like us, though, of course, they do better in business. I think sometimes that I should become a Jew, just for professional reasons." He goes on: "What I am against is Zionism, and this religious claim they make on a land where someone else is already living."

Julius, neither a Muslim nor a Jew and with no connection to the Middle East, feels uncomfortable:

> I wanted to tell him that, in the States, we were particularly wary of strong criticisms of Israel because it could become anti-Semitic. But I didn't, because I knew that my own fear of anti-Semitism, like my fear of racism, had through long practice become prerational. What I would impose on him would not be an argument, it would be a request that he adopt my reflexes, or the pieties of a society different from the one in which he grew up, or the one in which he now functioned. It would do little good to describe for him the subtle shades of meaning evoked in an American ear by saying "Jews" instead of "Jewish people." I wanted also to take him to task for attacking a religious ideal when his own central ideal was religious, but the skein of argument was beginning to feel like futility piled on futility.

Julius would like to have a substantive conversation about the politics of the Middle East, but he's not sure how, at least not with these Moroccans. Impacted taboos intervene. First, there is the possible coincidence of anti-Zionism with antisemitism, which triggers Julius' worry about indulging a political argument that is actually a racist one. Julius quickly realizes that something superstitious — in his words, something "prerational" — is at work in this fear. Indeed, his "reflex" against bigotry encompasses not only his "fear of anti-Semitism," but also his "fear of racism." The grammar is ambiguous. Does he mean his fear of expressions of racism from others — a plausible concern for an African who spends his time in the United States and Europe? Or does he mean his fear of being caught out, inadvertently, in some expression of prejudice on his own part? And who is he afraid *of*? What superego-like monitor is listening to his conversation?

Julius' fear of bigotry involves a heightened attention to verbal nuance, and accordingly to the possibility of mistranslation across idioms: "It would do little good to describe to him the subtle shades of meaning evoked in an American ear by saying 'Jews' instead of 'Jewish people.'" To talk politics, at least Israeli-Palestinian politics, is to embark on a fraught course where the landmines of bigotry are everywhere, even in the difference in case between "Jewish" and "Jew." In a less serious — but in its way just as precise — analysis, the comedian Louis C.K. has a routine about the word "Jew" that picks out its potential activation as a slur:

> "Jew" is a funny word. It is. Because "Jew" is the only word that is the polite thing to call a group of people, and the slur for the same group. Most groups have a good and bad [word], but [in this case] there is the same word with a little stank on it, and it becomes a terrible thing to call a person. 'Cuz you could say "He's a Jew" [in a neutral tone], it's fine, but, "He's a *Jew*" [with contemptuous emphasis], and that's all it takes.

When Julius winces at the failure to recognize the distinction between "Jews" and "the Jewish people" on the part of his Moroccan interlocutor, he is detecting, or worrying that he might be detecting, the "stank" that Louis C.K. says can be put on the word.

It is a sociolinguistic fact that, in English and in the right conditions, minor differences, such as the difference between "the Jews" and "the Jewish people," can in fact indicate prejudicial intent. But Julius' super-sensitivity to such potential maledictions exceeds any plausible situational warrant. It is a symptom of an American hypervigilance toward even inadvertent expressions of what could be taken for bigotry. For this detection system words are dangerous enough that they must be policed for their own intrinsic powers, entirely irrespective of inferable intention. They are like magical spells, or like primitive taboos. That is a part of what Julius means by "prerational," by "reflex."

These are the reflexes of the American liberal of a certain time and place. They are the reflexes, for instance, of the Americanist scholar who wrote "The N Word: Just Say No." What sets Julius apart from her, though, is his capacity to analyze the structure of the taboos whose violation he fears. Unlike too many humanities professors today, Julius recognizes that there is something dangerously "prerational" in the vogueish fear of words that wound.

Today, for us, such words partake of that magic — in the very reduced, very polite way appropriate to our own bourgeois etiquette rituals — with which anthropology from the nineteenth century through the time of Freud was so preoccupied: the religious superstition whereby certain objects, words, or people are invested with a kind of sacred dread. The Columbia linguist John McWhorter has sketched a brief conceptual history of tabooed words in modern English. He begins in the 1930s, when the lexicographer Allen Walker Read could write an entire etymological entry on the word "fuck" that never actually spelled out the word. In our own time, "f—" or "f—k" (or "fugg," as in Norman Mailer's novel *The Naked and the Dead* in 1948) seems quaint; taboo has settled elsewhere. It has "been transferred from the sexual and scatological to the sociological." These changes are of course not arbitrary. "What a society considers profane reveals what it believes to be sacrosanct: The emerging taboo on slurs reveals the value our culture places — if not consistently — on respect for subgroups of people."

This is an important supplement to Julius' reference to taboo as "prerational." In fact, the deep logic of any given taboo expresses important, and in some cases perfectly rational, societal commitments. The prerational aspect of any taboo isn't necessarily the social argument it reflects, but the disabling emotions that its violation elicits.

I have begun with slurs because they are the most concentrated, the most crystallized, site of our polite culture's concern with taboo. But that makes them only the neatest instance of a much more general phenomenon. For college students and professors, a huge range of things became troubling in the years since 2012 or so. Literary texts, historical events, and venerated institutional leaders marred by the sins of their times became occasions for complicated rituals of disavowal and purification. Depictions or representations of sexual violence, for instance, are an especially common target. The environment could become punitive enough that college teachers would routinely report feeling afraid of doing their jobs. A Reed College professor described feeling "scared to teach courses on race, gender, or sexuality — and I am a gay mixed-race woman." That was in 2016, during the first Trump administration; the professor was not anxious about surveillance by MAGA politicians seeking out wrong-think, but about Reed's left-wing student activists, whose militant campaign against the college's humanities core curriculum included outrage at the playful inclusion of a Steve Martin skit in which the comedian dresses up as King Tut. As one student said, "That's like somebody . . . making a song just littered with the n-word everywhere." The video deserved to be removed.

Demands of this sort have of course become a mainstay of the resuscitated culture wars of the last fifteen years. And they have become fodder for right-wing critiques of student "snowflakes." Such critiques, pretty plainly, are not exactly misplaced. There really is something pathological about the streams of activist sensitivity to the teaching of literature or art thought to contain harmful words, ideas, or depictions. But the interesting question, the one that demands a more persuasive social theory than it has yet received, is this: What does this sensitivity say about the place of the work of art more broadly in the psychic economy of students?

To be sensitive to a work of art should be a good thing; one of the goals of a college education should be to cultivate the capacity for such sensitivity. That includes the inculcation of a critical sensibility sensitive to a work's blind spots, omissions, political presumptions, and so on. But the sensitivity exhibited by the snowflakes — I'll use that slur for them, with apologies — is not the broad but discriminating sensitivity that tries to comprehend a work in all its parts, however contradictory or ideologically opaque. It is instead a kind of fetishizing fixation on a quite narrow and specific range of meaning, which has been promoted above all other possible meanings — more specifically, on a particular range of political sins whose concretization in the work are thought to be traumatizing to those who encounter them.

These students' overall economy of attention has been deranged. One or two presumptively objectionable features of a work loom large, and the rest seems almost to disappear in the shadow of the bad thing. This new hermeneutics — call it snowflake hermeneutics — is a way of reading specifically for sins. It is a generational refinement, or debasement, of the broader "hermeneutics of suspicion" from which it is descended, that suite of demystifying critical practices, deriving from Marx, Freud, Levi-Strauss, and Foucault and culminating in the work of Fredric Jameson, whereby the hidden motors and meanings of artistic and cultural production are brought into exhilarating view. At their best, the interpretive tendencies lumped under "hermeneutics of suspicion" are not just clarifying but also — by increasing the range and multiplying the kinds of meaning attached to any work of art — dignifying, rather than reductive, prescriptive, or mechanistic. (That the latter lapses were a risk has been clear at least since the Russian formalists rebuked the crudity of their Marxist counterparts.)

Snowflake hermeneutics, by contrast, is never dignifying. Sometimes, perhaps, students absorb these bad habits from their secondary educations or from other ambient forces in the culture and bring them to the college classroom. But to a substantial degree it seems obvious that students have picked up on cues from their college professors. With varying degrees of sophistication and vulgarity, snowflake hermeneutics is practiced by faculty members themselves, modeled for students in their writing and in their classroom instruction.

The most obvious area where this is so is in the vogue for trigger warnings, a vogue which now seems to be receding. And to be fair, it met with stiff headwinds early on; all the way back in 2014, the American Association of University Professors released a statement arguing that "mandated trigger warnings threaten academic freedom." I don't want to revisit trigger warnings now just to attack the professors, often well-meaning, who used them, or to attack the students who sometimes demanded them. But a brief look back at this recent trend can tell us something about the academic humanities' role in mediating taboos. Consider the list of topics which Oberlin University briefly contemplated requiring faculty members to include trigger warnings for, before dropping the policy after extensive public ridicule. An inexhaustive sample of potentially traumatizing topics: "racism, classism, sexism, heterosexism, cissexism, ableism, and other issues of privilege and oppression." Even Chinua Achebe's novel *Things Fall Apart* might "trigger readers who have experienced racism, colonialism, religious persecution, violence, suicide, and more." More than suicide?

The pseudoscientific emphasis on trauma triggers has a purpose: it is meant to proliferate taboos by expanding the range of topics to which "prerational" or "reflexive" responses might overwhelm the capacity for rational discussion. When McWhorter writes about the shift in our culture from the sexual and scatological to the sociological, including words that stigmatize disfavored social groups, he is describing something that happened, to a degree, organically, driven by large-scale shifts in societal sensitivity. But the taboo proliferation encouraged by the trigger warning movement was also a kind of conscious "norm entrepreneurship," in Cass Sunstein's useful phrase. The hope was that, with enough design, enough insistence, enough administrative coercion, these expanding lists of troubling and offensive topics would start to feel super-sensitive for more and more teachers, triggering a "norm-cascade." What is a taboo, after all, except a norm with an especially intense emotional charge?

Taboo proliferation of this kind is obviously a political project. The version at Oberlin and elsewhere draws heavily on political assumptions of various left-wing identitarian stripes. But it should always have been obvious that this kind of entrepreneurship was politically indeterminate. As early as 2015 some Christian conservative students began to object to representations in assigned works of literature that they felt demeaned their own political or religious identities. Last year, at Texas A&M, a professor was fired for teaching about queer issues in children's literature; the student-driven campaign against her accused her of attacking students' Christian identities. We can expect much more of the same in the months and years to come.

The rawest and most strident instances of snowflake hermeneutics have always been on social media, which has both exacerbated the tendency and provided a convenient window into the pathological interpretive consequences of the prejudices of the professoriate. Here is a favorite example, which will first require a little background. A couple of years ago, the scholar and critic Merve Emre wrote a review of John Guillory's *Professing Criticism* in the *New Yorker*. That review approvingly cited a phrase of Guillory's, "professional deformation," which was his rendering of an exactly cognate phrase in French. Originally, a professional deformation referred to a bodily deformation resulting from one's professional activity: carpal tunnel for typists, for instance, or the asymmetrical shoulders that coal miners develop, as described vividly by D. H. Lawrence in *Lady Chatterley's Lover*. But even in the nineteenth century and certainly after it, the phrase could be applied to the mental deformations attendant to certain professions. Different kinds of scholars might suffer from different kinds of epistemic, cognitive, and evaluative distortion. Intellectual historians might overrate the influence of Calvinist theology on the development of American political institutions, underplaying various economic causes. Or early modernist literary scholars might overestimate the influence of Shakespeare on the emergence of modern subjectivity. It was in something like this sense that Guillory used the phrase.

I paid more than usual attention to the reception of *Professing Criticism*, because I had written about it several times myself. I was interested to see what the folks at a popular public Facebook page devoted to "Remaking the University," hosted by a recent president of the Modern Language Association, would make of Emre's review. They didn't like it. And several of them — tenured professors of English, not naïve or overeager freshmen — were appalled by Guillory's use of the phrase "deformation," as well as by Emre's approving use of it throughout her review. The subject is introduced thus, by a distinguished Victorianist: "I just read this and I'm feeling dismayed" by the "flippant, careless, and damaging work, including the unspeakable use of 'deformation' here, not to mention the Anglocentrism, elitism, etc." This professor goes on: "It is horrifying that a person can use 'deformed'/ 'deformation' in 2023 in an article in a major magazine and nobody flagged it." Then another professor — like the first, a well-known scholar in her field — weighs in: "the ableism was stunning." And the first professor returns to the charge: "I just did a search for 'deformed' and felt physically ill. She uses it nine times in the article, starting with 'hideously deformed.' What the hell? How are disabled scholars supposed to feel when they read that? How is it possible that she could think it was cute to use such a derogatory term and that the editors didn't flag it? I don't even see how one can debate the merits of the idea with slurs like that sitting in the prose."

As a response to an essay by an important critic about another important critic, these hyperventilating non sequiturs are appallingly irresponsible. (They are also trivial.) But they do give a sense of the hair-trigger environment which some precincts of the humanities have become. This is a world in which the editors of the *New Yorker* are held to be incomprehensibly out of touch for failing to police the figurative use of "deformation." It doesn't occur to these professors that the discursive norms which they are demanding might seem odd, even bizarre, to verbal workers outside of their peculiar guild (and to a few souls inside their peculiar guild, too). Professional deformation indeed!

None of this is to say that metaphors of ability or disability are not legitimate areas of interest for scholars of literature and language. "From the crooked timber of humanity no straight thing was ever made": Kant's famous apothegm might well yield to an interpretative analysis drawing on the resources of disability studies. By the same token, it is almost impossible to imagine describing activities of cognition and perception, at least in any of the languages with which I am familiar, without recourse to metaphors of blindness and insight, opacity and transparency, lightness and dark. Those are interesting facts, and perhaps a literary-critical interest in "ableism" can yield insight about them.

But all that is somewhat beside the point. If I say "Finally, I see what you're saying," it does not mean that I have a problem with blind people. And after all, the angry professor who initiated the attack on Emre's alleged ableism might be accused of an analogous crime. Emre's sins, she says, are "unspeakable." In using the phrase "unspeakable," the professor would seem to be entirely insensitive to the fact that some people, for reasons either anatomical or neurological, are indeed incapable of speech. She should reckon with her own heart.

The tunnel vision — one of those metaphors again! — that caused this professor to home in so intensely on the word "deformation" that, in her words, it is not even possible "to debate the merits of the idea" is a nonpareil instance of snowflake hermeneutics, not just because of its extraordinarily partial and distorted approach to a larger and more complicated text, but also because of the extreme emotional intensity of the response. The professor word-searched for the offending word and reported feeling "physically ill." Physically ill!

Like the compulsive probing of a wounded tooth, there seems to be some gratification in the discomfort. It is sought after. This is an indispensable feature of snowflake hermeneutics. Something is very offensive, dismaying, painful to encounter, traumatizing even — but these very discomforts are virtues in their way. They are quickening, exciting. They get the blood up. They afford, in other words, some of the powers of art. "Slurs like that sitting in the prose" are in their way magical words, talismans of intensity and poetic transformation, dark jewels. They unite the ethical, the verbal, and the aesthetic in ways that might be called literary.

There is a connection between the moralizing extremism of the interpretive practice to which the eminent professors subjected Emre's essay and what the very non-extremist literary critic Wayne Booth called "ethical reading" — a practice which, as Booth himself recognized in 1988 in his book *The Company We Keep*, can in its own right have much to do with "suspicious" reading (the phrase is Booth's). His great book is bookended by a kind of allegory about ethical suspicion, in this case with regard to the teaching of *Huckleberry Finn*. The year is sometime in the 1960s; Booth is teaching in the University of Chicago's humanities core where *Huckleberry Finn* is one of the assigned texts. There is only a single black instructor among the faculty who teach the core, an art historian named Paul Moses. (Moses died at the tragically young age of 36; *The Company We Keep* is dedicated to him.) Alone among the faculty, he feels that *Huckleberry Finn* should not be part of the core.

Here is how Booth paraphrases what he calls Moses' "overt, serious, uncompromising act of ethical criticism," which shocked his colleagues:

> It's hard for me to say this, but I have to say it anyway. I simply can't teach *Huckleberry Finn* again. The way Mark Twain portrays Jim is so offensive to me that I get angry in class, and I can't get all those liberal white kids to understand why I am angry. What's

more, I don't think it's right to subject students, black or white, to the many distorted views of race on which that book is based.

In Booth's summary, Moses says explicitly that he is not objecting to racial slurs per se, but to "the whole range of assumptions about slavery and its consequences, and about how whites should deal with liberated slaves, and how liberated slaves should behave or will behave toward whites, good ones and bad ones. That book is just bad education, and the fact that it's so cleverly written makes it even more troublesome to me."

Booth's initial response is condescending. "I can remember," he writes, "lamenting the shoddy education that had left poor Paul Moses unable to recognize a great classic when he met one. Had he not even noticed that Jim is of all the characters the closest to the moral center?" Recalling with ironic distance his rejection of Moses' views, Booth remembers feeling that "Moses obviously could neither read properly nor think properly about what questions might be relevant to judging a novel's worth."

Toward the very end of *The Company We Keep*, Booth returns to *Huckleberry Finn* in order to vindicate Moses' critique, at least to a degree. He rereads the novel with Moses in mind and then offers an account of "how a fully 'suspicious' interpreter might view it." For that interpreter, the book reduces Jim to "simply a comic butt, suitable for exploitation by cute little white boys of good heart." Even worse, Twain "simply treats Jim and his feelings . . . as expendable, as sub-human — a slave to the plot, as it were." What's more, the novel endorses a racial ideology in which "black people, slaves and ex-slaves, are a special *kind* of good people — so naturally good, in their innocent simplicity, that the effects on them of slavery will not be discernible once slavery has been removed." Moreover, "black people are hungry for love . . . and they will be (*should* be) obsequiously grateful for whatever small favors whites grant them." Finally, "the consequences of emancipation will be as good as they can be, in this wicked world, so long as you (the white liberal reader) have your heart in the right place — as you clearly do because you have palpitated properly to Huck's discovery of a full sense of brotherhood with Jim."

Booth has much more to say about *Huckleberry Finn*, and the reading of the "fully 'suspicious' interpreter" is not the one that he himself ultimately settles on. But it is obvious to him, as it is surely obvious to us, that to the extent that the skeptical analysis offered by this fully suspicious interpreter was unavailable to Moses' colleagues in the early 1960s, those colleagues were missing something. Their blindness to aspects of the racial dimension condemns their understanding of the novel to an embarrassing incompleteness. The kind of ideological critique that Booth offers, one developed after the prompting by Moses' ethical rejection of the novel, clearly contributes to a more accurate and more probing understanding of what Twain had done.

I should put my cards on the table. I think Moses was wrong to refuse to teach *Huckleberry Finn*. And his sweeping rejection of the novel — it's "just bad education," in Booth's paraphrase — is simplistic to a fault. But Moses was obviously right that something had gone awry in the interpretative consensus around *Huckleberry Finn* in his time. The critical suspicion that made him the odd man out among his faculty peers in the early 1960s makes him look, in retrospect, like the only person to perceive how complicated a text, formally, ideologically, and politically, *Huckleberry Finn* is. Ethical suspicion of this sort is obviously a good thing, one of the good habits that literary study and the study of the arts generally is designed to cultivate. Yet I feel quite certain, by contrast, that much of the ethical suspicion of our own period, marred by the moralizing extremism (and overt politics) which is all too common in the literary humanities now, will not look prescient at any future point. It will look instead like a kind of derangement, a mania, a punitive fixation on discovered sins and a narcissistic wallowing in one's own capacity to feel wounded by a text — to feel, as one of Emre's critics put it, "physically ill."

Which brings us to the problem with Moses' stance, the part that was prescient in the wrong way. Moses was wrong not about the interpretative complexity of *Huckleberry Finn* but about its traumatic impact on some of its readers, including himself. Moses (again, in Booth's paraphrase) said that the book made him too angry to teach. But that just cannot be the role of the critic or the scholar. He should have striven to overcome it. Moses' anger, after all, was not just a private experience. He was a professor, a teacher; his reaction was a pedagogical act, and a destructive one. It modeled a kind of disabling vulnerability for students which the university simply cannot afford to harbor. To the extent that ethical criticism is rooted in a kind of therapeutic emphasis on a critic's emotional state, it is incompatible with the scholarly vocation. To the extent that those emotions are understood to have primarily political stakes, their invocation risks reducing the role of the critic to something very narrow and constricted. The mini-scandal that Moses' refusal to teach *Huckleberry Finn* caused in Chicago should thus be understood as provoked by two related but distinct concerns. The first was about the meaning of a specific novel, on which point Moses and his opponents were each partially correct. The second was about the extent to which emotional vulnerability toward texts or works of art should ground interpretation and even authorize revisions to the curriculum. On that, Moses was wrong.

The curricular sensitivity of our own time, and the therapeutic emphasis on the feelings not just of students but of professors as well, has met with far less resistance than Moses did. Why? I can speculate, but my speculations will be necessarily vague and telegraphic. The question comes down, I think, to a large-scale transformation in how and why we value literature and the arts, and to an accompanying change in which of the competing evaluative justifications are able to carry weight in our colleges. To put it very reductively, a certain set of political and civic concerns has come to seem like the most plausible justification for many areas of the high humanities, such as the study of literature and art history. Grounding the teaching of the humanities in these concerns reflects a profound revision of an earlier phase of institutionalized humanistic endeavor. The account of this transformation I have found the most compelling is the literary critic Simon During's — he labels it "the second secularization," a process whereby the substitutive religions of literature and art that had for educated people come to supplant the role of religion proper have themselves suffered a diminishment in power. For educated moderns, as I. A. Richards put it in the 1930s, the whole complex of metaphysical ideas — "about God, about the universe, about human nature" — that religion deals with had come to seem too tenuous or imprecise to keep religion vital — but they survived in poetry, which doesn't even pretend to deal with real facts. Literature could therefore act as a kind of replacement religion. "As poetry conclusively shows," Richards explained, "even the most important among our attitudes can be aroused and maintained without any believing of a factual or verifiable order entering at all." Literary education and the institutionalization of the humanities would constitute a training in this surrogate religion.

In our own time, university study devoted to what Richards calls the "pseudo-statements" that poetry no longer commands the same cultural prestige it once had. No one knows exactly why, but the high humanities have suffered a loss of power, and we are all trying to figure out how to recover from this diminution. But that fact can obscure a strange reality: what Richards calls the "arousal" of "the most important among our attitudes" — or what his Victorian predecessor Matthew Arnold called the "emotion" poetry attaches to ideas — remains a function of the literary even in the straitened form that is now encapsulated by trigger warnings and by what I have been calling snowflake hermeneutics. What Richards calls "the most important among our attitudes" has come to be understood as our identitarian attitudes toward one or another political situation.

It's as if the substitutive spiritual function that both Arnold and Richards ascribed to poetry, literature, and art has been chastened, for its modern secular adherents in our own hyper-political but also hyper-utilitarian moment, into a kind of restricted dark magic of the political word. The emotional charge of the aesthetic has been peculiarly channeled, attached to a set of therapeutic identitarian concerns with progressive political implications: not disenchantment but, perhaps, "misenchantment," to borrow a phrase from the religious historian Eugene McCarraher. The multifarious taboos around "slurs . . . sitting in the prose," to quote our angry English professor, depend on fundamentally political emotions and motivate a fundamentally emotional politics, disabling and constrictive however emancipatory it may feel. The cultic or magical power of the literary has been preserved, but in a kind of negative. This is the cultural situation in which, at no less a college than Oberlin, Chinua Achebe's *Things Fall Apart* — which, of course, brilliantly mounts a political argument — becomes the site of a series of taboos necessitating trigger warnings regarding "racism, colonialism, religious persecution, violence, suicide." In its ironic way, this vulgar politicization of the literary is also literature's astonishing aggrandizement, and even a kind of desperate wish. If only literature could mean so much.

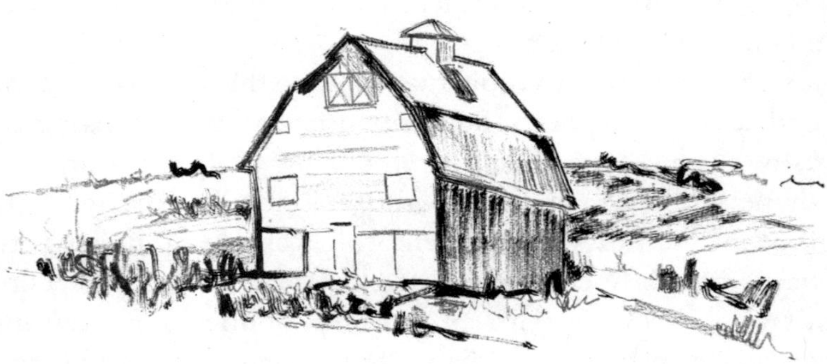

WALT WHITMAN

The Prairie Grass Dividing

The prairie-grass dividing—its special odor breathing,
I demand of it the spiritual corresponding,
Demand the most copious and close companionship of men,
Demand the blades to rise of words, acts, beings,
Those of the open atmosphere, coarse, sunlit, fresh, nutritious,
Those that go their own gait, erect, stepping with freedom and
command—leading, not following,
Those with a never-quell'd audacity—those with sweet and lusty
flesh, clear of taint,
Those that look carelessly in the faces of Presidents and Governors,
as to say, Who are you?
Those of earth-born passion, simple, never-constrain'd, never
obedient,
Those of inland America.

(1860)

KAI SINA

Thomas Mann's Exemplary Fury

When does a democracy tip into crisis? When is simply defending it no longer enough, and when does resistance become necessary? These were the questions that Thomas Mann (and many others) faced in the fall of 1930. For his "German Address," subtitled "An Appeal to Reason," he returned to Berlin's Beethoven Hall — the same hall where, eight years earlier, he had declared his decisive support for democracy in his speech "On the German Republic."Now, it seemed, his role as a political intellectual required a redefinition.

This redefinition came in the wake of a dramatic, almost explosive surge in votes for the Nazi Party in the Reichstag election of September 14, 1930. Nearly one in five voters had cast their ballot for Adolf Hitler and his party. Just two years earlier, in May 1928, they had garnered a mere 2.6 percent. When Mann gave his speech, the newly elected Reichstag had just met for the first time. Nazi deputies marched in wearing brown shirts and swastika armbands — a deliberate provocation and breach of parliamentary norms. In the days that followed, they and their supporters stepped up intimidation and violent attacks on political opponents. Jewish-owned shops and department stores came under assault as well. For Mann, these developments marked a turning point — not only for the country, but also for his own political thinking and commitment to politics. 18.3 percent: this figure transformed Mann, the committed republican and democrat, into a resolute activist and outspoken anti-fascist.

His address begins with an apparently unambiguous disclaimer. "I am no follower of relentless social activism," he told his audience. The age of aesthetic idealism was irretrievably gone, but that did not mean one had to accept an "activistic equation of idealism and frivolity." The disclaimer is a rhetorical gesture. Its function is to make the exception to the rule appear inevitable: "Nevertheless there are hours, moments in communal life when such a justification of art practically fails," he explained, "when the artist can no longer create from within, because pressing necessities push aside the thought of art — when the crisis of public distress shakes him to the core, so that the playful, passionate immersion in the eternal-human, which we call art, . . . becomes psychologically impossible."

"Immediate thoughts of necessity," "crisis of public distress": in the eloquent flow of his words, the sharpness and urgency of Mann's description of the situation in the fall of 1930 almost fade. But only against this background does the Lutheran resolve of his confession reveal its full pathos: *Hier stehe ich. Ich kann nicht anders.* Here I stand. I cannot do otherwise.

Above all else, the speech aimed to explain the rise of National Socialism and, at the same time, to rhetorically discredit the movement. "Purely economically," Mann began his analysis, Nazism could not be adequately understood — it was not merely the result of unemployment, hunger, and cold that shaped social life in the wake of the global depression. Rather, two tendencies converged. On the one hand, a pseudo-intellectual program "from the academic-professorial sphere," consisting of "mystical philistinism and extravagant nonsense," which, with "vocabulary such as racial, national, fraternal, heroic," had "flooded and glued together the brains of Germans in 1930." On the other hand, a "giant wave of eccentric barbarism and primitive mass-democratic fairground vulgarity" that swept through the modern world of consumption, nervousness, technology, and noise. From this fatal combination emerged a grotesque and orgiastic political style: "Fanaticism becomes a principle of salvation, enthusiasm epileptic ecstasy . . . and reason veils her face."

Having identified the activism in the speaker's confession, it is important to understand his manner of speaking as a manifestation of activism, too. In rapid-fire style, the speaker hurls vividly charged labels one after another, beating down the very subject he describes: "fanaticism," "principle of salvation," "ecstasy," and so forth. It is unmistakably a rhetoric of attack — fast, hard, precise. What is good and what is evil: in the "German Address" this distinction is framed in rhetorical and performative terms. And therein lies the most striking contrast with the speech "On the German Republic" delivered eight years earlier. There the speaker sought to "win over" his audience for his position, to engage them in a democratic contest of arguments. But now he was confronted with a political and social phenomenon that could no longer be debated — it had to be *fought*. In 1930, he no longer dealt with political opponents. They were enemies.

And they were enemies not only in an abstract sense. That October evening in Berlin, a group of disruptors had mingled with the bourgeois audience — including the brothers Ernst and Friedrich Georg Jünger, two leading figures of what would later be called the "Conservative Revolution." Joining them were twenty SA men, disguised in borrowed tuxedos, dispatched personally by Joseph Goebbels. What began with heckling soon grew into a tumult that required police intervention. A photograph documents the scene: while the audience turns, wondering what is happening in the back rows, Thomas Mann stands at the podium, his gaze fixed in stone. It must have been an uncanny situation: the very behavior he feared took shape in the moment he addressed it. Democratic debate was obstructed by force.

The Nazi press exploited the scene for propaganda. They claimed the audience had turned away from the speaker, that no one wished to hear his appeal to reason, that he stood isolated in his political views. In fact, the opposite was true: the audience's sustained applause had helped prevent the disruption from succeeding. The lie of Nazi propaganda served no other purpose than to recast the true failure of their actions as a triumph in the media. It is precisely the logic of fake news: turn reality upside down and present defeat as victory.

The Beethoven Hall speech marked a deep break in Mann's political biography. His status as a public adversary of National Socialism had become irreversible. When does a democracy begin to tip and what conclusions must be drawn? Thomas Mann had found his answer.

From the "Appeal to Reason" in the fall of 1930, we can trace a clear line showing how Mann's political activism took on different forms over time: beginning with his Open Letter to the Dean of the Faculty of Philosophy at the University of Bonn, which in the winter of 1936 — three years into his Swiss exile — stripped its honorary doctorate from him; through the Radio Addresses "Listen, Germany!" delivered from American exile after 1938, speeches that were both intended to inform the Germans about the reality of the Nazi regime and to call for resistance against it; and finally, his advocacy for Zionism, which after 1945 took the form of outspoken support for the founding of a Jewish state.

These three examples show a form of political activism that did not end with the Nazi seizure of power. Instead, it had to constantly adapt — in Swiss and Californian exile, in transatlantic dialogue, and in the face of a new world order after World War II. At the same time, they are documents of confidence. They present a writer who saw in the political catastrophe of the twentieth century not only a historical challenge, but also a personal duty. Facing this task became part of his lifelong process of political learning.

Jacob Grimm's pamphlet, in 1838, on his dismissal from the University of Göttingen and his expulsion from the Kingdom of Hanover is one of the most remarkable political testimonies in German intellectual history. He had protested in writing the king's perjury in suspending the liberal constitution and was therefore dismissed from his post — together with six other professors, including his brother Wilhelm. They entered history as the "Göttingen Seven." This protest was widely regarded as one of the earliest acts of modern German academic resistance. "I was compelled to yield to force," Jacob Grimm wrote in his account.

It is hardly surprising that Thomas Mann took Grimm's pamphlet as an inspiration when, in December 1936, he wrote his letter to the Faculty of Philosophy in Bonn, later published as a booklet, as his diary records. The analogy is clear. On one side stands a criminal regime with an ideologically corrupted university. On the other side stands the intellectual driven into exile. Even before his academic dismissal — on December 3 — Mann had already been stripped of his German citizenship. A double blow.

Although he did not explicitly mention this in his personal letter, Mann followed the nineteenth-century exile's example with striking precision: in the form of publication, in the self-positioning as a political intellectual, and in the style of his language. This was not just coincidence. Mann's personal library included Jacob Grimm's writings, which he had acquired in 1911 and annotated extensively, including the pamphlet on Grimm's dismissal. Mann followed his long-standing inclination to "live in parables," that is, to mirror his own situation in the lives of earlier historical figures.

That Mann's letter, like Grimm's pamphlet, had to be published abroad — in Zurich and Basel, respectively — only reinforced in him the sense of a historical parallel. His diary even calls Grimm's "form of publication" a "blueprint." Wilhelm Grimm had once predicted that Jacob's pamphlet, "written in such an urgent manner, will arouse great attention — more than you perhaps think." He was right. Even before the pamphlet appeared, Swiss newspapers printed excerpts, which soon circulated in Germany. This marked the beginning of an extraordinary history of impact — one that endures. Today, the pamphlet is considered a founding document of intellectual integrity in Germany.

Mann sought similar resonance when he devised his "plan for a pamphlet." And the plan succeeded: not only the exile community and the international press took note, but even the opposition within Germany, through clandestine printings and private copies. Three months after the initial publication, Mann recorded in his diary: "Reprint yet again of the letter, which is said actually to have circulated in tens of thousands of copies in Germany. Snowball system, multiplication of copies by each recipient." Like Grimm's pamphlet, Mann's letter was, as the scholar Steffen Martus has observed, "a polemic calculated for maximum public effect."

No one captured the profound consequences of this development for the persecuted more movingly than Marcel Reich-Ranicki, who, after the war, went on to become Germany's most influential literary critic. At sixteen, together with a group of communist friends, he secretly read the letter in a Berlin apartment. "Everyone was silent; in the half-dark room there was something uncanny," he recalled in his autobiography. The tension in that furtive reading was great: how would Thomas Mann, whom he admired, position himself toward the Third Reich? After the last sentence was read, the young Marceli Reich abruptly excused himself: "I mustn't be late getting home, I have an important test tomorrow." But the real reason was different: "In truth I wanted to be alone — alone with my happiness."

To "proclaim the German word in complete freedom" — this commitment, made in the Bonn Letter after Jacob Grimm, became the guiding program of Thomas Mann's radio broadcasts from his Californian exile. The sheer volume of insults and invective — uncharacteristic for the exquisitely proper Mann — is the most obvious demonstration of this commitment. Consider, for example, the broadcast of March 28, 1944, in which Mann ridiculed Nazi press talk of a "new socialist Europe," exposing it by pointing to the reality of German state capitalism:

> Hitler, as the principal shareholder of the Eher Press [the official publishing house of Nazi Germany] amassed a swollen personal fortune that surpassed that of most American multimillionaires. Reichsmarschall Göring, after establishing his industrial empire, the Reichswerke Hermann Göring [an enormous state-controlled industrial conglomerate producing war materials], and expanding it internationally through war, grew so corpulent with capitalist excess that he was likely the richest man alive. . . . Wasn't the driving force of Nazism always envy, greed, the lust for plunder — the unrestrained urge to wallow in power and wealth?

Mann abandoned all bourgeois restraint to portray the Nazi elite as vicious, aggressive, and fundamentally corrupt beasts. Hardly impartial, he even targeted Göring's physical appearance with the phrase "capitalist fat." Göring emerges as the grotesque embodiment of Nazi gluttony for power and money.

Between 1940 and 1945, Mann delivered fifty-eight such broadcasts to Germany. These were not literature but "actions," as he said, serving the purpose of psychological warfare. Never before or after did Mann step so far beyond literature. Despite the fact that listening to foreign radio was illegal and punishable in Nazi Germany, the BBC's German Service was the most listened-to "enemy station" in Nazi Germany. Mann's role was to undermine confidence in the regime and to spark resistance.

The BBC prescribed only the length of each broadcast; otherwise Mann enjoyed full freedom. Slight disagreements arose over tone, particularly concerning certain harsh polemical phrases and insults that the BBC deemed "far too abusive." Mann, however, insisted on maintaining his independence — especially when it came to personal attacks. They even gave him some leeway: "I cannot help it," he wrote in 1942, "it does me good to call Hitler a stupid maniac straight to his face."

To undermine trust in the regime, the speaker himself had to establish trust with his audience. In this, his voice played a crucial role. Initially, a British speaker in London read his texts, but from March 1941, at Mann's own suggestion, great effort was made to have him recorded directly. From an NBC studio in Hollywood, his speeches were recorded onto discs, sent to New York, relayed via telephone to London, and finally broadcast to Germany. "It is the voice of a friend, a German voice," Mann told listeners in his first personally recorded broadcast — a technical and logistical feat with profound psychological impact.

Nowhere was Mann's personal engagement felt more profoundly than in his references to the systematic murder of the Jews. After the Wannsee Conference of January 20, 1942, Mann denounced mass gassings that same month. He drew not only on international press reports but also on Allied intelligence. Most dramatically, in September 1942 he cited reports that 700,000 Jews had been murdered in the Warsaw Ghetto. His follow-up was direct: "Do you Germans know this? And what do you think of it?" Rhetorically brilliant and suggestive: however one answers the first, the second allows no moral wiggle room.

The "I" that addressed German listeners was never abstract. At times it appeared subtly, at times with striking directness. Consider his April 1942 broadcast on the British bombing of Lübeck, his hometown. About a year and a half earlier, the German Luftwaffe had devastated the English city of Coventry, causing massive civilian casualties; now Mann invoked this event to frame his reflections on Lübeck. His words shattered the self-image of Germans as innocent victims. Moral listeners, ethical Germans, he suggested, would accept — even welcome — the suffering of bombardment as an act of justice:

> The most recent raid over Hitlerland has damaged the old city of Lübeck. That concerns me, it is my hometown. The attacks were

> aimed at the harbor, and the installations of the war industry, but fires broke out in town, and I do not cherish the thought that St. Mary's Church, the magnificent Renaissance Town Hall, or the house of the Seamen's Society may have been damaged. But I am thinking about Coventry — and I have no objections to the lesson that everything must be paid for. Probably there are other people in Lübeck, in Hamburg, Cologne, and Dusseldorf who have no objections to it either, and when they hear the drone of the R.A.F. over their heads, wish them success.

The "Appeal to Reason," the Bonn Letter, the exile radio broadcasts — these are the classic texts when one thinks of the political Thomas Mann. But there was another side to his political activism that is less commonly remarked upon: his support of Zionism. From the mid-1920s he supported it, first as a member of the German "Pro-Palestine" association, later through a visit to Tel Aviv and Jerusalem, and finally, after knowledge of the Holocaust, as a forceful advocate of a Jewish state.

This lasting conviction grew urgent in March 1948, when the United States suddenly withdrew its support for the UN plan to partition Palestine into Jewish and Arab states, with Jerusalem as an international zone. Fearing immediate war, the Truman administration now favored UN trusteeship. The founding of Israel seemed indefinitely postponed. In his Los Angeles mansion, Mann followed events closely. Having publicly demanded a safe refuge for Europe's Jews, he now reacted with outrage.

His response to a survey by the émigré newspaper *Aufbau* appeared just one day after the American announcement. It expressed profound disappointment in American policy, drawing an immediate and dramatic parallel to the Munich Agreement of 1938. That agreement is remembered as the epitome of appeasement, when Britain and France allowed Hitler to annex part of Czechoslovakia in exchange for the illusion of peace. Almost no event had ever outraged Mann as deeply as Munich — a moment that he had publicly protested in 1938 before 28,000 people at Madison Square Garden. Now, ten years later, as a new American citizen, he wrote that the reversal on Palestine was "the most humiliating and outrageous political event since the betrayal committed by democracy against Czechoslovakia in 1938. It is an act of sordid and low expediency, a murder of faith and trust, and reveals with horror how ideals of democracy, truth, freedom, justice have become empty words." The article's effect was immediate, and it certainly played a role in the successful campaign to persuade the Truman administration to return to its original position. Thus, on May 14, 1948, David Ben Gurion was able to proclaim the creation of the State of Israel. The voice of Thomas Mann, alongside many other voices, had made a contribution to this outcome.

But why did Mann speak out with such moral fury on Palestine? For him, the issue posed a decisive question: had democracy learned from history? Would it once again abandon Jews, as Czechoslovakia had been abandoned in 1938? "How can one betray a people who have suffered deepest misery, who seek to build a democracy of industrious, culture-loving citizens," he asked, "in order to promote on the other side what is base, retrograde, rotten, hated by the nations — the feudalism of the Arab oil magnates?" The language carries a faintly colonial and Eurocentric undertone, of course, framing non-European powers in terms of backwardness and moral deficiency. At the same time, his diary shows that Mann perceived the threat to the Jews clearly and realistically: "15,000 well-armed Arabs threaten Jews in Palestine, who, under the eyes of the wretched UN, seem condemned to destruction." Once again, his concern was democracy and its ability to defend itself.

In the light of history, Mann's position was almost prophetic. What he said in the 1940s — about the Holocaust, about Israel, about Germany and democracy — resonates today. It connects directly to the weighty term, revived since October 7, 2023, and first invoked by Chancellor Angela Merkel in 2008 in a speech to the Knesset, regarding Germany's "special responsibility for Israel's security." That term is *reason of state* — in German, *Staatsräson*.

After his *Aufbau* article, Mann wrote in a letter that he had "let loose so violently" he might have to answer before the House Committee on Un-American Activities. The remark is telling. Over the decades, his political style expanded steadily: always ethically firm, increasingly rhetorically unrestrained. Already the "German Address" combined moral clarity with verbal force. What changed over the years was the tone: sharper, more direct, less inhibited. The bourgeois composure that Mann usually valued was shattered — not in anger, but with deliberate intent. He remained faithful to his humanistic ideals, but he understood that form had to adapt to urgency. That he pushed his language to its limits belongs to the story of a great political commitment: serious, uncompromising, never confined to argument alone.

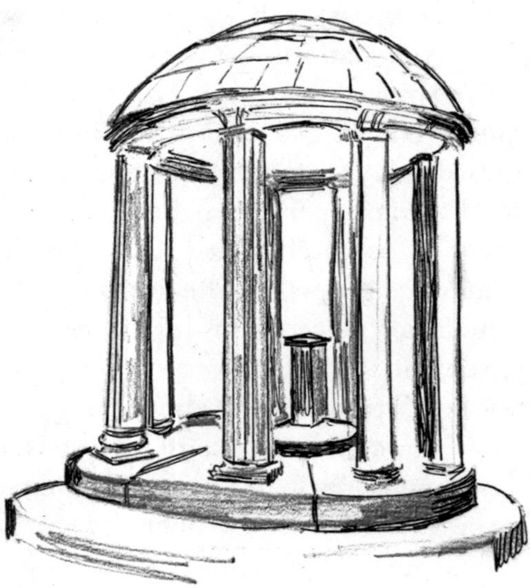

STEPHEN CRANE

Friend, your white beard sweeps the ground

Friend, your white beard sweeps the ground.
Why do you stand, expectant?
Do you hope to see it
In one of your withered days?
DO you hope to see
The triumphal march of justice?
Do not wait, friend.
Take your white beard
And your old eyes
To more tender lands.

When the prophet, a complacent fat man

When the prophet, a complacent fat man,
Arrived at the mountain-top
He cried: "woe to my knowledge!
"I intended to see good white lands
"And bad black lands —
"But the scene is grey."

(1899)

I AM JOSEPH, FATHER: RECOGNITION IN A POEM BY MAHMOUD DARWISH

NADIA JAMIL

Forty years have passed since Mahmoud Darwish released his extraordinary micro-allegory, *Anā Yūsufun Yā Abī*, "I am Joseph, Father." This was based, of course, on the biblical story of Joseph, widely appreciated for its psychological depth, acclaimed by Robert Alter as "the preeminent instance of biblical narrative as a fictional experiment in knowledge." It is a narrative that has inspired myriad works of literature and art. With *Joseph and His Brothers*, Thomas Mann transformed the story into a four-volume epic exploring human cruelty, responsibility, recognition, and reconciliation. What was a Palestinian poet doing when he reimagined it in a slim ten lines that culminated in an astonishing challenge to the patriarch Jacob? What is the enduring relevance of a poem that Darwish continued to perform in public till shortly before his death in 2008?

Anā Yūsufun Yā Abī appeared as part of the collection *Ward Aqall* ("Fewer Roses"), published in 1986 (Dār al-'Awda, Beirut) when Darwish was in Paris. He had moved there from Tunis after a four-year sojourn still managing the Palestine Liberation Organization's Research Center after expulsion from Lebanon with the 1982 Israeli invasion — a rupture compounded by the subsequent Sabra and Shatila massacres that haunted Darwish's writing thereafter, and precipitated his full transformation into a critical PLO insider. The shock, in the words of Fady Joudah, was "another glaring mirror of exile" reflecting the displacements he had already endured, beginning with the Nakba in 1948. The impact on his creative output seemed obvious: critics view his Paris period as the site of his transformation from resistance poet to an interpreter of exile as a universal condition.

Edward Said calls exile "an unhealable rift" and *Ward Aqall* is an exercise *par excellence* in wrangling the internal disorder caused by that rift in the form of a non-teleological journey — in Arabic, *rahīl*. Fascinatingly, Darwish's collection revolutionizes the most deeply psychological and liminal movements of the oldest Arabic poetry — also conventionally called *rahīl*. In these works poets externalize inner conflict — existential fear, bereavement, rage, chronic doubt — and metaphorically take to the saddle to process the experience. The poet's persona typically splits into two, rider and she-camel, figures which symbolize, respectively, the mind — *'aql* — and the heart — *qalb* — the premodern seat of the psyche. The two may function in perfect harmony; but descent into crisis — the norm — will catalyze fragmentation and the two will constellate, sometimes multiple times, into different conflicting parties, each new scene allegorizing alternative modes of confrontation with danger or failure, and the rejection of despair. These "journeys" generally have no arrival. They are performances of self-resurrection through the poetic word. The goal is integration. Darwish's *Ward Aqall* is a polyepisodic unity that follows such a psychological arc.

I will relay here the substance of *Ward Aqall*, with no pretense of adequately conveying its artistry, breadth, or sublime musical lyricism. The collection is comprised of fifty short poems of approximately equal length as stages of exhausting movement through time, space, and memory, in pursuit of a dream. Poetry is invoked to reconstruct the homeland, to puncture circuitous exits and entries through rock, sky, and sea; but there is no returning to the journey's start, and the end is always out of sight. Projections of war and loss echo with references to ancient histories and legend: Homer's *Odyssey* and the fall of Troy; the travels of Imru 'al-Qays, legendary poet-king, on the doomed trail to redeem his kingdom; the fall of al-Andalus, Darwish's *Paradise Lost*, somehow fusing with Lorca's "Song of the Horseman" on an abortive road to Cordoba. These are riveted with flashes of memory: sensory recollections of a mother's home; the few minutes allowed him before an international community that clapped and forgot; impatience with peer-group humbuggery. There is also descent toward fatal despair, fear of the voice falling silent — but this momentum shifts.

As the process nears its end, a daylight epiphany revitalizes the commitment to life, and affords the reprieve the poet desires to reconcile with himself, albeit "on the road to other folks' destinations": "Here am I, able to live till the end of the month, striving to write a plausible pulse into my heart, a believable existence for the spirit hereafter ... able to go to the end of life as a couple: my solitary self with myself alone." Moving forward, he begs the lightning to illuminate his way — "Brighten, Lightning, the night for us! Brighten even but a little" — once more channeling Imru 'al-Qays, and the most famous night-crisis in the Arabic poetic repertory, in which that poet urges Night to clear into a day that will likely bring no respite. He then emerges from his own "long night" into a state of unbroken defeat and into a desolated old age where poetry has in fact won nothing, nonetheless charging the "butterflies" of his poetic imagination to write the record of his land and identity: "We will write in order not to die; we will write for the sake of all our dreams." His identity at the close of the "journey" is a composite one: "Of us are the Messiah and Judas; and of us are the chroniclers of our wombs." This compound identity chimes with other reworked biblical narratives in Darwish's poetic *rahil*, most emotively his interpretation of Cain and Abel (Poem 15: "He Embraces His Killer"); and a metonymic retelling of Jesus' crucifixion from the perspective of Maryam, mother of Jesus, who wonders if God has indeed "divorced" her (Poem 39: "My God, Why Have You Forsaken Me?").

In his lightly veiled reworking of Cain and Abel (he mentions no names), Darwish ventriloquizes the figure of Abel to wonder what sin he committed to deserve to be murdered by his brother. But, once bereft of the hope of life, Abel resolves instead to grasp hold of his killer, to embrace his own death, translating the mark of Cain into an ironic promise of eternal constancy: "I will never release the twine of our embrace. I will never, ever leave you." The poet's interpretation of Maryam, meanwhile, lodges a fatalistic complaint taken straight to God: "Why did you promise the soldiers my single vine? . . . You descended in me as the Word; you made two branches to descend from a single seed. What, did you divorce me? Or did you leave to save another — my enemy — from the chop?" Maryam's experience of betrayal is grounded in a visceral sense of severance from a shared legacy; the pruning of her single vine — Jesus, descended through David from the root of "God's vine," Jacob, or Israel — to promote growth in a competing branch. Such biblical vignettes as these all intertwine at the levels of betrayal and injustice; but they also reflect the deep and tangled empathy that can exist in this no man's land between love and hate.

There is bitter empathy alive throughout the whole of *Ward Aqall*. Readers who understand this can better appreciate Darwish's Joseph, albeit that his predicament is more tragic than bitter. It is at the three-quarter mark of the "journey" — following a vision of metamorphosis and ascension through the agency of a falcon to which he consigns his cadaver (Poem 36: "To the Falcon Your Remains"), and preceding a protracted Last Supper, where he urges the Lord to transport those present to the beginning of all things (Poem 38: "The Last Supper Draws Out") — that Darwish chooses to place his singular Joseph.

I am Joseph, Fatherw
Translated by Nadia Jamil

Oh father, my brothers do not love me; they do not wish me among them, father.

They are brutal to me; they assail me with stones and words of reviling; they want me dead so that they can praise my life

They closed before me the way to your house; they drove me out of the field

They poisoned my grapes, father; and, father, they even broke my toys

When the breeze came and caressed my hair, they were jealous; they rose against me; they

rebelled against you; but what was my offence to them, father?

Butterflies would alight on my shoulders; sheaves of corn bent in homage to me

Birds hovered over my hands; so what exactly, father, did I do?

And why me? You gave me Joseph for a name; and they threw me down in the pit, and

blamed the wolf; but the wolf is more merciful than they.

Dear father, did I sin against anyone when I said: I saw one and ten stars, and the sun and the moon; I saw them bow themselves to me?

The poem begins at the end of the story, bypassing twenty-two years of exile — Joseph's enslavement and imprisonment in Egypt; his evolution from boy-dreamer to divinely favored interpreter of dreams; his rise to power in Egypt and deliverance of its people from famine; his reunion with the brothers who had betrayed him when they came to him to purchase grain; and his testing them before finally disclosing his identity and moving to reconcile. His dramatic self-revelation to them —"I am Joseph"— is replaced with an opening address to his long lost father. Time is collapsed on what remains of the story to permit a present-tense reprise of the injustices Joseph endured on his father's watch, including a fleeting allusion to his dream of the sheaves which enraged the brothers. The poem culminates in a question of politest reproach for the near-blind patriarch who failed to validate either of his prophetic son's dreams, both of which foresaw Joseph's ascent.

The poem is told in only one voice but it is polyphonic, a counterpoint of complementary tones. A biblical timbre colors Joseph's complaint of the poisoned grapes, for it raises the figure of the rootstock of "God's vine," represented in Jacob/Israel, and the fruit that it yields: his progeny. And it is a complaint consistent with the reasoning of Deuteronomy: "For their vine is of the vine of Sodom, and of the fields of Gomorrah: their grapes are grapes of gall." That is to say that, for Joseph, the moral ecology is corrupted by his brothers' sinful injustice such that his "grapes," his life and legacy, are existentially threatened through their communal interconnection in the "vine." This sin with its implications is, of itself, in tension with the meaning (and promise) of Joseph's given name, which augurs "increase," fruitful continuity — his brothers sought to rob him of his birth right. But it is a powerful testament to Darwish's internalization of biblical logic that he also goes on to draw directly the kind of ironic contrast between what "Joseph" signifies, and the deathly constriction implied by the pit into which his brothers threw him. ("You gave me Joseph for a name; and they threw me down in the pit, and blamed the wolf.")

Woven into this tapestry of sound are strands of Darwish's authorial voice, playfully intercalated like the cameos of a director walking briefly onto his set, shadowing Joseph's beautiful, slightly vain, coddled persona: The phrase "They want me dead so that they can praise my life" is lifted verbatim from an earlier poem in which the poet anticipates the hypocrisy of ill-wishers who will one day eulogize him. And the butterflies which alight on Joseph's shoulder are readily recognized by followers of Darwish as a recurrent, idiosyncratic motif symbolizing his own poetic inspiration.

But the pedal tone is the resonance of the Palestinian experience: violent displacement, vilification, and exile — all as if a penalty for the crimes of others; the existential threat of erasure; the talismanic dream of a return to the homeland; the earnest expectation of validation for that dream. And this is performed entirely through the total inhabitation of Joseph's voice — except for the climactic final question regarding his dream of the stars, sun, and moon, now proven true. This draws directly from the Qur'an's *Sūrat Yūsuf*; and the sudden impact of his speech mediated by divine discourse is startling: register and idiom are flipped. The distance between Hebrew and Arab is erased to produce a mirror of deep, if unforgiving, empathy demanding recognition.

The suspension of the story at this point is natural, for the extended lesson of Joseph's tale — that the recognition of injustice, the validation of the account, are necessary precursors for reconciliation and forgiveness — lay outside the perimeters of the poem in its time. The same remains true today, so that Darwish's retelling not only retains its power, but brings new urgency and nuance with each performance, at every shift in the political landscape. "True peace," he declared a decade later, in a powerful encounter with the Israeli poet Hilit Yeshurun,

> is a dialogue between two accounts. You claim that the land has always been yours, as if history didn't continue while you weren't there, as if there was no one there, as if the land had only one function — to wait for you. Don't force your account on me and I won't force mine on you. We must recognize that everyone has the right to tell his own story. And history will laugh at both of us.

MY DEAD ARE JEALOUS OF YOUR DEAD

TAMAR GLEZERMAN

It is very easy to bike into town to get provisions at the country store or at one of the farm stands, and appear like another Brooklynite up for the summer. The truth is that I am an interloper.

To me, the town looks like a Raymond Carver story, an Edward Hopper painting, or any of the towns on the imported American network shows I grew up on. "Dawson's Creek" and "Gilmore Girls" captivated my mind with images of a pastoral existence of quaint old wells and gentle brooding in gazebos. For immigrants to America, cultural shock is absorbed by the familiar blanket of simulacra. America is everywhere.

It is 2 PM on an August weekday, and few people are out as I pedal the flat terrain. Here beauty is unavoidable. Any mundane errand means traveling between creeks, rolling hills, and fields strewn with yellow goldenrod and purple loosestrife. The air smells of cut grass and sometimes of hot gravel, but usually it smells of nothing — a soothing absence of stench. I cherish America for its vastness and the possibility of privacy, but I don't belong to this inviting tableau of soft, deep greens. I belong to an aggressive mix of yellow and olive.

Before I ride back to my cabin, I loop around the large field in the center of town, cycling past the old Victorians and the small cottages watching over it.

Whoever owns the field rotates crops every year and sometimes grows nothing at all. A few years back, before marijuana legalization sprouted coolly designed dispensaries everywhere, hemp covered the field. That summer, increasingly desperate signs were taped to the fence: "Contains no THC!," "Will NOT get you high!," and — my favorite — "You WILL get a headache."

I find comfort in Americana: diners, motels with Googie-style signs, the majesty of Walmart. Here I make sure to be the nicest, cheeriest version of myself. Otherwise I might be found out. Directness is the most obvious mark of my alien origins, so I learned to sugarcoat and pussyfoot and not to say what I mean. I make small talk, commiserate about the road work on Route 23, and ask the locals if they know my elderly landlady. I tell them how much I love their town.

I don't tell them about my own town. I don't tell them about my aunt, who was shot dead at the beginning of this war at the age of eighty-eight. I don't tell them that my aunt's body is now going to be exhumed and reburied, because, at the time of her death, her kibbutz was still an active war zone: too dangerous for the living, too dangerous for the dead. Next week my aunt is to be dug out, driven south, and put back in the dirt. I don't tell them about that.

I don't tell them about Noor, my friend in Gaza, who just sent me a goodbye note for the hundredth time: "This is the third night without shelter, the sun is scorching during the day and cold at night. As I told you before, no one will survive this war. Good night sister." I have known Noor for eight years; we run a direct-aid program together. We message every day of the war, sometimes about the aid, often about the horrors. I am secular, godless even, but every day I tell Noor I am praying for her.

I turn the corner and pass a farm stand, where honest Americans can buy eggs, corn, squashes, and tomatoes by simply putting cash in the designated box. An essay by Joan Didion pops into my mind. The essay, "Notes From A Native Daughter," fills me with resentment, and for that reason it pops into my mind a lot. I resent how free Didion feels to call herself a "native daughter" of Sacramento. Or of anywhere, for that matter.

Didion also knows her familial history, going back many generations, and has masses of living extended family: "Dozens of great-aunts, year after year of Sundays." To my Jewish mind, this seems to be nothing less than a magical phenomenon; growing up where your great-grandparents, or even grandparents, were born and died, being undisturbed for enough generations to grow roots. Almost every branch of my own family tree was hacked off in 1940s Europe, save my grandparents, who fled in time. My family's story differs only in detail from that of most of my peers, unremarkable, nothing to write home about.

In the essay, Didion asks and answers:

> Q: In what way does the Holy Land resemble the Sacramento Valley?
>
> A: In the type and diversity of its agricultural products.

Didion is lucky that her home doesn't have holiness in common with the Holy Land. Diverse agricultural products are a far better thing to share with my country of origin. She goes on to describe her unholy home exquisitely: "All that is constant about the California of my childhood is the rate at which it disappears".

How wonderfully bittersweet it must feel to watch your hometown modernize, the cultural and physical terrain morphing with the times. I experience this too, but my terrain is not evolving; it is burning to cinders. It is imploding and exploding. It is saturating itself with a stain so deep that it will never come off; it will cover everything until the stain is indiscernible from the fabric itself.

Until it becomes the fabric.

I am a native daughter of nowhere because my identity, the very name of where I am from, is in the eye of the beholder. When I state my geographical origin, it doesn't read as an autobiographical detail; it reads as a political statement. In this, the Israeli identity is similar to the Palestinian one; others will decide, according to their personal stands, on the validity or even existence of these identities. So consider this, Joan Didion: no one ever says that Sacramento doesn't exist.

This year the field in the center of town is growing flowers, and its rows of carefully cultivated bright colors halts only a few feet away from the hordes of wild ones encroaching on them. Until the end of the eighteenth century, all the fields in the area and the surrounding 160,000 acres owed tithes to the Livingston dynasty. In 1715, Lord Robert Livingston the Elder purchased the land from the indigenous Mohican people, already nearly decimated by western-imported diseases, and received the deed from King George I. Livingston Manor became a feudal tract of land sprawling across what is now seven different towns. It differed from other British manors only in its avid exploitation of enslaved people. Livingston the Elder also went as far as investing directly in the transatlantic slave trade by owning shares of the slave ship *Margriet*. Amongst his descendants are the entire Kennedy, Bush, and Astor families, along with Michael Douglas, David Crosby, and Eleanor Roosevelt.

I bike past the house where, a few summers back, a couple who sold both cars and haircuts from their little porch helped me with a flat tire. Two houses down, sharing the car salesman and hairdresser's view of the field, lies the cemetery.

The graves jut out in moss-covered gray shards from the grass, which is dappled with bursts of purple wild thyme. There is no hard border, the graves just stop at a certain point in the green. The oldest tombstone reads 1757. Some of the epitaphs are barely legible, smoothed out by centuries of rain, the stones alive with mold and erosion.

Only a few hundred graves look over the field. Almost all of them must now contain very little — dead people allowed to remain unbothered for long enough that they returned to nothing. How beautiful it must be to be completely taken over by moss, surrounded by thyme, slowly disengaging until nobody who ever knew you is alive to see your grave, because they too have turned to moss. The cemetery belongs to the local Methodist Church. Built in 1854, the building is a white one-story wooden Greek Revival structure painted white with a red door, another comforting American image.

A row of quintessential American names — Harry, Frank, Fred — almost trips me, as these tombstones are no taller than two stacked bricks and bear only these first names. Small American flags billow over a group of graves at the far end of the cemetery. These are the graves of veterans. I check the dates — the soldiers buried here died in their eighties, decades after any battle they took part in was rewritten by the victors. They didn't burn in their tanks or get shot following orders given by someone just as terrified as they were. They didn't die killing people they knew were not their enemies. They died old and likely safe. Even the soldiers buried here are enjoying a peaceful death. How dare they?

A sound interrupts my inner tirade. It is the sound of a man speaking softly, and it is coming from the entrance to the graveyard. The man has a ponytail and a border collie, whom he is coaxing to do his business. I nod my head to show that I see him and am not afraid of him. He nods back, probably oblivious to the possibility that someone might consider him scary. The border collie urinates on Fred. This horrifies me, although at this point Fred has been dead for over 150 years and has fully left the building, corporeally speaking. Pissing anywhere, at this point, would be pissing on Fred. But I can't look away. I don't want the man to think I am judging him — although of course I am — because I don't want to make a strange man angry while I'm all alone in a field full of dead people. I look around, hoping that I am coming across as lost in thought, and wander away. A few minutes later, on my way out, I pass the man with the border collie again. I say, "Have a good one." But what I really want to say is: "My dead are jealous of your dead."

I get back on my bike and turn the bend. I think of Noor's dead, who are jealous of my dead. Noor's dead are under the rubble, in mass graves, or nowhere to be found. Noor believes that every day is her last. During the previous war, she once wrote to me, "I hoped to die in my house; I have many fond memories of it." In this war, this sounds like a fantasy. Noor's home was turned into rubble months ago, along with the home of every other person she knows. For a moment, images of dogs eating corpses blind me to my surroundings, but then my eyes readjust to the beauty. How dare this beauty?

CAPITAL MAGIC

ANI CHKHIVADZE

My grandmother sent us to catch a frog when I was about thirteen. Down to the riverbank we went, me and my cousins, tingling with the unease endemic to being assigned a task you don't quite understand. In those days we used to catch frogs for the sport of it, and cruelly inflate them and turn them into balloons, but the activity earned us rebuke from our elders. Why my grandma — who always warned us against the practice and often enforced the prohibition with a stick — suddenly insisted upon the forbidden activity was unclear.

Her son, my uncle, was thirt-five and still unmarried. This, apparently, required intervention from higher powers at the expense of a common frog. We were conscripted to provide the goods for a ritual. The frog was placed beneath my uncle's pillow without his knowledge and we waited to see if he would dream of his future bride.

Over breakfast, grandma probed him casually. She asked whether he'd dreamed anything interesting the night before. My uncle first couldn't recall exactly what his dream had been about — he had been drinking with his pals earlier that evening, you see. This irritated her, a communist woman and the wife of the *kolkhoz* chairman, well versed in interrogations. She pressed for answers like a good government inquisitor, insisting he jog his memory. Under pressure, my uncle said he may have seen a snake or a reptile of some sort. The laughter that followed is what I remember best. Soon thereafter my uncle was roped into an arranged marriage and my grandma's lifelong struggle with her daughter-in-law began. For the rest of her life, she called her daughter-in-law a "serpent."

Recently the serpent slithered up from the murky recesses of my childhood memories, summoned by an invitation I received from friends in Washington, DC. "Sip and See Your Future," the subject line read. A tarot card reader was selling us the opportunity to glimpse our romantic futures.

Back home in the former Soviet Republic of Georgia, Turkish coffee fortune telling was a common activity. We would drink our coffee thick and sweet, turn the cup upside down on the saucer, wait for it to cool, then press our thumbs into the dark deposit and read the shapes and patterns left behind. That is how we passed the time. And there were other such methods. The women I knew growing up had elaborate rituals for seeing their future husbands. They would tie a ring to a thread with a small cross, drop it in water, then hold it up to a mirror, hoping to see the face of a future spouse in the reflection. Or they would eat salty bread baked by a happily married woman before bed, believing their soulmate would appear in their dreams.

Men used the occult differently. Among teenage boys, there was a widespread belief that if you smeared lizard blood on your eyeglasses, you could see through girls' clothing. And there were supernatural strategies that were equally useful to everyone. Students believed that placing a snake's tongue under your pillow the night before an exam would make you dream the test questions. (What is it about human nature that tricks us into believing that hunting down and cutting out a snake's tongue is easier than studying for a test?)

I never imagined that this sort of superstitious thinking would follow me to America, or that I would find myself in Washington, DC, about to have my cards read. After all, I had left all that nonsense behind: the bad coffee, the bargaining with fate, the superstitions of a collapsing Soviet experiment. I had moved to America, to the rational capital of the world, where people made decisions based on evidence. Right?

The Pew Research Center, that ultra-American oracle, published a survey in 2024 that found that 30% of American adults consult astrology, tarot cards, or fortune tellers at least once a year. Women are nearly twice as likely as men to engage in such practices (35% versus 18%). Among women aged 18 to 49, the numbers are higher: 43% say they believe in astrology and 46% consult it at least annually. The revival of this brand of spirituality and of witchcraft is often explained as a consequence of declining traditional religion. In 1972, just 5% of Americans described themselves as religiously unaffiliated. Today that figure stands at roughly 30%. Churches weakened, but the need for meaning did not. At the same time, marriage, friendship, and sex have all become less common. In 1960, 59% of Americans aged 18 to 29 were married; by 2010, that number had dropped to 20%. The median age of a first marriage has risen by about seven years since 1960.

But hope springs eternal, doesn't it? Maybe tarot would succeed where Hinge had failed. Even a rational person prefers magic to uncertainty. We knew this all too well in the former Soviet Union. Communism was intended to create a new man, a rational, scientific man who would not dabble in magic or religion. Occultism and witchcraft were criminalized. Fortune tellers, often accused of "anti-state activity," were prosecuted.

Faith, it turns out, is harder to kill than Romanovs. In 1989, as the Soviet Union unraveled, a psychotherapist named Anatoly Kashpirovsky appeared on state television, staring into the camera and performing mass hypnosis to calm a panicked population. An estimated 87% of viewers tuned in, streets emptied, and people insisted they were healed while Kashpirovsky conveniently called for renewed faith in the government and communism itself. The Soviet state, supposedly built on rejecting spirituality, spent its final days broadcasting mass hypnosis to save itself.

Across fifteen newly independent republics, as the old order dissolved, people turned to anything that promised salvation, including magic and sorcery. When one of my relatives left his wife for another woman, his family knew why immediately: she had cast a spell on him. How else to explain it? They searched and found the evidence: clothes and feathers sewn into the lining of his sportcoat. Someone who knew the old ways had cunningly put them there. They took his photograph and drove all the way to the Azerbaijani border, where the old Zoroastrians, the fire-worshippers, lived. They were rumored to be the most powerful practitioners of the occult. The spell was removed. The man came home. For two weeks. Then he left again, back to the other woman. Maybe, someone suggested, they should have paid the witch more.

But extra money to spend on altering fate was in short supply in newly independent Georgia, unlike here in the West. My friend, let's call her Mariam, spent no less than $3,000 to have a curse removed by a fortune teller to get back together with an ex-boyfriend. One day she was walking with her friends in Dupont Circle, heartbroken and tipsy, when they stumbled upon a sign on a sidewalk and a small shop. "We thought it would be fun to try it," she said. But what she learned convinced her that $3,000 dollars was a bargain. A witch named Victoria told her that she carried a generational curse. That her father had broken a woman's heart, and that woman's mother, naturally, cursed him. "She said I was paying the price for what he did," Mariam told me. The bit about the father happened to be true. It turned out he had indeed broken off an engagement to marry her mother. "That was what got me to trust her — because it was true," Mariam said.

The curse was removed. But maybe Mercury was in retrograde because the ex-boyfriend proved resistant to the magic. "It's easy if you see a girl who is in her thirties out single and tipsy to guess what her story is," she said. "They work on generalities and insecurities that they sense and make educated guesses. I mostly got hope and comfort out of it."

I did not want to go to the tarot reading. Stars tell you nothing. *Que sera sera*, whatever will be will be, I always believed. The only time I had come close to tarot and witches was when I heard that my ex-boyfriend had gotten married. And to a fortune teller! Which made me dislike the practice even more, though I took some comfort in the fact that she was evidently not a very good one. They divorced quite quickly.

But I went to the reading anyway.

In ancient Greece, if you wanted to know the future, you made a pilgrimage to Delphi. The journey itself was part of the ritual, its length and difficulty shrouded prophecy in mystery and significance. Now the oracle comes to you. Witchcraft and related spiritual services have grown into a $2 billion-plus industry in the United States. Scroll on TikTok and #WitchTok — with over 30 billion views — will materialize between cooking tutorials. My algorithm feeds me manifestation rituals, birth chart readings, and crystal healing. We lonely hearts consume cosmic guidance the same way we consume everything else: passively, endlessly, while lying in bed at 2 AM wondering why we're still single.

The tarot reader was scheduled for a Friday evening in a Dupont Circle apartment. We drank wine while waiting for her to arrive. "Can she put curses on people?" someone asked. "Because I got a list." Then the tarot reader settled in and began laying out the cards. She was soft-spoken, with pointed elf ears, but apart from that did not seem in any way manifestly witchy. She had gotten her esoteric education in Salem, Massachusetts, as one does, and had taken up tarot reading right before the pandemic. It was catnip to the Capital crowd: she'd once read cards at a DNC side event. But her magic didn't do the Democrats much good.

Over the course of her readings, she mentioned that her clients were mainly women. Most ask about their careers because people are ashamed of inquiring about their love lives. Or maybe her patrons suffer from the common DC myopia in which admitting you care about finding a partner is somehow more embarrassing than admitting you want to be an undersecretary of state.

Most of the people in the room were women in their late thirties, all successful, good careers, well-traveled, cat owners sprinkled liberally throughout. They had climbed the ladder, checked the boxes, done everything right. Everything except the one thing that apparently requires supernatural intervention: finding someone willing to split the rent.

The witch offered nothing as concrete or damning as what Oedipus got at Delphi. No prophecies about murdering your father or marrying your mother. No unavoidable fates. Instead, her readings were conveniently vague. The cards offered reassurances: a period of transition was coming (isn't it always?), trust your intuition (so why are we here?), the universe was aligning in your favor (the universe is procrastinating). Nothing specific enough to be proven wrong nor dramatic enough to make you change your life. Just enough meaning to feel meaningful.

Someone asked about the war in Ukraine. She laid the cards out. The Judgement card: a crossroads, she explained. The Pentacles reversed, or lack of money, and another, I can't remember, that points to an uncertain future. The cards, like the rest of us, were confused.

One woman asked about her romantic future. The reader laid out the cards: the Two of Swords, the Strength card reversed, the Five of Wands. "This is about having a choice between two different paths," she explained. She paused at the Five of Wands. "This card is about conflict. I see this as talking about the past, having a lot of conflict and being like, 'I don't want to do that again.'" In other words: You're single because you've had bad relationships before. Groundbreaking.

Back home in Georgia, Turkish coffee readings and the sorcery that my friends practiced with mirrors and rings were games, really. Looking around the room in Dupont Circle at women in their late thirties, I understood that this felt less like fun and more like what made my relatives drive to the Azerbaijani border. When rational methods fail, you try the irrational. Maybe no matter where a person grows up, the hope that someone somewhere is keeping cosmic score is irresistible. Anyway, catching toads is fun.

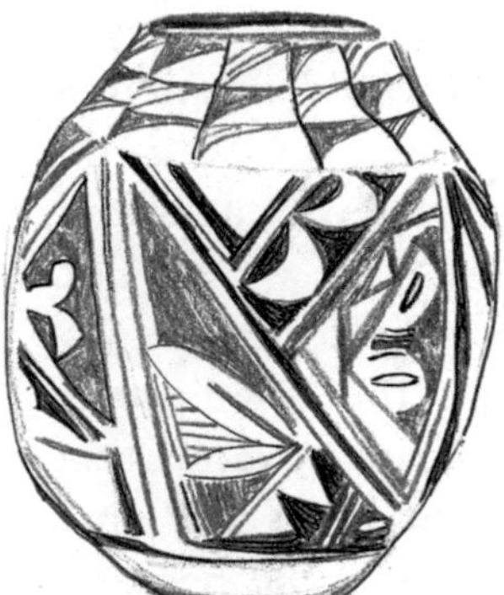

CELESTE MARCUS

Phallocracy All the Way Down

The Epstein Phenomenon ought to foist the subject of sexual cruelty to the forefront of our consciousness. It is a common cruelty, so common and so awful that we have had to find ways to blind ourselves to it so that we may be relieved of the jagged responsibility of interrogating our own complicity — our own comfort — with its prevalence in our culture. It would unknit our social order to take this evil seriously.

In this instance, our strategy has been to feign that Jeffrey Epstein's cruelties have nothing to do with us, that we are not implicated by what his story demonstrates about human habit. We have localized his evil and sequestered it within the "The Epstein Class." The progressive Ro Khanna, for whom Epstein's monstrosities are a confirmation of Khanna's class politics, uses the term "Epstein Class" to refer to a group of "elites" who, he hectors, "play by a different set of rules." Those repulsive elites! They have their own rules! That blasted One Percent with its impenetrable carapace of privilege and power! The "elite," the moneyed powerful whose names we all spent hours looking up with delicious voyeuristic glee in early 2026, has nothing whatever to do with us. We scanned the Epstein files as if it was a kind of game with no discomfiting lessons for the plebs. It was even fun. Did you know anyone in the files? Were you yourself inscribed? Can you believe it about Larry Summers? Can you believe it about the saintly, justice-seeking Noam Chomsky? *Noam Chomsky*. And my word, can you believe that they all knew?

Knew what? What was this awful secret to which these elites were all privy? Did they know something that we did not know? Did they do something that we would never do? They got away with rape or forgave it — but don't we? Surely most people — certainly most women — have forgiven worse sexual cruelties than anything Larry Summers has allegedly done.

Are you so certain, reader, that you have not attended dinner parties at the home of an abuser or a rapist? Are you so certain that you would scrupulously distance yourself from anyone so much as plausibly suspected of such debased behavior? Do good liberals, or good God-fearing and hard-working citizens of good democracies, really care all that much about rape?

I have, alas, reason to doubt our sterling records and intentions. I'm afraid I have reason to believe — to know — that ordinary unEpsteined non-elites of every creed, color, and political fealty care staggeringly little about rape. People choose to routinely rub shoulders with rapists with no power or money to speak of, and they are borne by simple, uncomplicated, uncalculated desire. They want to. There are so many rapists, you see, and most of them are just our neighbors or business partners or brothers-in-law living in small towns, the scandals of which would never grace the front pages of any newspaper. Most abusers are not famous. They are merely guilty.

Rape is too horrific a crime to believe anyone would actually commit it, and too mundane a crime to care about even if it is likely that someone has committed it. That, I can tell you, is what victims learn, and it is what readers of national newspapers deduce from coverage about cases symptomatic of this oxymoronic law. People are unfazed by rape and they are horrified by it. It is the ur-crime, absolutely unforgivable in soldiers except that it is to be expected, repellent in men with enormous power except that it is their inevitable wage, a black stain on a shimmering intellect except that brilliant men must be allowed their transgressions if society is to progress. As for the anonymous rapists — boys will be boys and what are we supposed to do, skin the bastard? There would be so many skinless bastards! There would be so many disarranged friend groups, so many sidelong glances and prudish or prurient staring. And what business is it of ours if something horrible may or may not have happened to some woman who may or may not have invited it? Why does she insist on talking about it? Even if it is true, each of us is more than the worst thing we have ever done, as Bryan Stevenson taught us. Time cleanses reputations even when it does not mend decimated spirits.

We say that Epstein was permitted to indulge his evil predilections for as long as he did because of how much power he had. This is true with respect to the judicial system's repeated incapacity to punish him. His power certainly accounts for the legerdemain which got him out of legally bolted cages time after time. "I own the Palm Beach Police department," he used to say. But this is not the only reason that he escaped social opprobrium for as long as he did. Epstein got away with rape because people get away with rape. Far more people get away with rape than get punished for it. This is a hideous and inconvenient fact. If all ordinary people were decent people they would be compelled to act on this fact, to alter society. But society — by which I mean us — resists alteration. So we avoid drawing out the implications of Epstein's sordid story.

He got away with it because he was powerful, but he also got away with it for the same reasons that men we all know have gotten away with rape. We all know men who have gotten away with rape. I know more victims of rape than I can count with two hands and I do not know a single one who has secured justice. The same — statistically — is more than likely true for each of you.

Virginia Roberts Giuffre's name is well known because she was among the most outspoken and courageous of Epstein's victims. But Giuffre, like so many of the girls whom Epstein and Ghislaine Maxwell sniffed out, tormented, and emotionally disfigured, was abused by many other men and betrayed by many other women before she met the notorious evil pair about whom we have all been gossiping. The real villain of Giuffre's deeply affecting memoir, *Nobody's Girl*, is not Jeffrey Epstein. It is Sky Roberts, who was Giuffre's father. In her haunting book she wrote that her father began assaulting her when she was seven years old, that he raped and abused her for years, and that he invited a friend of his to do the same. She wrote that her mother, Lynn Trude Cabell, whom she remembered to have been loving and warm before her daughter reached the age of seven, suddenly became cold and cruel at about the time the paternal abuse began. Giuffre intimates that she saw her mother as an aging beauty who longed for the attentions of a man lusting after a helpless child. She believed her mother was jealous of and embittered by her adolescent daughter's erotic provocations. Giuffre claimed to have detected the same icy jealousy in Maxwell — who hunted down teenaged girls for Epstein and as they aged toward twenty hissed that he would soon lose interest in and discard them — a decade later, but in her own mother the cruelty was formative.

How could a mother allow her husband to abuse her daughter under her own roof? What causes the wives, the lovers, and the mothers of abusers and abused the world over to turn a blind eye, to pretend not to see? Cruelty is not more or less common in elite or ordinary circles. It is a human sin, a human failing. We have been made to reckon with the cruelties that Giuffre endured because two of her abusers were famous, but not all of her abusers were famous. Sky Roberts was not less likely to abuse her than

Jeffrey Epstein was merely because he was not a celebrity. Lynn Trude Cabell was not less likely to betray and permanently wound her daughter than Ghislaine Maxwell was merely because Lynn Trude Cabell was not a celebrity. And while Virginia Giuffre's life story is inordinately horrifying, the horrors that she endured are not otherworldly, not at all. One woman I know was raped by her husband after telling him she wanted a divorce. When she told her mother about the rape, her mother said, "Well, he says he didn't, and I believe him." I know another woman who confided to her mother that she had been raped by a friend and her mother told her not to talk about that kind of thing. A girl I went to high school with had been abused by her father and his friend in her home and her mother did nothing to stop it. None of these rapists or their passive accomplices had astronomical power. None of them were members of any elites. They were just people, with power over their victims and with the capacity for committing or tolerating criminal cruelty.

Sky Roberts was never punished for abusing his adolescent daughter because his daughter loved him and needed him, and because she never considered the police — or anyone else — a plausible source of protection from a man she loved and could not learn to hate. Virginia Giuffre spent much of her life, before her suicide last year, trying to mend her relationship with her father. She cared about this man who raped her. Most women care about the men who rape them.

I'm going to tell you the stories of three different women whose alleged rapists sit somewhere between Sky Roberts and Jeffrey Epstein on the ordinary/elite spectrum. All of these alleged rapists are men of above-average fame and influence. They have been awarded honor and respect in their communities. If you were to hear each of their names you might recognize them from a book jacket or a lecture notice. All of them, even the ones publicly and credibly accused of rape, have remained welcome in some of the most distinguished intellectual venues in the world.

The first of these women went straight to the police to seek justice; the second went to the police and then appealed to other authorities for support; the third woman — me — went to private authorities and appealed to the public to strip her rapist of the high status he had won before the rape.

Taken all together these three accounts are a useful thought experiment for the question that the Epstein story demands we ask ourselves: who really gives a damn about rape? I propose that there are two kinds of people: those who believe that rape is an unusually horrific crime and that just the possibility that it has been committed by or against someone we know places a moral obligation upon us to take the possibility seriously and to act on that knowledge as reason and compassion demand; and those whose immediate reaction to the possibility of rape having been committed is to say, like the mother of my friend did, "let's not talk about that kind of thing." Only the first of these two types is the moral one, obviously, and the rare one. Society stubbornly resists their influence.

The first of the women whose stories I will share, I'll call her Samantha, went to the police immediately after she was raped, bleeding and covered in bruises. A rape kit exam was administered and photos were taken of the black and blue marks on her body. The police told her that a man who rapes in the way she had been raped was likely a repeat offender. They told her that she should try and find his other victims to strengthen her case. That, oddly, was how she found me. Her social media sleuthing had yielded evidence that she and I might share an abuser. As it turned out, she was mistaken — my rapist and hers were not the same person — but I was lucky for it. In the years since we found each other she has become a kind of sister. When she and I first met she had just been told by the police that her rapist's arrest was imminent and she was instructed to prepare herself emotionally for what would follow in the coming weeks. But nothing happened. One season fell into another and her anxiety looped back on itself like a circular electric current. That was over three years ago. There has been no arrest. Her rape kit was finally processed a few months before this writing, but he still has not been charged with any crimes. To this day, every official and officer she can get hold of promises her that the case will begin soon, as they have for years.

I read about the second woman in the publication *Poets&Quants*, which reported that Bent Flyvbjerg, an emeritus professor at Oxford University, had been accused of raping a junior colleague, that he was arrested in early 2024 on suspicion of rape, but that the police let Flyvbjerg out of jail on bail and then did not bring charges because they believed a jury would be unlikely to convict him. *The Cherwell*, Oxford's independent student newspaper, reported that the university did not launch a formal internal investigation into Flyvbjerg after police decided not to bring charges, and took no steps to restrict his access to campus or remove his emeritus status. And it went on to report this: "The case later intersected with the misconduct inquiry that led to the resignation of Soumitra Dutta as dean of Saïd Business School. The complainant has said she then approached Dutta seeking protection regarding her safety concerns. Instead, Dutta made a sexual pass at her. A five-month university inquiry substantiated three harassment findings against him, and partially substantiated a fourth."

The public attributes impartiality to formal investigations, the authoritative aura of objectivity. When victims turn to official avenues to report rape, it is often because they hope that formal investigations will shield us from being called liars or worse, and will show that we are able to provide evidence and make cases that will withstand objective, rigorous scrutiny. That is what we want. We have the benefit of telling the truth, so we believe — however naively — that we have the ultimate advantage. But of course every investigation is conducted by human beings and so is therefore subject to the same biases that govern every other human attempt at impartiality. The woman who had accused Flyvberg had been able to provide police with sufficient evidence to arrest him, but the police had tossed out the case because they believed that the jury would not be likely to convict him. Then she went to Dutta seeking the safety and compassion that her narrative should have inspired, and Dutta did what Duttas sometimes do.

We, victims of rape with credible evidence and credible narratives, hope ardently that the people we trust to evaluate our cases will be girded by a profound sense of the urgency with which we feel and think about justice. The very possibility of rape should bind investigators with a sense of duty. And yet Dutta preyed upon the woman who had turned to him to help her shield herself from her abuser, and the authorities responsible for handling Samantha's case are not interested in the injustice that she is alleged to have endured. Not interested.

As I say, the third woman is me. Samantha and I talk often about our respective hells. In the beginning of our friendship, our phone conversations took place in a reality that I was fortunate never to have encountered before, one in which the buttons with which society has equipped us to press in the event of an injustice do not trigger a response. I had avoided outrage at a culture that countenances rape by concealing what had happened to me. I never pressed a button, I never asked for help. No one had failed me but me.

I had watched Samantha twist herself into a condition of ever-burgeoning anxiety for months when I finally felt compelled to act. We had just had another in a series of phone calls in which I found myself in the familiar but always uncomfortable position of asking whether the case had moved forward. I didn't want to make her feel guilty that she could report no such good news. I knew that she felt she was letting down the people she loves by failing to be lifted out of limbo and restored to a world that made sense. She is a truly formidable woman and I did not wish to embarrass her with a reminder of her helplessness. After this conversation, stoked by the adrenaline of my impotent concern for her, I decided that I would do for me what I could not do for her: I would force fate's hand. She had done everything right, she had gone to the police immediately, she had gotten a rape kit, she had gotten a lawyer, she had made a legal claim. Before she and I met I thought that I had missed my chance at justice because I had done none of these things. But look — she did all of them and justice was no less elusive.

I contacted *The Atlantic*, the magazine for which my rapist regularly wrote, and notified them that one of their writers, whom I named, had raped me. I received an email in response to my allegation assuring me that my allegation would be taken seriously and then I waited for a month for future contact, expecting that an investigation would be undertaken and that at least one of the witnesses would be me. After waiting exactly four weeks in which I received no communication from *The Atlantic*, I tweeted a screenshot of the email containing my allegation and my rapist's name, hoping that that abstract, all-powerful mass The Public would be moved by the sense of compassion and duty to which Dutta and the criminal legal system to which Samantha had turned had proven wholly immune.

After I made my allegations public, two institutions with which my rapist was associated reached out to me. One, the Council on Foreign Relations, notified me via a lawyer from the law firm Debevoise and Plimpton that they would be conducting an investigation with or without me, but they invited me to participate so that the investigation could be as thorough and fair as possible. Another, Johns Hopkins University, let me know that if I wanted to file a Title IX complaint the option was open to me despite not having any affiliation with the university. I chose to participate in the Debevoise and Plimpton investigation because they were going to conduct it anyway. I did not pursue a Title IX complaint with Hopkins at that time because I did not want to do both at once and because I had promised myself before coming forward that I would not waste my days pickling in rage, pursuing revenge. It was not my job to spend my life proving that I had been raped.

After an hour-long interrogation, the lawyer from Debevoise and Plimpton told me that, whereas she had been hired by the Council on Foreign Relations and therefore worked for them and not for me, she would do me the courtesy of calling me at the close of the inquiry to let me know how her client would choose to act on the basis of her investigation's conclusions. There would be no evidence of the Council's decision in writing, no formal statement, no communication of any kind between them and me. A few months later she called to tell me that on the basis of her investigation the Council had chosen to sever ties with my rapist. This was certainly a relief. But I cannot report that I was overjoyed, because such a "verdict" was what I deserved and what I expected, since I knew that I was telling the truth, and that I had solid evidence to support my claim. And that, I thought, was the end of the story.

I was wrong. For reasons I will explain, I was persuaded to file a Title IX report with Johns Hopkins University a few months later. I gave Hopkins all the same information and evidence that I had given the Council on Foreign Relations. I also offered to give them the contact information for all the witnesses whom the Debevoise and Plimpton lawyer had spoken to a few months earlier. Hopkins' lawyers told me they were not interested in speaking to anyone who hadn't actually been there on the night of the rape and so they never reached out to the publisher of the journal for which I work, the man whom I told first thing on the morning of the workday after the rape, about what had happened. Bill had helped me pay for the thousands of dollars worth of therapy that I needed in the months that followed, which is why I had given his contact information to the Debevoise and Plimpton lawyers. Other than him, though, Hopkins and CFR got the same information from me. At the conclusion of the Title IX investigation I was informed that Hopkins would not sever ties with my rapist on the basis of their inquiry. Just as with CFR, no notice of this was made public, but in this case apparently word got around. For obvious reasons my rapist had good reason to let people know about the results of this investigation but not about the results of the other one.

In the time since then I have been contacted several times by women at various institutions that have hired or otherwise engaged my rapist. One of these women asked me whether it was true that her institution had reached out to me to ask for my side of the story before announcing his affiliation. I hadn't heard of her institution before she contacted me and I searched my inbox to make sure I was correct in replying that they had never reached out. She told me that when she asked her superior about the fact that he had invited a man credibly accused of rape to join their program, he had told her that they had conducted an investigation and concluded that I had lied for the sake of attention.

On April 26, 2016, a "Katie Johnson" filed a complaint against Donald J. Trump and Jeffrey Epstein. It reads, in part:

> On the third occasion involving the Defendant, Donald J. Trump, the Plaintiff, Katie Johnson was forced to engage in an unnatural lesbian sex act with her fellow minor and sex slave, Maria Doe, age 12, for the sexual enjoyment of Defendant Trump. After this sex act, both minors were forced to orally copulate Defendant Trump by placing their mouths simultaneously on his erect penis until he achieved sexual orgasm. After zipping up his pants, Defendant Trump physically pushed both minors away while angrily berating them for the "poor" quality of their sexual performance. . . . The Plaintiff, Katie Johnson, alleges she was subject to extreme sexual and physical abuse by the Defendants, Donald J. Trump and Jeffrey E. Epstein, including forcible rape during a four month time span covering the months of June–September 1994 when Plaintiff Johnson was still only a minor of age 13.

According to Julie K. Brown's book Perversion of Justice, Epstein and his ilk abused twelve- and thirteen-year-olds in this way at parties attended by many men. In conversation with a male friend of mine, I expressed revulsion at the possibility that men who would not themselves rape adolescents could have witnessed such horrors and done nothing to stop it. He shook his head slowly and said: "I know exactly what men like that would say. They'd say 'She didn't look twelve.'"

When I was ten years old, a group of men at the Orthodox synagogue which I attended approached my father. They told him that, whereas girls below the age of 12 are allowed to sit in the men's section of the synagogue, I, a 10-year-old, did not look 12 — I looked like a woman. I looked too mature, they said, to continue sitting next to him, and so I would have to relocate to the women's section behind the customary partition in the same sanctuary. And so, two years ahead of schedule, I was ushered unceremoniously into womanhood.

When I was thirteen years old, I wore a sequined, strapless cocktail dress to a bat mitzvah party from which my father took me home. We walked from the building in which the party was held to our car alongside a friend of mine and his father. When we got back to our house, my dad told me that this friend's father had whispered to him: "Your daughter's a fox." My dad instructed me that I was not to wear sequined, strapless cocktail dresses anymore.

When I was seventeen years old, a group of boys in my small religious high school spread a rumor that I was sleeping with a rabbi — the head of our Judaic Studies department. I babysat for this man's children. I idolized his wife, who was also a teacher in our school. The school, to its credit, conducted a formal investigation to establish whether or not the rumor was true, and the ensuing public humiliation occasioned my first dalliance with depression and suicidal ideation.

When I was nineteen years old, I was sexually intimate with a partner for the first time — my first boyfriend. On one of the first of these sessions, he took the watch off his wrist, held it up at eye level, and said "you have thirty seconds to make me come."

When I was twenty-one years old, while on semester abroad, I was assaulted by a stranger with whom I had hitchhiked from the college campus gym to the main building of Hebrew University. When I tried to get out of the car he used one hand to grab me by the throat so that he could force his tongue into my mouth, and the other to try and pull my skirt off.

When I was twenty-five years old, I was raped by a man who had, before that crime, been a dear friend of mine. He did his violence in my own bed while I was sleeping — after telling him several times to go home — after a birthday party that I had thrown for him on the roof of my apartment building. He had just turned thirty-nine.

A decent person who overheard or witnessed any one of the instances in the above chronicle would have been provoked to defend and protect me. The humiliations that girls and women are forced to endure by sexual predators are compounded a thousand-fold by the silent protection that society offers the abusers. No official investigative body can offer these girls and women the redemptive healing that a horrified and protective onlooker can.

The reason that I finally chose to pursue a Title IX complaint is that one such onlooker asked me to do so. A man I had met once before, a widely respected figure in Washington circles, contacted me a few months after the CFR investigation culminated in the phone call that I described above. I will call this man Gabriel. Gabriel was hesitant to reach out for fear of presuming a right to knowledge about the specifics of my innermost deliberations, but finally he felt that he had no choice: he was on multiple boards with the man I had accused of rape and noticed that suddenly these and other institutions were inviting him back into polite society. "It's like they waited out the storm and decided he was kosher again." Gabriel muttered over coffee. He was disgusted at the thought of sitting side by side with a man who had been credibly accused of rape, and this disgust was among the greatest antidotes to my devolution that any outsider was able to administer. "Did you file a Title IX complaint?"

I told him about the CFR investigation, but he said that he had approached the chairs of various boards with regard to this issue and they had told him they were waiting for a Title IX verdict from Hopkins. Later he relayed the information about CFR, but the board chairs repeated that it was a Title IX verdict or nothing. I was deeply moved by Gabriel's concern, and shocked by the medicinal effect it had on me. He was acting precisely how I had hoped that all people in his position would act. He never pressured me and he never insisted that I provide him with the evidence that I had of the veracity of my claims since he did not believe it was his right or responsibility to conduct the investigation himself. He simply wanted to behave decently.

The Gabriels of the world see injustice and are compelled to combat it. The fact that their community may have wronged an innocent person is a fact that they feel implicates them. They believe that inconvenient, awkward conversations are not so terrible an evil as living alongside banal, stable cruelty. The Gabriels know that a person's dignity is a sacred thing and that it can be cleansed and mended by being treated with respect. Time does not always heal decimated spirits, but kindness can.

There is a sexual etiquette which governs polite society. People who deviate from this etiquette quietly, without insisting on public approval for their deviant appetites, are permitted to remain full and honorable members of the collective. Society resists instability and punishes those whose true testimonies about their own experiences shake the communal boat — the outspoken victims and the Gabriels alike. That is why the Jeffrey Epstein story has been widely interpreted as a story about the elites — the attribution of his turpitude to his social class was our collective defense against a more encompassing and crushing truth, our sophisticated mechanism for containing the threat to our own everyday indifference and cruelty. We all agreed that those epicene elites have their own rules, so that the crisis did not force us to reckon with the fact that their rules are the same as ours, and that they are unjust.

There is no button one can press to secure justice. Even if all victims had the benefit of judicial or otherwise official systems that handled their cases with the requisite care and intelligence, no conviction of any kind can give the victim of rape what she deserves: to never have been violated in the first place. Jeffrey Epstein's victims feel that he cheated justice by dying in his cell. I cheered when I heard he was dead and I cheer every time I remember it — that *is* as close to justice as they will ever get. But what those women — what all women, all people — deserve and need most of all is a society of Gabriels.

I remember where I was every single time a Gabriel reached out to or stood up for me. I remember where I was sitting when, after "news" of my rape spread, a man with whom I'd only ever exchanged emails called the number in my email signature to ask how I was doing. I remember the strength of the sun in the sky when a colleague nixed the possibility of collaborating with a certain famous and powerful woman because she had called me a liar. I know the street I was walking down when a friend texted to tell me that, when a stranger offhandedly mentioned my rapist's name at a fancy event at which she was speaking, she replied in a firm voice, "He raped a friend of mine" and damn her interlocutor's discomfort.

The specter of discomfort or ostracism is enough to keep many a potential Gabriel from rocking boats. In some ways small decencies, rather than grand flourishes, are the hardest to agitate for, but they are the ones that alter culture. Dinner parties and after-work cocktails are the arenas in which acceptable behavior is conditioned, sanctioned, and transformed. Every one of these Gabriels has inconvenienced themselves for the sake of another person's dignity. Each of them bestowed these small blessings without expecting accolades or even thank yous in return. For the most common and intractable evils, the greatest antidote is not heroism but kindness. Society-altering kindness. Is that too fanciful to aspire towards?

LEON WIESELTIER

The Patriots' Ball

A preliminary example of what not to wish for our country on its semiquincentennial

One of the consequences of the American crisis has been a countrywide obsession with the definition of America, as if there will ever be only one. Political philosophy is now a national sport. The madness of our political circumstances has returned us to the inflammatory realm of first principles. This is not an unsalutary development in a polity that bases its governments on the opinions of its citizens, and therefore may be undone from within by bad thinking. Yet still we bless the founders who concluded that the establishment of a republic upon good thinking — upon good thinking in the mass! — was a splendid idea. Is there a more idealistic notion? It breaks new ground in reckless idealism. Or are we fools to commit our fate to the thoughtfulness of millions of people? The founders lived in the age of media innocence, of course, when facts and ideas were communicated by simpler instruments whose corrosive impact upon what they were communicating was not yet an insuperable obstacle to meaningful social discussion. The distortions that we confront make the distortions that they confronted look like typos. In our present-day wrestling with the American definition, it is a life's work just to clear the field of the rubbish.

Opinions have become our opioids, our cheapest indulgences. The spread of the conspiratorial mentality is only the most extreme instance of our mental looseness, in which plausibility no longer has to answer to reality. No philosophical principle, no matter how foundational it once was, can any longer be taken for granted — which is a formula for a terrible confusion, but also a consequence of the glibness that liberals themselves visited upon our national liberalism. (In our social and political arrangements, and in our founding charters, we *are* a liberal country, and we have only ourselves to blame if we are surprised to discover that it includes also illiberal tendencies.) Anyway, principles must regularly be revisited if they are not to become high-minded alibis. What do we stand for? How do we stand for it? The freedom to be wrong is one of our glories, but the freedom to be stupid, well, there is nothing particularly glorious about that. Whereas all the holders of opinions are equal, all their opinions are not. They all await critical evaluation and none are exempt from the ordeal. Yet we are now marking 250 years of national contentiousness and our long patrimony of democratic experience appears to have made us no better at the art of reflective and respectful contention. There are pages and pages of Mencken that seem abundantly vindicated by what presently passes for democratic deliberation. We are still democratic amateurs.

The best one can do in such a degraded democratic environment, if one is a writer, is to remain fiendishly wakeful, to give up some sleep, and to challenge nonsense, especially pernicious nonsense, with the speed of a first responder. The new technology is certainly conducive to such an alacrity of response, except that it is itself a stain upon the reputation of alacrity: its speed can thwart a genuine debate as efficiently as it can launch one. Its avowals may be indelible but they are not lasting. A first response cannot be a last response, if your objective is to persuade and then to rebuild, to move beyond destruction to construction, and the second and third and fourth and fifth responses, the programs of restoration and reconstruction, will have to be more patient, more steadfast, more discursive. Firefighters, bless them, are experts only on emergencies, and we aspire to lives, and to a social order, that do not consist only, or chiefly, in emergencies. Have you noticed that all news is now breaking news, and that all events have been promoted to the status of emergencies?

Intellectuals are also first responders, and they can begin their contribution to the recovery of our equilibrium by pleading that not all ideas with which one disagrees are emergencies. Absolute truth and foul treason are not the only paths before us. Hysteria validates nothing and denotes only a razing of reason, which is anyway a sinister instrument of the elite. A fanatic is a person who is completely certain of himself because he is completely uncertain of himself. Our politics has been crippled by the prestige of fanaticism, by the desperation of Americans who cannot quite escape the ugly rumor that they are worthless. Why do so many Americans think so little of themselves? A man who denies his own worth, and the rational capabilities of his own mind, cannot aim high. And composure must be counted among the democratic virtues, because panic is inconsistent with wise self-determination.

Yet sometimes one is rightly ruffled and calm really is out of the question. Sometimes one comes upon a traduction of an idea or a tradition that one deeply cherishes — not that umbrage is ever a proof of truth or falsehood — and one feels a bit firefighter-like oneself, and down the pole you go in order to prevent a sinister notion from proliferating. There we were not too long ago, for instance, the tillerman-intellectuals, calmly reading *Notes on the State of Virginia* upstairs at the firehouse, when the alarm sounded. An influential writer had proposed that the United States is, and should be, a Christian country! We are ready. The meaning of America is under attack. We suit up and slide down and hit the siren.

Here is what the chatty and phony reasonableness of Ross Douthat loosed upon the land on the day in question, in the *New York Times*, on the subject, urgent for him, of "whether what you might call a Christian center can be restored in American life." By "center," he explains, "I mean a set of religious beliefs and institutions that are embraced and respected in the broad middle of the country, cultivate a widely shared interpretation of the American story and operate effectively at the elite level, informing political conduct and intellectual arguments even among nonbelievers. "Broad middle," "widely shared": it sounds so affable, so anodyne. But what if that lovely place includes people who are not Christians? The expectation seems to be that they should accept direction from a creed in which they do not believe, from a "faith tradition" that is not their own. And the tenderness of Douthat's remark about "nonbelievers" disguises his assumption that no moral principles of any significance are to be found in the godless traditions — that only God, whose political role in history has generally been to divide people, can bring us together and make us good.

Douthat cites with enormous enthusiasm this perfervid passage by a professor of political theory at Georgetown University, writing in a journal that "aims at equipping evangelical Christians to confidently and forthrightly defend Scriptural truths and natural law in the face of widespread cultural capitulation":

> America is the New Israel, the city on the hill, the light to enlighten the nations, a battleground on which Satan and his legion tirelessly seek to undermine the promise of God's New Israel. Did not King's speech on the steps of Lincoln's temple in 1963 call on America to live up to that promise? ... Errancy and return: This is the New Israel's perennially erratic path through providential history. America is not Aristotle's polis, nor is it the faint glimmer of Plato's iridescent city set up in the heavens. America is the 40-year wandering of Exodus, searching for the American dreamland of milk and

> honey (Exodus 33:3). Is not *the frontier* — from its "westward" iteration in the 19th century to Musk's expansive vision for Mars in the 21st century — an American recapitulation of Exodus for the New World, and for other worlds, without end?

As an Israelite I must say that this "Hebraic Christianity" is very flattering, even if it is more Christian poaching. I must also suggest to the professor and his journo acolyte that they have another look at the Biblical account of the ancient wanderings in the sands. For a start, the journey was directly supervised by God and led by a prophet who saw God face to face, whatever that means. Not so America! America in 2026 would be a terrible responsibility for God to bear, and I discern no evidence of divine afflatus in our squalid politics. We will never enjoy the certainties that the Israelites in the desert enjoyed. And see what those certainties accomplished! The Israelites were a whining materialistic lot with a slave mentality who were spoiled by miracles; their faith could not withstand the forty-day absence of their leader and they expressed their relationship to God mainly by clamoring and complaining. They represent the antithesis of a proper model for a redemptive politics, except that they were redeemed — but not by their own merit: what saved them was God's own plan and the merit of their forefathers, and owing to their incapacity for freedom, the exodus notwithstanding, only their children were granted the privilege of entering the promised land. I would not dismiss the Aristotelian polis quite so peremptorily. It must feel wonderful to find Moses in Musk, in the way that hallucinations feel wonderful.

"All these generalizations are sweeping and poetic and of course highly debatable," Douthat genially continues, "but let me do the pundit's job and repurpose them into a simpler typology." The typology is three-fold. First, "to really lead and shape America, a religious tradition would need to be, first, *worldly* in the sense of relating in a serious way to a complex cultural and political and intellectual landscape where many people do not share its beliefs." Check, though the claim that America must be led and shaped by a religious tradition remains to be proven. (As for the worldliness of American Christianity in our age, the less said the better.) Second, "it would need to be *American* in the sense of believing in a national mission and sacred destiny." But is the American narrative any less moving and any less inspiring when it is read secularly? Indeed, the opposite is more likely the case. If God is guiding you through the dark and unknown frontier, you will be less afraid but also less courageous. Lewis and Clark were not led by a pillar of fire. Third, "it would need to be *Christian* in the sense of believing in God and Jesus Christ and not just some kind of secularized 'arc of history' version of the Christian narrative — a version that gives way, under duress, to nihilism and despair." Excuse me, but how dare you?

I am an American and I do not believe in Jesus Christ. I have extremely thoughtful reasons. Also I have a profound and gorgeous prior tradition that has a strong claim on my allegiance. I am prepared to make sacrifices for America, and for my Christian friends, but not for Jesus Christ. My right to deny the alleged divinity of your savior is precisely your right to deny the alleged chosenness of my people. Truth to tell, I have some trouble with that legend myself, though irony requires me to note that your belief in the superiority of your religion, so that it deserves to be nothing less than the public philosophy of our entire country, is not completely dissimilar from my religion's sense of its specialness, though we have the decency to apply the bewildering conceit only to ourselves.

There is a missionary quality to Douthat's case for the moral and cultural supremacy of Christianity in America, a kind of soft conversionism — I say soft, because in the place of forced baptism and the other old cruelties, to which he most certainly does not aspire, there is the old weather of exclusiveness and exclusion, a promise of alienation and marginalization for Americans who are not Christians and Americans who are not theists, who will feel alien in a country that is supposed to have made this variety of alienness magnificently obsolete. It was my impression that Christianity teaches us to welcome strangers, not to create them.

I certainly do not intend to be "tolerated" in my own country. Douthat does not require me to be Christian, to be sure; only my society and maybe my government.

Douthat is selling snake oil also to his fellow Christians. How can anybody who has read in Christian literature, from Jesus at Golgotha to Hebrews 6:4 to the medieval mystics to Kierkegaard and the dark Christian moderns, the extensive canon of Christian abjection, contend that Christianity is a cure for despair? The fact that the story usually ends well — in what Douthat slickly calls "resurrection scenarios" — does not in any way vitiate the sting of the despairing believer's torments. Devoutness brings more than good cheer. The experience of the hiddenness of God is common to all the theisms, and the spiritual and intellectual respectability of all our traditions depends in part on acknowledging the difficulties that they present. There are no humans who are perfectly armed against despair, the gospel of jolliness notwithstanding.

Douthat's proposal, his birthday wish for our confused and iniquitous country, is not quite the establishment of a state religion — the First Amendment seems safe from his laptop, though its safety may not long be guaranteed in the Christianizing nation of which he dreams. What he does not grasp is that the introduction of a particular religion into culture as its controlling philosophical framework strikes far deeper than its introduction into politics, which would be damaging enough. (And damaging to the impertinent religion as well.) Or perhaps Douthat grasps precisely this, because he seeks an America that is Christian all the way to the ground. There is of course an aspect of his proposal that he omits to mention, which is that it is a program for a rank majoritarianism, as if the power of principles is owed not to ideas but to numbers. On the numbers, certainly, my kind loses and his kind wins. (Please note the intrinsic divisiveness of quantitative considerations in a democracy.) The tyranny of the majority is what Tocqueville and Mill accurately called this threat.

Does Douthat really have so much confidence in American Christianity's interest in social peace? As he runs through the qualifications of various Christian denominations for philosophical precedence — evangelicalism, Catholicism, old-line Protestantism, woke post-Protestantism — his exercise begins to look sectarian and small. Why is he holding the definition of our country hostage to his shul politics? The burning issue before us on this anniversary is really not which Christian sect should be selected to constitute the national teaching. (Nor is it this: "Note that I am setting aside a scenario where a truly post-Christian religious consensus takes shape; that would require a re-founding or perhaps the Singularity." By all means, set it aside.)

Who needs a Christian America? Only Christians whose faith needs help, and requires to be fortified by numbers and by power. (Social power can be even more total, which is to say, oppressive, than political power.) It has always been my understanding that the American revolution in these matters was that finally a country comprised mainly of Christians elected not to call itself a Christian country. Such a contraction had been unimaginable. (There was no Enlightenment program of toleration that did not exclude somebody from the end of exclusion.) The world has seen many Christian countries, with mixed moral results, but it has not seen many democratic countries, and it was the historical role of the American founders to insist upon a shift from the one order to the other, and in a particular arrangement of liberty that would not inhibit or prohibit any practice or profession of religion. Was that not miraculous enough?

The self-satisfaction of some of our Christian pundits knows no bounds. Here is another example by another patriotic Christian American. Explaining the spiritual advantage of his own faith, David French, another God-fearing graphomaniac at the *Times*, recently declared: "Christians aren't the only people who believe that man has a soul, that this life is not the sum total of our existence. We do, however, make a startling assertion, that God himself defeated death — that he entered into history, lived on this earth, was crucified and then returned to life." Brother, this is uninformed and unintelligent. There was never any need for God to defeat death because no intellectually acceptable concept of God ever expected God to die. When you promote a man into

God it may indeed seem astounding that this God and this man do not die; but who could ever call an evanescent being God, or worship what passes? Eternity has been an inalienable feature of any sophisticated understanding of God at least since the burning bush. And the notion that it was Christianity that introduced God into history is pure chutzpah. It is plainly belied by the entirety of the Hebrew Bible, in which God's involvement in human life — not only melodramatically at the Red Sea but also in its most mundane activities (Psalm 127:1, for example) — is ubiquitous. If Christianity introduced God into history, then who was Abraham arguing with and who was Job's interlocutor? This is all just newspaper theology.

These Christian friends who want the best for us think that they are what we should be. I am reminded of a delightful story. When Lionel Trilling's son was born, he insisted to the doctor at the hospital that he wanted the baby to be circumcised. The doctor was shocked. Professor Trilling, the great Freudian, the avatar of the Enlightenment on Morningside Heights, the rational explorer of unreason, wanted the primitive ritual, the barbaric cut, to be performed on his own son. They argued the point until Trilling, in exasperation, ended the conversation: "Doctor, I want my son to be circumcised because I want him to look exactly like me!" I imagine him chuckling wickedly. The best prescription for an ideal of citizenship is surely not to generalize solipsistically from oneself. In a multiethnic society — is there any other kind? — one's first obligation in the endeavor to find a moral and practicable criterion for membership is to look beyond oneself, so that premises may be devised that can be shared across differences. The sharing is everything.

Why a Christian center? Why not a center that we will each join for our own reasons? You bring the later testament and I will bring the earlier one (or none at all) and together we will defend voting rights. After all, the ethical and social values in our respective traditions are not so different, and they are derived from kindred metaphysics, if indeed they require any metaphysical basis at all. I count secularism as one of our traditions, incidentally. It is emphatically not spiritually worthless, as our churched pundits keep saying it is. It is incontrovertible that many souls are seeking and finding deep interior satisfactions in non-religious meanings and experiences, just as it is incontrovertible that many souls leave their houses of worship bored and hungry for lunch. Anyway, sin is hardly synonymous with the secular.

It is discouraging that there is still an occasion to make these points a full two and a half centuries after the Declaration of Independence, "endowed by their Creator" notwithstanding. (The Enlightenment Christian who composed that document — the same one who cut and pasted his own version of the Gospel — did not have a Christian country in mind.) The belief that one is in possession of an exclusive truth makes a person restless, I suppose. Revelation eventually seeks dominion, benign or otherwise; it is hard for its bearers to see why they should confine their news to themselves. They must be reminded of the democratic reasons that make it imperative that they remain, in this matter, somewhat thwarted. The greatest of those reminders is called liberalism. Christian liberalism represents a misapprehension, whereas the liberalism of Christians is, well, a godsend. The American compact's simultaneous hospitality to religious life and distrust of religious politics has always been one of the pillars of my own patriotism.

I love the country but I can't stand the scene.

LEONARD COHEN

Many millions of Americans will mark this anniversary with a mixture of gratitude and melancholy, of ardor and distress. As for the millions of Americans who will celebrate it in a state of unalloyed happiness, I can only remind you that all of us love this country that you are ruining. I understand that for a long time you have held the view that it was I, and those of my persuasion, who were ruining it; but still I would have you assent that the liberal dream of America, the one that prefers opportunity to authenticity, equality to hierarchy, decency to rapacity, governance to revolution, fairness to privilege, reflection to paroxysm, work to grandiosity — that this dream, too, is a patriotic dream. Of course I will not sit by the phone for you to call with such reassuring acknowledgment of any larger commonalities between us. We are patriots at war with each other, not for the first time and not for the last. The least that we should be able to agree on is that this epic battle between our visions should be conducted according to Mr. Madison's rules of engagement, but at this writing even that seems too much to ask.

For this national anniversary, which at this low and debilitated moment in our history ought to refresh everybody's sense of America's reason for being, I offer a small and incomplete typology of patriotisms.

The patriotism of justice

There is no such patriotism, because there is no just society. There is not and there has never been a just society; history provides not a single example. Anyone who prides himself on the moral perfection of his society is a fool or on the payroll. All the countries that have ever commanded the allegiance of their citizens have been unjust polities.

Patriotism, therefore, is, to borrow a phrase, the last refuge of relativists. It takes place in the realm of "better than" and "worse than;" the celebration is always comparative. And it should be uncontroversial to say that some countries have more to be proud of than others. Forgive me for getting into the unholy business of distinctions, but some societies are more just than others. (Not all distinctions are invidious.) I am relieved to owe my devotion to my country in part to its democratic character, though I do not claim that its democracy is remotely perfect; and I make the argument in good faith, having done my best — honestly, my best — to police within myself the intellectual corruption known as ethnocentrism. Democratic societies, even with the anti-democratic tendencies that they always contain, really are better than undemocratic societies.

"Better" is of course a triggering word, but I mean it to refer to universal and rationally examined criteria for moral conduct, though "universal" and "rational" are also triggering words. For some poor souls there is no way out of this semantic prison — so kick back with a kombucha and get triggered! — but those of us who still believe in the possibility of increasingly objective thought must insist that such judgments are not a power-seeking exercise in "standpoint epistemology," at least if they disclose and examine their assumptions.

The problem with "civilizational" discourse is that it is too often animated by disrespect for one of the civilizations under discussion; and speaking for myself, and with a vivid awareness of how my own people have fared over the centuries in debates about the alleged superiority of cultures and religions, I feel no burning wish to crown my own. I detest the exercise. There is something pitiable about needing to be Number 1. There are great civilizations that are not my own; and the world-historical contributions of the West, whose tradition I am honored to serve, include not only liberal and democratic politics but also Nazi and Communist totalitarianism, which together slaughtered more people than any other causes in history.

And yet, if it is the increasing welfare of more and more people all over the world that is our goal, it is still right, and unironically right, to prefer more just places to less just places, whatever the national and regional inflections of the language of justice. In a world without perfection we can do no more than select intelligently between imperfections, and unecstatically affirm flawed but fairer patrimonies and places. The question is how to make the selection among the imperfections, by what standards, and how to prevent the celebration of the less imperfect, the Fourth of July, from excluding shame and humility.

The patriotism of reason and unreason

The premise of such a way of thinking about patriotism is that national pride should have a basis in national reality — that it must to some extent be objectively justified. "To make us love our country," Edmund Burke observed, "our country ought to be lovely." Which is to say, patriotism should possess some degree of rationality. But sometimes no basis at all is found for the national vanity, and sometimes one discovers that one is a member of an evil society. (Which is not the same thing as a society all of whose members are evil: such a society has also never existed.) The disillusioned and disgusted citizen has a choice: he can secede, spiritually or physically, and find a new country that is worthy of his admiration, or he can revert to a type of patriotism that has nothing at all to do with reason and reality — a well-documented type. I have known extraordinary examples of the former, exiles and emigres from tyrannical states who bravely came to these shores and to their dying day despised their country of birth and stridently called themselves, in their almost hilariously heavy accents, Americans. (Joseph Brodsky's notion of rhyming in English nicely illustrated the charms of an adopted patriotism.) A dissident is a patriot in grave crisis. My friends chose not only defection but also conversion. They demanded a life of justified loyalty. It was a matter not of politics but of integrity.

But I had other friends from totalitarian societies who now and then could be heard to speak tenderly about their old countries. I do not mean to be harsh about them. Nostalgia is unavoidable, and comforting, in exile: I was raised in a long tradition of nostalgia in exile. And yet what I heard sometimes sounded like something more — a vestigial patriotism, a warm remnant of a still living loyalty. The conclusion was obvious: the veneration of the imperfect implies that in the absence of complete justification the boast about belonging must base itself outside the realm of reason. It is anyway a stretch to think that patriotism, even in the finest of moral circumstances, can be entirely, or even mainly, rational. It is, for a start, an emotion, and what do emotions have to do with reasoning? (Tell me, somebody!) If patriotism were rational, chauvinism and jingoism and ethnonationalism might not have scorched as much of the earth as they have.

Patriotism, in other words, is love in the domain of history. If you have ever been brought to tears by a national catastrophe or a national epiphany, or just by the sight of the flag or the sound of Martin Luther King, Jr's voice, then you know that patriotism is a form of love, with all its joy and gratitude and intensity and volatility — and blindness. Love is often the enemy of clarity, it is a glittering exemption from reason, a mental holiday, which accounts in large part for the pleasures of its swoon; there are no poems about falling in and out of objectivity. I confess that even a Sousa march can choke me up — this country saved my parents' lives; and who is not a sobbing French patriot when they sing the *Marseillaise* in Rick's Café Americain? When the cynical Yvonne, played by the refugee Madeleine Lebeau, re-discovers her *patrie* and sings its anthem like no song has ever been sung, our American hearts are hers, owing not to their fickleness but to their range. Only the wrong sort of patriot is moved only by his own country.

Stephen Decatur, Pablo Neruda: in 1816 Decatur famously uttered the words "our country, right or wrong" in a toast, and Neruda once declared that his love for his beloved was so great that he no longer cared what she was like. I used to admire the radicalism of such a passion; it promised a reprieve from the tasks and the duties — from the prose that follows the poetry — of love, a free and pure unaccountability. Is there anything more intoxicating than a respite from the constant scrutiny of one's sense of reality? But a nation cannot afford such a respite. (We are wrestling with one now.) About half a century later, therefore, Senator Carl Schurz of Missouri sought to introduce a more sober spirit into American patriotism and added a stringency to Decatur's exonerating license: "Our country, right or wrong; when right, to be kept right; when wrong, to be put right."

A critical patriotism, in sum, a patriotism with open eyes, a patriotism that drinks without drunkenness — which asks a lot of the love of country and has never made the life of any politician any easier. The blindness of love is not its glory but its undoing. No lover should be afraid to look or to see. The art of swooning lucidly must be developed in the individual and in the collective. A commitment that does not examine itself cannot be trusted, not in the bedroom and not in the halls of power.

The patriotism of provenance
Do accidents have moral meaning? As Ludwig Boerne, an affecting and caustic Jewish writer in nineteenth-century Germany, once remarked about the assimilationist anguish of his time: "You can change your religion but not your grandfather." (This Jewish grandson converted to Lutheranism, which was his way of asserting that inherited conditions can be bested. In the end, in this instance, they were not.) Patriotism is most commonly determined by accidents of birth — indeed, patriotism is a method for making the arbitrary into the necessary and randomness into luck. The most tragic feature of human existence must be the extent to which lives are determined by locations, and life prospects by life givens, and this, I suppose, is one reason why disadvantaged people can be ardently patriotic. The nation — the combined social whole, its solidarity, its dignity-conferring symbols and practices, its sense of agency — is nothing less than a retort to fate, an empowering and ennobling way of playing a bad hand.

For this reason, the poverty of poor people is often not the most salient aspect of their existences to themselves: they prefer to define themselves in other terms, by their religion, their culture, their customs, their music, their food, their parents and their children, by anything but money. Economic inequality, especially over generations, is not a purely economic problem, and proposals for mitigating it must be accompanied by more than a merely economic understanding. (For over a century, here and in Europe, liberals and social democrats have been regularly astonished by the frequency with which poor people vote for right-wing parties. They cannot imagine that poor people would vote on any grounds but economic ones, while it is aboundingly plain that they do. Trump was elected twice by people down on their luck for whom he offered nothing but coal. But he ratified them even as he duped them; he had the con man's practiced intuition of a mark.)

"I love my country because it is mine." I have uttered the words myself. There is no disgrace in them, only an absence of reflection. An attachment to origins is natural, even if it begs the question of the extent to which origins should have the last word. Often a natural state of affairs must be rectified or rejected, but not always. We are not plants but we have roots, and the affections and dispositions that they inspire can be significant for the creation of character. Our racination can also be a source of wrenching sweetness. And so, like belonging, alienation too must be justified.

Yet scrupulousness in this matter requires that we not exaggerate the allure of our own sway, our possession and sovereignty. In itself, the first person singular and plural hallows very little. Nothing is better or higher or deeper merely because it is mine. The admirable qualities of an object or a worldview are not owed to its circumstances. When a beautiful painting hangs on my wall, I am the fortunate one, not the painting. Even though I own it, I do not own it. Beauty and the other attainments of the spirit can never become property. The Torah was not lucky, the Jews were lucky.

The literature on patriotism is a long debate on the moral worth of the local. It was Orwell who most notably defended the local as the proper grounds of patriotism. In his view patriotism is not primarily a political emotion and it threatens nobody. "By 'patriotism,'" he wrote in 1945, "I mean devotion to a particular place and a particular way of life, which one believes to be the best in the world but has no wish to force upon other people." He contrasted patriotism with nationalism, which he despised because it is "inseparable from the desire for power." Nationalism flourishes in enmity, he says, but not patriotism. It is a somewhat baffling distinction, since patriotic feeling has certainly been as responsible for cruelty and aggression as nationalist feeling, and the patriot may be guilty of the same trespasses as the nationalist. Orwell's little lexical game is owed, I suspect, to his infatuation with Englishness. There is a touching passage in *Down and Out in Paris and London* when he is returning to London from his years of hardship in Paris:

> I was so pleased to be getting home, after being holed up for months in a foreign city, that England seemed to me a sort of

> Paradise. There are indeed many things in England that make you glad to get home: bathrooms, armchairs, mint sauce, new potatoes properly cooked, brown bread, marmalade, beer made with veritable hops — they are splendid, if you can pay for them.

Are these things trivial? Not if they are your customs, and everybody has their customs. Are they narrow? Of course they are. ("A foreign city," as if that is all you need to know about Paris.) Yet I would think twice before condemning the local as simply provincial. In the struggle for human meaning there are no privileged locations — no centers and no peripheries. The human epic is global; that is, the local is global. We live on a planet's worth of localities, which is why we can have foreign teachers. There is no greater refutation of ethnonationalism than a foreign film — not because it depicts a universe utterly unlike ours but because we recognize ourselves in its depictions. There are people in Kazakhstan with greater wisdom than people on Park Avenue.

Yet Orwell's patriotism of home, his early notion of *heimat* and *habitus*, is sorely lacking as an account of human allegiance. I do not refer only to his failure to consider that in his beloved England bread was baked in many varieties. There is also the problem that he saddles the sentimentalist with the knotty question of national characteristics, those gross generalizations that are impossible to establish with any rigor and are as useful to hating as they are to loving. Orwell's own patriotism battened on stereotypes: "the English are not intellectual," they "have a certain power of acting without taking thought," they have "a love of flowers." (There are anti-Semitic stereotypes in *Down and Out in Paris and London.*)

Yet the principal difficulty about Orwell's reverence for the local is that it distorts the relationship between the particular and the universal. It leaves the universal out. I imagine that he acquired his aversion to universalism from his horror of communism, but it nonetheless excises half the story. There is no particular that does not reflect a universal and no universal that does not imbue a particular. They are everywhere together; twins, not binaries; and one of the most typical and most injurious mistakes of our age is that we call them binaries. The moral hazard of local patriotism is that it will ease the patriot's conscience by endorsing the contradiction between the particular and the universal, and by denying the relevance of abstract principles, global principles, human principles, to which we all must answer even as in our own way we cook our own potatoes. Orwell himself acknowledged the practical effect of this moral trap: "There is almost no kind of outrage — torture, the use of hostages, forced labor, mass deportations, imprisonment without trial, forgery, assassination, the bombing of civilians — which does not change its moral character when it is committed by 'our' side."

This anxiety about the foul potentialities of particularism is what inspired, in the ancient world and in our own, the all-encompassing patriotism, the citizenship of the world, known as cosmopolitanism. It is a patriotic feeling about the entirety of our species; or, if you wish to speak more strictly, it is the end of patriotism. I know of no cosmopolitans (except Diogenes of Sinope, who lived in a barrel and was the first to call himself a citizen of the world) who do not somewhere include a codicil about our obligations to the family and the community with whom we live — cosmopolitans, too, lead specific lives — but their bonds with their own do not seem to affect their altruistic priorities, the sequencing of their causes and their acts of kindness, as if the humanity of someone close to you is somehow diminished by their proximity and their intimacy. Camus' vexation about the moral status of his mother during the Algerian crisis expressed a more intact conscience than the ethical preciousness of those who believe that the most rigorous test of your conscience is its ability to transcend your heart. There are situations, of course, in which the conscience and the heart conflict, but sometimes there is no conflict at all, and the highest ethical behavior may be demonstrated in your own kitchen. Surely it should not be held against someone in trouble that you happen to love them. Humanitarianism should begin at home but it should not end there. If it ends there, it has been stunted by lesser animal or tribal considerations. But there must be a universal dimension even to filial devotion, even to the case of *maman*; to be a good son is to be a good man.

"What is patriotism?" asked a political philosopher named George Kateb in a famous and virulent essay. "It is a readiness to die and to kill for an abstraction: nothing you can see all of, or feel as you feel the presence of another person, or comprehend." This is backwards, and not only in its absurd identification of patriotism with bloodlust. It is the cosmopolitan, not the patriot, who is promoting an abstraction, not that there is any dishonor in it. The more local is your allegiance, by contrast, the more concrete is its beneficiary. I imagine that it was precisely this sense of the nation, of his own nation, as too impersonal an entity, as an emotionally unsatisfying abstraction, that provoked Forster's renowned observation in 1939 — not the best year for broaching the moral preferability of treason — that "if I had to choose between betraying my country and betraying my friend, I hope I should have the guts to betray my country." He awarded his loyalty to something he could indeed see all of. But what doctrine of belonging can be derived from such an almost infantile immediacy? Do we derive our convictions from our senses? Are we not to exist within larger wholes unless they can be taken in easily and entirely, and who ever took in the entirety of a country or a culture? Ethically speaking, the great writer was incomplete, a purely local hero, and somebody had better remember to fetch him if war breaks out. (And his friend, too.) This is the sort of exquisiteness that relies on the services of the less exquisite.

The scholarly and activist project that in recent decades has come to be called "global justice" is a tribute to the extraordinarily wide reach of our ethical concern, to the growing expanse of human suffering that we now include in the purview of our duties and our policies. Global emergencies, such as the spoliation of the environment or genocide in a distant land, demand a measure of cosmopolitanism from every village idiot. And so I was ashamed, as an American, when Trump and Rubio unconscionably terminated USAID and similar programs of assistance far away from home. We made the deaths of vast numbers of Africans inevitable — more simply, we killed them; and this heartlessness does not comport well with my construction of American *amour-propre*, of American patriotism. Isolationism is, among other things, the belief that non-American lives are worth less than American lives, and that indifference beyond our borders is a sign of our moral health as a nation. Alas, I do not yet see what it will take to persuade my fellow citizens, in both political parties, that we always carry, as a result of our powers and our principles, two sets of obligations: the obligation to the near and the obligation to the far. In space and in time, the near and the far; over here and over there, for now and for later. Otherwise we will slowly, or not so slowly, become Little America, a giant who is a dwarf, a self-defeating self-enclosure, and American patriotism will become a puny calling.

The patriotism of mixture

This patriotism does not yet exist, at least in large numbers. This is because mixture has not yet been widely accepted as a social ideal and a social reality. Too many citizens of heterogeneous societies entertain fantasies of homogeneity. How many catastrophes of sameness, from legal discrimination to physical destruction, must we witness until we realize that otherness is precisely what may save us from ourselves? The fervor for likeness leads only to illusion, anger, and grief. Too many Americans inhabit the America in their mind rather than the America outside their front door. They regard multiplicity, and any version of America with the infamous prefix "multi," as the problem, when it is the solution. If we were all alike we would respect nothing.

There are many reasons for this bias. One of them is the simplification of focus known as identity, which pays lip service to pluralism but is in fact just a pageant of monisms. I once wrote a denunciation of identity that included a snarky comment about the perfectly commonplace proposition that A = A. In logic, yes; but in human existence? Never. (Liberalism begins with A = B.) "Identity" is a confusion between self-reliance and self-sufficiency. It holds that any dependence outside your own group, any significant influence from a tradition not your own, is a sign of weakness, and so it preaches a protective psychological and cultural isolationism. (In this isolationism we must even take care that others not be influenced by us, which is known as "appropriation.") The real infirmity, however, lies in the unspoken suspicion that one's own tradition will not withstand an exposure to other traditions — that it can flourish only in the absence of alternatives. For this monopolistic temperament, as for its counterpart in the marketplace, competition means nothing but danger. A retreat into the desert is obviously impractical. And so buffers are built and walls are erected and conformities are enacted. Never mind that somehow the water always gets under the door.

One of the ironies of this subject is that the people who most loudly proclaim difference, the "multis," are the ones who are most wary of mixture. But where can difference flourish except in a mixed society? Or more precisely, in a mixed society that is free. Since we are compound and multivarious beings, the deliberation about sameness and difference must always begin with this question: with respect to what? The same or different, with respect to what? Patriotism in our mixed society is an answer to that question: the same with respect to America. We are alike in that we are all Americans. We have many attributes, and many commonalities, and our country is one of them; and when together we call ourselves Americans, we do not annul our other attributes, or renounce our individual interpretations of Americanism. To borrow the trenchant twelfth-century words of Maimonides, "our natural diversity will be hidden through the multiple points of conventional accord."

As with all our characteristics, we emphasize or consecrate them on certain occasions. Every day is not the Fourth of July. But on the Fourth of July, we express, or we ponder, the love of country — even, or especially, the love of a country in free fall. In 2026 anxiety becomes an American patriot. We may each have our own reasons for patriotism, and we do not all share an identical image of our country's past — you bring Frederick Douglass and I'll bring — actually I'll bring Frederick Douglass too — and that fellow in the red baseball cap, the one with the beat-up copy of Patrick Deneen, he should also join us on the Mall, because we stand under one canopy and inhabit a single over-arching category.

But what about that Howard Zinn book in that *New Yorker* tote bag over there? Never mind. It's Independence Day! Tomorrow is another day. Patriotism is a social truce, a hopeful simulation of the unity that we lack, a wager on the sympathy and the benevolence that remain after our quarrels; and a diversified patriotism is patriotism of the highest kind.

The patriotism of sorrow

There are times when the truest expression of patriotism is sorrow. After all, we mourn only for what we love. *Ubi lacrimae ibi patria.* Sometimes infidelity is made most clearly manifest in the absence of grief.

I do not grasp Americans who shed no tears for America and Israelis who shed no tears for Israel. Shame on the dry eyes! They, the dry eyes, are emblems of complacency or delusion or prejudice. Historians will explain how the countries took their sickening turns and surrendered so many of the stirring values upon which they were established, but we cannot postpone the attempt to comprehend why so many of their citizens are satisfied with the new national courses. I have heard no adequate defense of all the violence that has been committed, all the unending and unreluctant brutality.

Some of the finest patriotic compositions in history have been lamentations. I dare say that there is no language in which they have not appeared. Who will write our own? We do our political work in sackcloth. We wear black to the ballot box. At the patriots' ball this year let us not omit the heartbreak waltz, if we can bear it. Strike up the band.

CONTRIBUTORS

SEAN WILENTZ is the George Henry Davis 1886 Professor of American History at Princeton University and the author most recently of *No Property in Man: Slavery and Antislavery at the Nation's Founding*.

ANDREW DELBANCO is Alexander Hamilton Professor of American Studies at Columbia and President of the Teagle Foundation.

LEWIS HYDE's latest book is *A Primer for Forgetting: Getting Past the Past*.

ROXANA SABERI is a correspondent for CBS News. In 2009 she was held prisoner in Iran's Evin Prison for 101 days under accusation of espionage.

ARMANDO CHAGUACEDA is a political scientist and historian. He is currently Karl Loewenstein Fellow and Visiting Professor of Political Science at Amherst College.

MEG VLAUN is a writer who lives in a log cabin in rural North Carolina.

IHAB HASSAN is a Palestinian writer, researcher, and activist.

CARISSA VÉLIZ is an Associate Professor at the Faculty of Philosophy and the Institute for Ethics in AI, as well as a Tutorial Fellow at Hertford College, at the University of Oxford. Her most recent book is *Prophecy: Prediction, Power, and the Fight for the Future, from Ancient Oracles to AI*.

MICHAEL C. KIMMAGE is director of the Kennan Institute and the author of *The Abandonment of the West: The History of an Idea in American Foreign Policy*.

ARASH AZIZI is a writer and a lecturer at Yale University. He is the author of *What Iranians Want: Women, Life, Freedom* and *Shadow Commander: Soleimani, the US and Iran's Global Ambitions*.

LEN GUTKIN is Associate Editor at the *Chronicle Review*.

ROBERT ALTER is the author of many literary studies and professor emeritus of Hebrew and Comparative Literature at University of California at Berkeley.

KAI SINA holds the Lichtenberg Professorship for Modern German Literary Studies and Comparative Literature at the University of Münster and leads the Thomas Mann Research Center.

TAMAR GLEZERMAN is an Israeli writer, director, and editor living and working in Brooklyn.

NADIA JAMIL is a senior researcher in the Faculty of Asian and Middle Eastern Studies at the University of Oxford.

ANI CHKHIKVADZE is a journalist focused on international politics, security, and American foreign policy.

CELESTE MARCUS is the executive editor of *Liberties*.

LEON WIESELTIER is the editor of *Liberties*.

The insignia that appears in the pages of *Liberties* is derived from details in Botticelli's drawings for Dante's *Divine Comedy*, which were executed between 1480 and 1495.

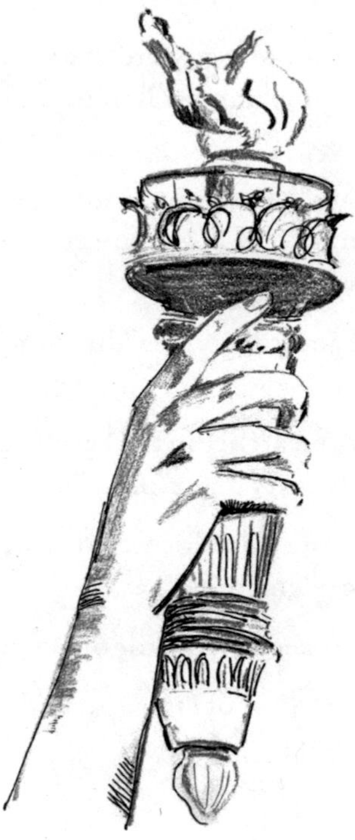

Liberties

POETS

BENJAMIN FRANKLIN's first published works were poems.

PHILIP FRENEAU is sometimes called the "Poet of the American Revolution." He was the editor of a Jeffersonian newspaper in Philadelphia.

CARRIE WILLIAMS CLIFFORD was an African American poet and an activist for women's and civil rights in the United States.

FRANCES ELLEN WATKINS HARPER's first poetry collection *Poems on Miscellaneous Subjects*, which appeared in 1854, made her the most popular African American poet of the day. She was an abolitionist, a suffragist, and a temperance activist.

JOHN GREENLEAF WHITTIER was a renowned nineteenth-century poet and a staunch Quaker abolitionist.

HERMAN MELVILLE stopped publishing novels in 1857 and spent the last decade of his life writing poetry.

PHOEBE CARY was a poet, as was her sister Alice. The two published a joint anthology of their poetry in 1849, on the earnings of which they moved from Ohio to New York City where they lived for the rest of their lives.

RALPH WALDO EMERSON believed that the poet was the highest form of writer and (incorrectly) that he was not one.

AMBROSE BIERCE was a poet, a journalist, an author of fiction and horror, a literary critic, and a scourge.

EMMA LAZARUS was a poet and a social reformer and an activist for Jewish refugees and immigrants in New York.

WALT WHITMAN was Walt Whitman.

STEPHEN CRANE was a poet, a novelist (*Maggie: A Girl of the Streets*, *The Red Badge of Courage*), and a war correspondent. He died of tuberculosis at the age of 28.

CAN'T GET ENOUGH LIBERTIES?

Visit our website for new writing, every week.

Subscribers and first-time readers alike can find more *Liberties* on our website, **libertiesjournal.com**.

For a taste of what you've missed online, an excerpt from "Natural Medicine" by EMMETT RENSIN:

It's easier, at any rate, to accept that you're taking medicine from a doctor. The others drugs I have taken in the past dozen years — lamotrigine, carbamazepine, cariprazine, olanzapine, aripiprazole, quetiapine, and on and on — were developed by pharmaceutical corporations in laboratories; they are tasteless, marked by little alphanumeric codes, carry the dull reassurance of a deliberate empirical design, of a rational and secular world. Lithium is a great deal stranger. Lithium asks you to accept that you really are mad, that there is a particular kind of madness that is not, despite what you've imagined, like the vagaries of human life as experienced by other people, that this madness comes from some invisible defect of the brain, and further: that all of this is best treated by the ingestion of a magic rock, of a trace of the Earth itself, found in stones and soil and hot springs. This cure is a kind of bargain, like something out of a fable: Take just enough to settle the spirit. Take too much and you'll fall into a deep sleep. Take more and you'll shake and shake and die.

To continue reading "Natural Medicine" and new essays every week by authors including **HIRSCH CHITKARA**, **JONATHAN ZIMMERMAN**, and **CHRISTINA CACOURIS**, visit **libertiesjournal.com**.

MIDDLEMERCH

We couldn't resist.

Wear your intellectual passions proudly, from the library to your living room with *Liberties* merch.

Featuring crewnecks, t-shirts, mugs, ball caps, and a tote bag, every *Liberties* reader's can find something that fits their reading habits. Whether you read the journal at home, curled up in a crewneck with the *Liberties* insignia, or finish your favorite essay at your desktop with a cup of coffee from your *Liberties* mug, our merch is just like our journal: something to return to, again and again.

Peruse our merch options by scanning this QR code or visiting our website, **libertiesjournal.com**.

ENTER THE WORLD OF LIBERTIES

Subscribers get more Liberties *in 2026*

A subscription to *Liberties* is more than a delivery every three months — it means membership in an intellectual community.

Subscribers gain exclusive access to *Liberties* seminars, included in the cost of your subscription. The inaugural seminar, Reason, Religion, and Integrity in Belief: A Liberties Seminar with Leon Wieseltier on Moses Maimonides' *The Guide of the Perplexed*, ran this spring. The next seminar, led by our European liaison Morten Høi Jensen, will be Does T. S. Eliot Still Matter? Enrollment for this seminar will open late summer and the course will run through the fall. Further details will be shared in our newsletter, *Liberties Weekly*, and on our website **libertiesjournal.com**.

In addition to seasonal virtual seminars, Liberties subscribers also gain access to subscriber-only events in our Washington, D.C. offices. Take full advantage of your subscription and check the events page on our website. Don't see anything in your city? Contact **events@libertiesjournal.com** to share your interest.

HELP ENSURE THE FUTURE OF LIBRTIES

Liberties: A Journal of Culture & Politics features essays from award-winning writers, significant scholars, the next generation's rising talents, and poets from around the world. There's a reason why cultural warriors, political leaders, opinion makers, and engaged citizens from across the political and cultural spectrum read and cherish *Liberties*. Through this quarterly in-print publication, new weekly online content, podcasts, vodcasts, and in-person events, *Liberties* champions liberal democracy and the humanities.

As a matter of principle, Liberties does not accept advertising or other funding sources that might influence our independence.

In addition to subscriptions, we look to our readers and those individuals and institutions that believe in our mission for contributions — large and small — to support this nonprofit publication.

If you are interested in making a donation to Liberties, please contact us by email, **publisher@libertiesjournal.com** or by phone, **202-891-7159**.

libertiesjournal.com

Printed in Canada.

Liberties: A Journal of Culture and Politics is distributed to booksellers in the United States by Publishers Group West; in Canada by Publishers Group Canada; and internationally by Ingram Publisher Services International. It is available by annual subscription and by individual purchase from bookstores and online booksellers.